1983

*One never does evil so thoroughly and so gaily
as when one does it for conscience's sake.*

PASCAL

IN GOOD CONSCIENCE
Abortion and Moral Necessity

DAVID MALL

KAIROS BOOKS, INC., LIBERTYVILLE, ILLINOIS

Permission has been granted by the publishers to quote from the following:

Epigraph, p. 153 "An Irish Airman Foresees His Death," from *Collected Poems of William Butler Yeats* (copyright 1919 by Macmillan Publishing Co., Inc.; renewed 1947 by Bertha Georgie Yeats).

Table, pp. 60–61 "From Is to Ought: How to Commit the Naturalistic Fallacy and Get Away with It in the Study of Moral Development," by Lawrence Kohlberg, from *Cognitive Development and Epistemology*, by Theodore Mischel, editor (copyright 1971 by Academic Press, Inc.).

Epigraph, p. 117 "On Teaching," from *The Prophet*, by Kahlil Gibran (copyright 1923 by Kahlil Gibran; renewed 1951 by Administrators C.T.A. of Kahlil Gibran Estate and Mary G. Gibran), Alfred A. Knopf, Inc.

Excerpt, pp. 42–43 "Understanding the Hidden Curriculum," by Lawrence Kohlberg and Phillip Whitten, from *Learning*, December, 1972 (copyright 1972 by Pitman Learning, Inc.).

Published by Kairos Books, Inc.
P.O. Box 708
Libertyville, Illinois 60048
Printed in the United States of America
1 2 3 4 5 6 7 8 9 10
Library of Congress CIP data is located
on the final printed page of this book.

To
my mother and father
who taught me to cherish life

CONTENTS

PREFACE

This book is written by one committed to a cause, one who has observed a persuasive campaign from the inside and has helped to shape that campaign as part of a broad social movement. It is the product of a rhetorician at work.

To be lastingly effective, persuasion must tap the deepest wellsprings of human motivation and must be grounded in an accurate view of human nature. If a rhetorical theory does not describe people as they really are, the possibilities for its lasting success are exceedingly poor. This is why any sound rhetorical theory has a built-in safeguard irrespective of the architect.

Although activists within a social movement are ideologically committed, the rhetorical theories they apply should be generalizable to other movements. Where such theories do not exist, I shall attempt to show that they can be fashioned. All that is needed is a rhetorical imagination prompted by firsthand knowledge and wide reading.

As part of a proposed trilogy about the rhetoric of the abortion controversy, this book is written to make persuasion easier for those who uphold the "pro-life" position. It presents no arguments against abortion per se. Instead, it attempts to establish the most favorable psychological climate for such arguments. As a preliminary to argument, however, it may yield its own persuasion in its effort to create a common ground for both bystanders and participants.

This book is a meta-rhetoric—a way of looking at, or thinking about, rhetoric. As such, it can be considered a tool of rhetorical analysis. I believe that, while talking about the issue directly is always effective, we cannot rule out the possibility that the most powerful arguments for a point of view are often made by simply describing a rhetorical process. I also believe that at this time in history a firm grasp of the process itself will help delineate the philosophical and psychological bases for some of the bioethical problems now plaguing humankind.

More questions may be raised by this book than it answers. As part of a search for a unified theory of persuasion for social movements, it contains ideas that are both complex and interrelated. My primary aim is to try to uncover important clues to a new model that will contribute both to a scientifically based understanding of rhetoric in general and to an effective way of presenting the moral arguments surrounding the question of abortion.

I believe that the rationale here expounded is consistent with recent research findings and can withstand logical criticism. This rationale— a developmental approach—is only one of many possible models of persuasion which might have been used. (See Appendix, Section A for a list of sources from which other models could be derived). As a practical tool, it should be viewed as an entrée to communication, not as a panacea. The theory is an attempt or a beginning and can be modified or fleshed out as necessary. The theory might also be universalized beyond the abortion question to apply to other areas of moral concern. But perhaps the chief justification for the theory is that it always pays to see things in a new light. This book is not an archaic armchair rhetorical analysis; it was formulated in the trenches by a social activist of long standing. It is a way of clearing the underbrush so that we can see the trees.

The organization of the book is simple—theory followed by application. In addition to an introduction and conclusion, a tripartite division is used. Part I deals with important theoretical considerations such as the relationship between religion and morality, the principles of mental development, and the sequence and evolution of moral stages. Part II applies this theoretical information to the problem of abortion. Seven modes of moral discourse are used to categorize and evaluate the pertinent arguments, both pro and con, in the abortion debate. Part III extends the theoretical application to the practical task of changing attitudes by means of effective communication. While the progression of ideas in the book moves from theory to practice, there are two key notions which resonate throughout. One is the notion of justice; the other is the notion of the shape or form of moral judgment, or the reason why a moral judgment is made. Both are central to the moral-developmental school of psychology, and together they constitute a foundation for the use of the theory as an analytic tool.

The reader will soon discover the great debt I owe to cognitive-developmental psychology and in particular to the pioneering work of Lawrence Kohlberg of Harvard. Though I have tried to be faithful to Kohlbergian thought in every essential respect, I have not hesitated to point out conceptual and methodological shortcomings. In the process I have tried to separate the good from the bad and to consider only that which is useful to my purpose. I cannot accept his theory without first modifying parts of it in light of my own investigations and experiences. Still unresolved in my thinking are the limitations posed by three areas recognized by Kohlberg himself as "1) the stress placed on form rather than content 2) the focus on concepts of rights and duties rather than issues of the good [and] 3) the emphasis on moral judgment rather than behavior." [KH77f-58]* Perhaps my own contribution will be in placing these troublesome dichotomies within a real-life context where they reside in dynamic tension. At any rate, I will be discussing them throughout the text.

As impressive as the scholarship of Kohlberg has been, and as worthy of universal admiration, I am compelled to agree with Kohlberg's own admission that his theory is only "*a partial guide to the moral educator*" (italics added). [K78e-14] It offers clues, but it should not be oversold or studied in a vacuum. Lengthy case studies are needed to make his theory effective, and to illuminate and extend its application. A detailed analysis of the moral issues involved in the question of abortion based on a Kohlbergian developmental model should be an effective way to test the theory while giving it flesh and blood.

In applying the moral-developmental model to the question of abortion, it is certainly not my intention to make anti-abortion ideologues out of Kohlberg and his school. Yet we do not live in a morally neutral world and an objective study of morals cannot really be indifferent to certain moral outcomes. In fact, there is strong evidence that Kohlberg's model is based upon assumptions with clear links to the doctrine of liberal moral philosophy as propounded by John Rawls and others. I will contend that a pro-life position is both consistent and compatible with the core of these assumptions.

This book will be successful to the extent that it removes bitterness

---

* Throughout this book all direct references to Kohlberg's work will be bracketed and placed in the body of the text. The first letter(s) in upper case is/are the last-name initial(s) of the author(s). This symbol is followed by the year of publication sequenced alphabetically (lower case) in relation to others of the same year. After the hyphen, each citation ends with a page number. The complete reference can be found at the back of the book in the first section of the bibliography.

and recrimination from the abortion controversy and allows logic and justice to prevail. It is written for all who have an open mind.

———————

The credit for whatever good may come from this book must be shared with others. My investigation was sparked by the advice of William Hunt, a friend of long standing, who suggested that I read the developmental psychology of Lawrence Kohlberg and Jean Piaget. This suggestion was followed diligently and led eventually to further extensive reading in such areas as cultural anthropology, theoretical biology, educational psychology, and general systems theory. The relevance of my own background in rhetoric became increasingly clear to me. It is an art whose boundaries extend to the whole spectrum of human motivation and performance.

Among the many activists who engaged in dialogue and helped shape my thinking, I hold three in special regard: Ralph Folkers, Kenneth Kaplin, and Roger Mall. Their Judeo-Christian moral outlook attests to the ecumenical nature of the pro-life cause and, I hope, to the potential appeal of this book.

A special note of appreciation is due Juli Loesch, Burke Balch, and my editor, Janice Feldstein, whose helpful criticism has made this a better book. Also, I would like to thank Virginia Reuter, whose clerical skills enabled me to keep on schedule. To the many who read copies of the manuscript, as well as to all who assisted with obtaining reference materials, I offer a collective thanks.

Finally, I wish to thank George Mall for his uncommon help and encouragement. This project could not have been executed without the generosity and support of family and friends.

Chicago, Illinois
January, 1982

INTRODUCTION

In this and like communities, public sentiment is everything. With public sentiment, nothing can fail; without it, nothing can succeed. Consequently, he who moulds public sentiment, goes deeper than he who enacts statutes or pronounces decisions. He makes statutes and decisions possible or impossible to be executed.

LINCOLN

THE TASK OF RHETORIC

Human abortion is certainly not new, nor is it of overriding concern to most people. Anthropologists remind us that every known culture, whether literate or preliterate, primitive or modern, has engaged in it. The highly personal nature of the abortion act itself, burdened as it is with a tangle of human emotions, including fear, shame, and guilt, has kept it from close public scrutiny. It is not one of those issues people like to talk about, so it resides below the threshold of common public concern. Opinion polls, when treating the subject along with others, have consistently shown that people are more concerned about war and peace and the immediate problems of earning a living. For most, however, even individuals who give it only a passing recognition, the abortion topic is one of those intimate moral questions which, because it touches upon the very meaning of human existence, cuts deeply.

It is not my intention here to fuel the debate with my own convictions on this complex and explosive issue. Rather, I wish to expose its underlying rhetoric in an effort to help communicators to understand and frame their own arguments. One must master whatever one should know before one persuades. With time, the right cast of mind will give precision to persuasion. The theory in this book is a preliminary to argument; it precedes debate and lays the groundwork for persuasion. It can be an effective tool for social change only if it stimulates reasoning, inquiry, and critical thinking, and only insofar as it becomes an aid in categorizing arguments, in relating them to each other, in fitting them into a coherent whole, and, ultimately, in simplifying an understanding of the reasoning process. This is not a "self-improvement" or "how-to" book, but an outline of how one might utilize a complex moral reasoning process. The basic problem-solving strategy it employs is to help people make sense out of their moral experiences. More specifically, my purpose is to increase the reader's awareness of and sensitivity to the moral reasoning patterns used in the abortion debate, to isolate these moral components and look at them in a sophisticated manner.

In many respects the current abortion controversy rages in the public mind because each side lacks a clear understanding of how people learn and are persuaded. Admittedly, heretofore there have been many attempts, both verbal and pictorial, to make audiences face "reality." But there has been no comprehensive attempt to define what it means to be rational. It is not enough to consider the philo-sophical assumptions behind the rhetoric (or how well we think); we must also consider the psychological assumptions behind the actual way we think. We must look for the messages behind the messages or we will all end up only half persuading. What is worse, we might not persuade at all.

I believe that the abortion propaganda consumed by the general public inadequately taps the wellsprings of human motivation. Both sides unwisely assume that the indifferent or uncommitted really have taken a position, albeit an undisclosed one, and that more informa-tion will crystallize their thinking; the right fact will round out their natural inclinations. I submit that such a view is a gross oversimplifica-tion. It is the thinking process itself that must be explored.

THE MEDIA VS. THE PEOPLE

Anti-abortion activists of long standing interpret the abortion con-troversy as a struggle between a grass-roots movement and an elite which has successfully cultivated the nation's print and broadcast media. They have known from the very beginning of their activism that the lower-income groups are generally opposed to abortion, as are those on the lower rungs of the educational ladder. And this conclusion is not theirs alone. One university researcher using complicated statistical techniques found much the same thing. Low income and education were better indicators of a person's objection to abortion than were age, sex, race, or marital status.[1]

Judgments about the grass-roots nature of the anti-abortion crusade are more than just intuitively or empirically based. It is my repeated experience that the pro-life ideology will receive a warmer reception in the ghettos of the inner city than in some affluent suburban neighborhoods or, more pertinently, in the editorial board rooms of most large metropolitan dailies. While working for Americans United for Life, a national pro-life educational foundation headquartered in Chicago, I edited material for an information-retrieval service which was distributed to pro-life organizations on the state and local levels. With the help of a large clipping bureau, the service carefully inspected the nation's print media every twenty-four hours. The clippings for an eighteen-month period, numbering many thousands, showed quite clearly that newspapers from the nation's largest cities favored abortion editorially, but that small-town newspapers for the most part did not.

Although there is some indication that major print media sources are now including more information favorable to the anti-abortion position (the 1978 *Chicago Sun-Times* abortion clinic exposé is the best example),[2] those who are deeply concerned about the impartiality of American journalism must still agree with John T. Noonan that with few exceptions the American pro-life movement fights against print media that are either hostile or indifferent.[3] Except perhaps on college campuses during the late 1960s, pro-life activists believe that the pro-abortion ideology has never been a true grass-roots phenomenon. And by their continued support of a Human Life Amendment to the U.S. Constitution, they are determined to prove that the Supreme Court in its 1973 abortion decision never really did reflect the wishes of the American people, the attitudes of the nation's major print media notwithstanding.

Through a knowledge of persuasion, that instrument which can change minds, the grass-roots activist can prove the rightness of any worthy cause. And rhetoric, the theoretical study of persuasion, when put into practice becomes the great equalizer in any moral controversy. The rhetoric of abortion can be handled by anyone capable of perceiving moral distinctions. A person's socioeconomic status need be no barrier, for morality is everybody's business. And the study of ethics, the theoretical study of morality, is not the exclusive province of the rich and powerful. Only an elitist would contend that poor people are not fully capable of engaging in an intelligent moral discussion. To reason morally one does not have to be an editorial writer for the *New York Times* or a news director for a major television network. Big media may hold a good hand but they do not have all the cards. Although, most assuredly, they are the keepers of the gate in communicating on a grand scale with the American public, they do not control the basic power to persuade. That, fortunately, derives from the inherent moral truth of one's position.

THE RHETORICAL IMAGINATION

Successful communication in a social movement requires a rhetorical imagination. Such an imagination must be preceded by the recognition that rhetoric is important in human affairs. To the rhetorically imaginative there can be no such thing as "mere" rhetoric, for all rhetoric worthy of the name can justify itself in terms of some social good. It is only noise or nonrhetoric that justifies criticism.

In my view, true rhetoric is associated only with the good; its highest purpose is to help the individual mature within a universal culture and thus ameliorate the human condition. Rhetoric is transformational; it takes us as we are but strives to assist our natural inclination to become better morally. And while helping people to grow morally, rhetoric also helps build a sense of community. The process is interactive. "Community" is more than a simple uniformity at any level; it is really a smoothly functioning system of moral relationships. The more mature the relationships, the stronger will be the individual's sense of belonging and the more efficacious the support given by the community. True rhetoric signifies one's triumph over personal alienation and the specter of social disintegration.

From a more personal view, the realization that rhetoric is important, coupled with a strong desire to understand and use it effectively, gives rise and free play to the rhetorical imagination. When put to practical use, the work of this imagination is to understand what motivates us to think and act as we do. After all, that peculiar composite of people called an audience is an exceedingly complex entity quite difficult to comprehend. The rhetorical imagination looks at the world *sub specie orationis*, under the guise of rhetoric. To understand rhetoric is to give oneself a firmer (and more confident) grasp of reality as well as a deeper understanding of humanity and the social universe.

☐

Linked closely with the need for a rhetorical imagination is the need for a clear concept of valid knowledge through which the rhetoric can be observed and evaluated. Such an epistemology, or theory of how we know what we know, if not selected wisely can obscure the rhetoric and distort the observer's perspective. The theory of knowledge advanced in this book is derived from the field of developmental psychology or, more specifically, from the work of the renowned Swiss biologist and philosopher Jean Piaget. Drawing heavily as well upon the work of the Harvard educational psychologist Lawrence Kohlberg, the book represents an extension of the developmental model to the ordering of values within a social movement. The important governing assumption of the book is that in the real world, facts and values interact and are controlled by a basic logic. The rhetoric of the abortion controversy represents an amalgam of moral discourse and scientific discourse, both of which are rational and can be analyzed objectively. Piaget himself, in a classic statement regarding the primacy of human reason, noted that "reason works over morals, as she works over everything."[4] What we present in the following pages is a theory of persuasion designed by nature and circumscribed by a biological metaphor.

For a clearer understanding of this biological metaphor, it would be useful to review briefly the Piagetian theory of mental development. Piaget's answer to the question of how a child learns—a product of over sixty years of research—utilized ideas transferred from his observations of organic growth. As a biologist he was intrigued by the idea that adaptation also plays an important part in how the human mind comprehends the physical and social environments. To account for what he perceived to be distinct changes in the thinking of each individual, Piaget postulated a series of invariant stages. These stages represented structured wholes which were the result of the learner's attempt to organize information and to adapt mentally to changing environmental circumstance.

In Piaget's view all of nature strives for equilibrium. Every living organism (including, where applicable, its mental functioning) grows through interaction with an environment. What makes this idea so revolutionary is that it rejects the traditional views which support either the primacy of heredity or the primacy of the environment. Piaget's view holds that neither dominates. Cognitive mental growth is accounted for by what he calls the twin actions of assimilation and accommodation. Just as the digestive system attempts to assimilate whatever food the organism provides, so also that same digestive system modifies itself through changes in shape and chemical action to accommodate the special type of nourishment consumed.

What Piaget expounded was an embryology of intelligence in which structures of the mind are built up through successive stages that are qualitatively different. Mental growth like physical growth exhibits differentiation and integration, which is to say that the parts become increasingly specialized while functioning ever more smoothly to attain a more completed whole.

Piaget's great insight was that mental growth is, by analogy, an extension of organic growth. The epigenesis of cognitive functioning implies a ceaseless striving for higher levels of equilibrium. The higher the equilibrium, the better will be the individual's mental adaptation. Logic, in this sense, then becomes an elaborate system of autoregulations. As Piaget stated in one of his more important works, "Cognitive functions are reflections of the essential mechanisms of organic autoregulation."[5] Carrying it a step further, and using Kohlberg's moral-developmental scheme as a base, I have grounded my understanding of rhetoric in the same biological metaphor.[6]

The model spun out in the pages to follow constitutes a theory of how moral ideologies are communicated. As an extension of Piagetian-Kohlbergian theory to the ordering of values within a social movement, it assumes that humans are persuadable animals and that through the process of communication they can be induced to think, and ultimately behave, in certain ways. An important corollary of this assumption is that to behave justly one must first understand what is just, and that any failure to act morally usually represents a failure in the developmental life-span of the individual. In a word, either someone did not send or someone did not receive an appropriate moralizing message—or both. And, finally, since our very place in nature carries enormous moral implications, it will also be tacitly assumed in these pages that nature defends herself from cultural assault largely through moral discourse. (Although this last statement may be self-evident to some and overly optimistic to others, it would probably take another book to prove.)

Whatever else the abortion question has or will become, its immediate and all-pervasive character, albeit subtle and hidden, is that of a great moral debate. That the basic moral character of the debate is not universally acknowledged is the main reason, in my judgment, why the issue has become so confused in the public mind. Though people decide to accept or reject abortion chiefly for reasons that are moral, they would prefer to think that they reached their decisions on some other ground for fear of being accused of imposing their private morality on others (an accusation which is itself a moral argument). Such thinking further aggravates misunderstanding because it tricks the unwary into avoiding some serious moral reasoning. Thus, the one area of knowledge accessible to everyone which can bring sense to the abortion controversy and augment its much-needed rigorous investigation is placed far in the background. What is required to cure this mass schizophrenia is not less moral reasoning but more. Just as the cure for bad democracy is not dictatorship but better democracy, so also the cure for bad moral reasoning is more and better moral reasoning. Despite the risk of discovering some basic and irreconcilable differences about the very nature of ethics, the moral thinking process must be brought to the foreground.

Moral arguments for or against abortion do not derive exclusively from a conventional religious perspective. Rather, they derive from the way in which the human mind perceives (or misperceives) the social world. Humanists, both secular and religious, have much in common as they engage in the process of forming moral judgments about abortion. They can respect the merits of reasoning, inquiry, and critical thinking. They can agree on a cognitive yardstick that will measure the kind and the quality of the moral reasoning that is to be used in the debate. In this endeavor the tenets of developmental psychology can provide an important meeting ground. Through the Kohlbergian paradigm, ideological strangers can be reconciled and bitterness can be alleviated. The full spectrum of moral arguments can be approached with greater clarity and understanding.

This short preview would be incomplete without a few sentences regarding the content of moral reasoning, a concept interwoven with the idea of justice, but a shadow concept in Kohlbergian theory. Content is the substance of moral judgment or what a person believes. It is the substantive material to which moral reasoning is applied: abortion, capital punishment, slavery. While Kohlberg is largely silent about the moral questions that can be plugged into his theory, some choices fit better than others; some, in fact, do not fit at all. Obviously, then, without a content there can be no moral reasoning. What is said in the pages to follow will therefore consider the process of relating form to content.[7]

$\square$

Not enough people understand persuasion and its purposes. Like almost everything else in the universe, we know very little about it, at least compared to what we could and should know. One fact, however, is now becoming increasingly apparent: the process of persuasion has a pattern built into our very natures. This pattern is an integral part of the individual's becoming aware of the correct rules of interpersonal behavior. The very minimum that can be said about persuasion is that it must coincide with how the human mind works; it must be tied to and express naturally occurring thought patterns.

There is an intimate connection between language and morality. The very words we choose to express a behavioral commitment toward others help make that commitment appear good or bad, desirable or undesirable. It is not enough to observe that all morality is embodied in language, however. New attention must be paid to the role of rhetoric in developing moral attitudes. Communicators must study the progression of ideas in moral discourse. Those who wish to understand the abortion debate can be no better advised than to acquire a knowledge of how morals grow and are expressed through social movements. After all, it may well be true that the primary function of a social movement is to facilitate the involvement of society in moral discourse, and that to understand the rhetoric of a social movement is to understand the physiology and pathology of morals. In any effort to effect fundamental social change, it is the task of rhetoric to turn society into a school without walls and to open moral dialogue.

Although definitions might be more wisely left to the end of the exposition, this much can be said here. Rhetoric will never be defined completely. All that can be reasonably expected is an ever-closer approximation. This, of course, is no scholarly flaw but an acknowledgment of the dynamic nature of the rhetorical enterprise.

Each investigator approaches his or her inquiry from a different perspective. My perspective is from the vantage point of social-movement activism and a deep interest in developmental psychology. I have come to believe that the function of rhetoric is to help individuals grow into new patterns of moral thinking. Over the individual's lifespan, these patterns are sequential, with each pattern tending to represent an increase in moral maturity. In this respect, rhetoric (and the symbolic) help free up or release the developmental inclination to grow morally. Rhetoric therefore introduces action and commitment to general moral education. And so conceived, it is, as we have said, inherently transformational.

□

The social organism does not often recognize the disease which afflicts it. With the best of intentions we do things now that prove harmful later. Vietnam and the environmental crisis are among recent examples. History is replete with others. Slavery became woven into the fabric of even the most civilized cultures before a determined few decided to put an end to it. Humanity's conscience learned to live with this monstrous injustice until the discrepancy between belief and act became too painful for further graceful accommodation. In America, for example, it took over a generation of concerted effort by a mere handful of zealots to rid the country of slavery. And it is noteworthy that, with few exceptions, the intellectuals did not flock to the abolitionist crusade. Most who read these pages probably could not mention more than a small handful of respected abolitionist thinkers: Whittier, Thoreau, Lowell, Emerson, Beecher. Where were all the others? Through timidity or ignorance they watched from the sidelines. The call to justice came from those sensitive few who saw the harm and accurately perceived the future. Through the rhetoric of the anti-slavery movement, society finally responded decisively, and America's actual behavior also became its ideal behavior. Would that the future consequence of mass abortion could now be foretold (and clearly understood by those who mold public policy).

America and the world are undecided about abortion. This uncertainty is reflected in opinion polls, in legislative voting patterns, and in the consciences of most citizens. Even the U.S. Supreme Court decision of January 22, 1973, and the more recent decision upholding the Hyde amendment have been unable to allay the widespread concern and deep divisions over the issue. Whatever final action is taken, however, one thing is certain: it must reflect a genuine national consensus or the agonizing debate will only continue. Education, the cornerstone of significant social change, must respond to the need for consensus building. As the epigraph by Lincoln pointed out, education, or the molding of public opinion, is fundamental to legislative and judicial action. Likewise, an uncultivated public opinion makes both impossible.

Why write another book about abortion? Not just because for the first time in history the question has become the focus of a heated national debate. Probably no other issue of values since slavery has been fought with such determination for so long a time. Not just because political careers have been launched, sustained, and ended by this issue. According to one poll, in the fall elections of 1978, 7 percent of the American voters said they would change their votes solely because of a candidate's stand on abortion.[8] We write here because those who are motivated enough to read this book—especially those who are uncommitted—have the capacity to change history. It is because just enough active people are concerned to make a difference. After all, the future is hardly shaped by the indifferent. Abortion is one of those rare issues that clearly reflects a national malaise. And dealing as it does with life and death, this issue tells us, perhaps more graphically than any other single issue, what we are as a people.

PART I

The Development
of Conscience

If you treat a person as he is, he will stay as he is; but if you treat him as if he were what he ought to be and could be, he will become what he ought to be and could be.

GOETHE

MORALITY AND RELIGION

To the detriment of clear thinking, the abortion debate has taken on a distinctly religious coloration. This, of course, is not to say that religion is inconsistent with clear thinking, but that what should be plainly argued on the basis of social intelligence and wisdom has now become confused with denominational theology. The "religious connection" is probably the most troublesome feature of the entire debate; it deserves our most careful consideration.

Twenty-five centuries ago, Western culture received one of the earliest philosophical explorations of the religio-moral relationship. In a well-quoted passage from one of Plato's dialogues, the relationship is summarized in a question asked by Socrates: "Now think of this. Is what is holy holy because the gods approve it, or do they approve it because it is holy?"[1] In more pedestrian language, is an action immoral because God forbids it, or does God forbid it because it is immoral? George McGovern in the 1972 presidential primary in Wisconsin faced this question obliquely in a characteristic and dramatic way. When asked by a questioner about his stand on abortion, he said that although he did not regard abortion as a federal matter, he did consider a fetus to be human. He added, however, that he was "not equipped theologically to discuss when the soul enters the fetus."[2] Clearly, the presidential hopeful had suggested that the question of when life begins is a religious issue, rather than a simple fact about the physical world. Such confused thinking is not an isolated example. More recently, presidential aspirant John Connally, in reconsidering his position on the Human Life Amendment, told a group of evangelical clergymen that "if convinced of 'a Biblical basis' for the anti-abortion cause, he would 'take another look' at the amendment."[3] The abortion controversy compels us to clarify some essential meanings. Without a better understanding of the relationship between religion and morality, ambiguities between them are bound to increase, and their natural affinities will become hopelessly snarled. In addition, any improved understanding of the relationship is necessary for a better grasp of certain important rhetorical principles.

Perhaps the greatest single challenge to an unimpeded view of the abortion debate is understanding the role played by religion. In general, the American public has always been more than a little confused about the role religion plays in a pluralistic society. William K. Frankena, a respected contemporary philosopher, has, in fact, called this role confusion "one of the central issues in our cultural crisis."[4] When the problem is carried over to the abortion controversy voices become dramatically intensified. One side faults the other for being irreligious, or, conversely, for being a pawn of some religion (usually Roman Catholicism). Such accusations add no light to the debate, only a considerable amount of recrimination which obscures the issue even further. Fanaticism on the side of religion or irreligion hampers rational discussion and stokes the fires of bigotry. An objective assessment is needed.

A common misconception about morality is that it is somehow a poor stepchild of religion. People often think of matters concerning sex or the use of alcohol as typical moral concerns. While moral judgments are certainly made in these areas, for most people they involve only a very limited sphere of moral activity. Of greater moral importance are judgments relating to justice and injustice. A strong case can be made for the claim that one coldhearted, unjust person could do more harm to society than a thousand inebriates or violators of sexual custom. In our contemporary world, moral judgments relating to war and peace or to the breakup of the home through divorce and desertion might be better candidates for social concern. Historians might even say that until fairly recently the issue of slavery was the most serious moral issue ever faced by the human race. Now, many would argue, as I do, that abortion is humanity's most important moral problem. But in any case, caring for one's offspring is universally regarded as an essential moral task.

Some of the religio-moral confusion in the abortion debate is caused by the fact that a purely rational approach to morality has been submerged or abandoned. It is not enough merely to call attention to this imbalance; I have attempted to rectify it by giving what is purely moral a greater emphasis, an attempt reflected in the title chosen for the book. "Conscience" is an ambiguous bridging term which suggests the inner life of religion as well as the inner voice of morality. In popular usage, it represents a guide to behavior without identifying its origin or path of development. Both the believer and nonbeliever will recognize it, with the former contending that it is given by and answers only to God. Righteousness, responsibility, sin, repentance, and confession also have religio-moral overtones and, as we shall see later, represent a reciprocity that is critical for a mature morality. I will contend along with Kohlbergian scholarship that morality is partly teleological, or goal oriented, in that it strives for the development of one's true nature: autonomous moral thinking.[5]

OBJECTS AND SUBJECTS

The abortion issue can be better understood by dealing separately with two dimensions of the problem: (1) the impersonal world of objects, or the physical world; and (2) the interpersonal world of subjects, or the moral world. When we consider the two questions that derive from these two dimensions we see that they are interrelated: "Is it human?" and "Should we abort it?" The first question is decidedly scientific: "Is intrauterine human life human?" The next question enters the moral realm: "How should this developing human life be treated?"[6]

Moral decision-making is a functional characteristic of the human mind which coordinates the point of view of moral agents or subjects. Strictly logical reasoning, on the other hand, which assists the moralizing outcome and remains at its core, is more recognizably involved with the myriad relationships found in the physical (scientific) world. The way we look at these two worlds, either singly or in combination, can be rational or irrational, but irrationality in the moral world is much more serious than in the physical world. Viewing the earth as flat and the center of the universe, for example, is not as tragic a misconception as support for slavery or abortion represents. Moral reasoning is a matter of deep human importance.

Although the physical and social worlds embrace different realms, both hold a common allegiance to logic. Moral thinking depends upon the logic of interpersonal relations, while its physical counterpart depends upon the logical categories of space and time, causality and chance, etc. Developmental psychology tells us that while the earliest periods of human mental growth are devoted to exploring the physical world, the natural process of aging is primarily a process of moral maturation. Also important to the normal process of maturation is the fact that human beings are not purely passive receptors in what they feel, think, or decide. They meet the moral world as active agents who assimilate until the logic of circumstance forces them to accommodate. The central feature of this approach is that "the human subject is a *creator*, not just a creature, *of meaning*" (italics in the original). [GKCS76b-39]

From the standpoint of developmental psychology, these twin dimensions of how one views the object and subject worlds are said to be isomorphic in that both, though clearly distinct, develop in parallel fashion. Morality, as we've said, deals primarily with interpersonal relations or conflicts arising from human interaction. It is cognition applied to social things. On the other hand, how we manipulate the object world is cognition applied to physical things. To say that someone is 5 feet 10 inches tall is to make a statement about the physical world. To say that someone is a suspected child molester is to make a statement about the sociomoral world. Both dimensions are commingled in the abortion controversy.

Although both object and subject worlds contain elements of emotion, the former arouses far less. The continuum in Figure 1 shows this. "Should I cheat on my upcoming exam?" is primarily a moral question, while determining the trajectory of a comet is mainly a scientific one. Of course, a comet's trajectory has emotional significance when it is learned that it will come perilously close to the earth.

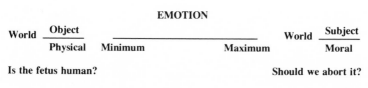

Figure 1.

The moral or socio-emotional involves directly human concerns which can inspire great passion. Object and subject are but two aspects of a single mental act. They are separated here for clarity of analysis. To understand the abortion debate adequately, one must be willing to make this distinction.

Recently a poll was taken by the American Institute of Public Opinion which exemplifies the dichotomy we have been discussing. When the respondents were asked about the beginning of human life and about the Supreme Court decision that allows a woman to obtain an abortion, a close correlation was apparent. Of those who thought that human life begins at: (1) conception—27 percent favored the court ruling, 66 percent opposed it, and 7 percent had no opinion; (2) birth—73 percent favored the ruling, 20 percent opposed, and 7 percent had no opinion; and (3) some point between—70 percent favored, 21 percent opposed, and 9 percent had no opinion. Quite clearly this indicates that two categories of questions were asked concerning (1) when human life begins and (2) one's attitude toward abortion. Taken together, these categories reveal the dual mental functions of knowing and feeling. Answering the first category—Is unborn life human?—demands a physical explanation, while answering the second category—Should unborn human life be aborted?—calls for a psychological explanation. The results of the poll were not surprising. Those who believed that human life begins at conception also tended to oppose the Supreme Court decision; those who did not, tended to favor it.[7]

Results such as these are hardly very startling. It would be surprising to find the opposite true: i.e., that those who felt life begins at birth also felt that human life should be protected from conception by means of a constitutional amendment. Conversely, it would be unlikely that those who felt that human life begins at conception would not be disposed to protect it, given the opportunity.[8] What this and similar polls suggest is that how we view the physical world somehow influences our view of the moral world. While the reverse might also be true to some degree under certain conditions (how one views the moral world might affect one's view of the physical world), the relationship is not clearly understood. Further empirical research is needed to bring this intriguing relationship into sharper focus.

THE NATURAL LAW

The testable characteristics of a psychology of moral growth and the presuppositions about rhetoric which inevitably flow from it force one to consider a Natural Law Theory of Morality. In Western thought the natural law is known as the universal law applicable to all humans; in rabbinic teaching it is akin to those minimal moral duties embodied in the Laws of the Sons of Noah, or the Noachide Laws. In this regard, my position is that of Aquinas. What is right and wrong, including abortion, is not dependent on God's will; however, because of God's inherent nature, He always does right and could never approve of wrong, including abortion.

Natural Law Theory stipulates that moral truths, for example that killing and lying are evil, are independent of culture and experience; they can be discovered by reason alone, and their discovery needs no assistance from revelation. In much the same vein Kohlberg writes, "The natural law perspective holds that there are universal or natural principles of justice which should guide all societies and which are known to man by reason independent of specific religious revelation." [K74c-5] Whatever the Bible or any other sacred book may say about abortion, the conclusion derived from such sources belongs to the realm of moral theology. On the other hand, whatever the mind unaided by revelation concludes about abortion belongs to the realm of moral philosophy. Aquinas summarizes the matter succinctly by saying, "The theologian considers sin chiefly as an offence against God; and the moral philosopher, as something contrary to reason."[9] All that a rhetoric of moral philosophy demands is that, in shaping morality through persuasion, an individual consult human reason first before consulting any sacred book.

It is not my intention to go further into the Theory of Natural Law beyond simply calling the reader's attention to the United Nations Declaration of the Rights of the Child, which advocates legal protection for both the born and the unborn.[10] The UNDRC is important because of the great diversity of religious and moral outlooks among those who were involved in its creation. It certainly comes as close as any political document can to a Law of Nature in regulating human conduct.[11]

A knowledge of natural-law thinking can help one acquire a fuller understanding and appreciation of cognitive moral development. In addition, the theory offers a common ground for humanists and nonhumanists on both sides of the abortion controversy. It also provides an approach to moral reasoning which can unite believers and nonbelievers. I find it easy to agree with Macquarrie, who advocates rethinking the meaning of natural law and who feels that the rehabilitation of natural law is "an urgent task today."[12] He calls it "foundational to morality" and an "inner drive toward authentic personhood . . . presupposed in all particular ethical traditions."[13] Echoing Kohlberg's moral developmentalism, he views Christian moral education as an "unfolding of the 'natural' morality of all men."[14]

The abortion controversy has reflected some alarmingly defective thinking which confuses religion and morality. As an antidote, what needs to be stressed is that morality and its expression through rhetoric should be grounded in human nature. What is normative to the orthodox Judeo-Christian tradition is that God's will is moral. He commands actions because they are right. Morality considered from the viewpoint of religion is, and should be, autonomous. God wants us to be autonomous moral agents because that is our true nature. In short, like the medieval Scholastic concept of nature, morality is simultaneously autonomous and God-directed.

     ☐

Kohlberg and his associates tell us that a logical mind, or one adept at dealing with abstractions in manipulating the physical world, is a necessary but not sufficient ingredient in moral reasoning. In one study, Kohlberg reported that although 60 percent may reach the highest tiers or registers of logical thought, only 10 percent may reach an equivalent level or degree of moral thought. [KG7li-1071] It may very well be that moral reasoning is a more reliable index of logical reasoning than the opposite. History, after all, is full of intelligent scoundrels as well as those who were morally gullible and misguided. A recurring theme in the analysis to follow is that we are all selectively insensitive in certain areas of our moral decision-making. From a purely objective viewpoint, those who accept abortion as morally right, regardless of their general intellectual abilities, have failed to exhibit maturity in a vital moral decision-making area—respect for human life. And, conversely, those who reject abortion absolutely, fail to exhibit mature moral decision-making in not considering the plight of the distressed woman.

As applied to the abortion debate, an important lesson to be learned from the Kohlberg findings is that one should not be impressed with the intellectual credentials of noted individuals who speak out in favor or disfavor of abortion. Academic degrees or Nobel Prizes do not make a person moral. The obvious fact is that not all intelligent people teach at universities or have lengthy publishing records. The sons and daughters of the poor have consciences as finely wrought as those of the rich, the well-born, or the so-called egghead. What should be emphasized is that while moral development presupposes general intellectual development, moral reasoning does not arise automatically from intelligence; evidence indicates that it develops independently and in parallel fashion. Logic and morality are certainly correlated but not causally. Impressive intellectual credentials can be misleading measures of moral functioning. Evil may be done with great maturity.

Polls can never substitute for morality, because morality is not determined by head count. At best, polls can only reflect how moral or immoral a nation is. Apart from such reflections of public opinion, however, an objective morality is that which concerns the degree of respect we hold toward ourselves and our fellow human beings. Activities like abortion or slavery, which are marked with a disregard for those rights which all humans possess, are moral activities. The choice of behavior flowing from them is a matter of judgment or reasoning. To constitute a moral problem, one activity must be in conflict with another activity and usually involve a second party (i.e., to live or die, to be free or enslaved). In this sense, most social situations are not moral but discretionary since there is no interpersonal conflict. Morality is a shared system of expectations for regulating human behavior—an action guide for persons and groups. As will be seen later, individuals have been observed to develop morally through predictable stagelike episodes of reasoning. And although the episodes are sequential, they may also be viewed as concurrently existing styles of thought.

Dissociated from the actual judgment made, for example that abortion is right or wrong, the moral thinking used to arrive at the judgment is a patterned or structured process. Kohlberg draws this distinction clearly when he asserts that "the concrete choice made by a person is the *content* of one's moral judgment" and "one's reasoning about the choice defines the *structure* of one's moral judgment" (italics in the original). [KW80f-561] Developmental psychologists claim that over the individual human life-span there is an evolutionary process at work similar to that which occurs in society as a whole. I contend that the forms of moral judgment, at least in the more advanced categories, are linked only to certain moral outcomes. There are correct and incorrect moral choices, and the ideal form of reasoning fits certain choices better than others. One commentator asserts that "the higher one moves up the developmental scale, the greater the likelihood that the behavioral choice will favor one side of a two-choice conflict."[15] Kohlberg himself shows how his empirically based developmental theory supports the idea that capital punishment is unacceptable to morally mature individuals. [K80a-67] He writes that ". . . our conception of moral principle implies that one cannot ultimately separate form and content in moral analysis." [K71c-60] To this, we would add, and we will contend throughout the pages to follow, that whatever form the moral reasoning may take, abortion is always morally unacceptable except when involved with the absolute dilemma of having to choose one physical life over that of another.

☐

An important question to be asked is: Does one have to be religious to be moral? This, of course, depends on one's definition of religion—a question this book does not treat. Does religion even imply a theistic concept? Those who claim to be atheists may in fact be unconscious believers, while believers may unconsciously resist their religious affiliation. This may also be true with attitudes toward abortion. Atheists who oppose abortion may be unconsciously receptive to religion.[16] In the face of these unprovable hypotheses, we are forced to consider certain facts. Of particular importance is the recognition that an awareness of justice and injustice preceded any revealed religion. The ancient Hebrews, for example, acknowledged that Gentiles could be righteous and share in the kingdom of heaven. And equally important is the knowledge that the common intelligence of humanity

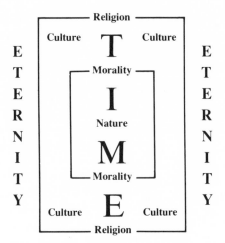

Figure 2.

has nearly always considered abortion to be less than noble. Western civilization received its secular attitude on abortion in part from the Hippocratic Oath, which rejected the practice some five hundred years before the Christian era. Both of these historical facts would appear to argue persuasively against any essential connection between morality and religion, especially in the context of human abortion.

Strictly speaking, the moral, wherever possible, enters into an alliance with the religious—an alliance found in many social movements concerning basic human values (slavery, prohibition, etc.). Religion adds a new or extra dimension to morality. It helps make morality personal and functional. It gives morality greater motivation, inspiration, or vision—"a courage of participation which sustains community in confrontation with privatism and totalitarianism." [PK80c-367][17] A religious outlook, along with Kohlbergian developmentalism [K71b], helps to link *is* to *ought*, or the facts of the moral situation to what one should do about them. (For example, abortion *is* killing, and it is something one *ought* not to do.) Ironically, abortion is one of those issues that both clouds and accentuates the differences between religion and morality. It is an issue touching both structures intimately. The diagram in Figure 2 expresses this relationship. The two boxes represent the spheres of morality and religion, with morality guarding the relationship between nature and culture (what people do with nature) and religion guarding the relationship between time and eternity. Each, as it were, interfaces or bridges the two great chasms in human experience.

Considered as a subset of religion, morality is necessary but not sufficient for a genuine religious outlook. This does not imply that religion causes morality, but that it adds to the moral message a repetition and intensity the message would not otherwise possess. A world without religion would be a world of people who might never hear the moral message, or at least might never hear it clearly and completely. A realistic assessment of the human condition requires that moral messages be repeated often and be of sufficient volume to compete with human frailty. This is why effective communication in social movements is so critical to moral education. Without its religious amplification, the pan-human abortion proscription, which has been called a near constant in history, would remain below the threshold of human audibility. Religion is critically important to the promulgation of the universal moral code.

Although religion and morality are intertwined and should be considered inseparable, they can be viewed independently for purposes of analysis. The following paradigm, by no means exhaustive, discusses several points of intersection. Bear in mind that what is strictly moral or strictly religious is difficult to determine.

MORALITY	RELIGION
1. Emphasizes how one treats others (human to human)	1. Emphasizes how one treats God (human to God)
Includes or fosters a proper love for the other	Includes or fosters a proper love for the self
2. Relates to the here (this world)	2. Relates to the hereafter (other world)
Encompasses the finite (accommodates)	Encompasses the infinite (assimilates)
Interfaces nature and culture	Interfaces time and eternity
3. Stresses obligation in human action—"having to"	3. Stresses commitment in human action—"wanting to"
Concerns the problems of existing (synchronic)	Concerns the problems of growing (diachronic)
Pursues justice	Pursues love
4. Represents shape or organization of response (moral)	4. Represents intensity and frequency of response (moral)
5. Relies upon reason (derivative)	5. Relies upon revelation (nonderivative)
Reflects religion (an effect)	Grounds morality (a cause)

In short, religion as a more expansive entity becomes the background or frame to the foreground or picture of morality.[18] And, to use a convenient metaphor, if religion is the general long-range climate, morality is the specific short-range weather.

It is a truism that how one treats the *other* determines one's relationship to God. To promote justice is for the religious person to participate in a divine activity. Yet, before one can relate to another morally, one must have a self to share. How we view the self affects intimately how we view the other. Hence, religion teaches one to be true to the self. As Shakespeare the poet had Polonius say, "To thine own self be true, and it must follow as the night the day, thou canst not then be false to any man." And again as Andrew Greeley the priest has written, to be moral one must get out of the self but have a self to get out of.[19] Religion helps build a profile of the healthy self. While not actually neglecting duties toward the other, it emphasizes how to treat the self.[20] It defines what it means to be human and answers the question, "Why be moral?" Without religion, morality is in danger of being oriented totally to the other. One merits the world to come by fulfilling one's obligations in this world. And as religious thinking would assert, since God is a moral being, to break a moral law is to displease God. Morality, like everything else, depends on God. Finally, as the great biblical story of Abraham and Isaac graphically illustrates (my interpretation), our relationship to God is more important than our relationship to other people.[21]

JUSTICE

Experiences of moral conflict abound in the abortion debate. Such conflicts must inevitably occur because the debate focuses upon discrepancies in what we value. Religion recognizes these discrepancies but transcends them by also requiring commitment, care, and compassion. If justice is the process of giving each his or her due, there is no justice that is due compassion, since compassion transcends justice. Yet, in the absence of a genuine love, the outcome of the struggle between the right-to-life and the right-to-choose can be decided only through the principle of justice. Kohlberg asks "Where human claims compete, whose claim does the loving person choose?" [K77e-194] Whose role we should assume, with whom we should identify, are conflicts only a clear sense of justice can resolve. We now turn to a brief consideration of the moral principle of justice.

The physical and social worlds discussed earlier are translated respectively into the realms of science and justice. Abortion, in violating the normal human perception of the physical world, also violates the requirements of justice. And it is this latter violation, so difficult for those who feel outraged to tolerate, that sends people into the streets, puts fresh batteries in bullhorns, and spawns large-scale social movements. In a strictly logical sense, there is an inability, while holding humanness constant, to move backward in time from the hiatus of birth to the moment of conception. Abortion of human offspring represents a socially sanctioned response to this inability. The very word "offspring" takes on a much narrower meaning, since born and unborn as descriptions of offspring are no longer conceptually interchangeable. In justice, the failure in reciprocity between the inalienable right-to-life and the stern duty to protect it is seen simply in what abortion accomplishes—the destruction of human life. Any right-to-life grounded on a universal principle of justice inheres in the mere fact of being human. When innocent life is destroyed, the reciprocals of rights and duties are abandoned, and in turn the basic understanding of the social contract is violated.

Justice, of course, is related to logic and is independent of any specific religious tradition. The relationship is found in the fact that both justice and logic are expressions of a judgment in equilibrium. In simplified Piagetian terms, the structures of human thought must be matched with the structures of the social and physical environments for truth to emerge. This relationship is further expressed in the notions of equality and reciprocity. Logic claims that all human beings are created equal, since the same basic genetic material is possessed by all. Homo sapiens, without exception, belong to the same breeding stock. A unique chromosomal structure sets them apart from the rest of animate nature and proclaims that they are what they are, namely, human. Cognizant of this scientific reality, justice therefore claims that the interactive affairs of humans ought to be conducted in complete reciprocity, or treating like for like.

According to Kohlberg, the core of any moral system ought to be the principle of justice. It is the best index to morality and is its highest expression. As a universal guide for human conduct, its function is to address competing claims in such a way that all humans are given their due (including unborn humans). Society is founded on this principle: it is central to moral judgment and constitutes a practical organizing concept for moral education. Justice, as will be shown later, is refined through a series of stages. In the American context, it frequently appears under the guise of fairness or fair play. Only justice can resolve human conflicts adequately. Only justice can provide an adequate basis for determining what is moral and what is immoral.

A blindfolded woman with scales balanced is the familiar symbol of an idealized justice. Sightless impartiality becomes the symbolic equivalent of an equilibrium between opposing parties and between crime and its punishment. The metaphor associates a disinterestedness in judgment regarding the reciprocity between competing claims. Whose claim is satisfied can best be determined by the principle of justice. In treating like for like and giving each his or her due justice generates the ultimate equilibration—a universalized reciprocity. And the study of justice becomes the study of symmetrical interpersonal relations.

A sense of justice is a natural emergent in life which inheres in the human experience. In order for it to arise, however, social interaction is necessary. Piaget emphasizes this by saying: ". . . [T]he rule of justice is a sort of immanent condition of social relationships or a law governing their equilibrium."[22] Kohlberg agrees that it is an "ideal equilibrium of social interaction" [K71b-194; K71c-53] and further observes that "when a society has arrived at a relatively just solution to a conflict, that solution tends to be maintained, whereas a situation of injustice is always a situation of disequilibrium." [K76d-12] When rights and duties are in balance or cancel each other out, justice prevails. The speed and certainty with which justice emerges as an equilibrating factor in human society are the responsibility of all those who seek a just world. Human actors within the context of social movements are the leaven that facilitates this emergence.

In an open and pluralistic society, the principle of justice lies behind the social order. In democratic societies it is the warp and woof of constitutions from which they derive their basic moral character. Justice is the soul of morality and of a civil society morally based. It is the only principle in the abortion debate that can be truly universalized. Morality, expressed by justice, dictates to law and is its final judge.

The principle of justice must be tied to the law of nature, or the legal system when deciding any moral issue will be plagued by endless inconsistencies. For proof, the reader need only witness the mounting court challenges to *Roe* v. *Wade*, the watershed U.S. Supreme Court decision of 1973 which swept away most legal restrictions regarding abortion.[23] These will surely increase as the pro-life movement gains momentum. To propose the inviolability of human life, on one hand, and then on the other hand to violate it through abortion is to spurn an equality and reciprocity that are the bulwarks of the natural law of morality and of any universal sense of justice. Both distributive and commutative justice are undermined, thereby placing the weak at the mercy of the strong. Without recourse to a true sense of justice, the abortion debate will remain unsolvable.

□

The aspect of the abortion controversy which receives the greatest public, and therefore rhetorical, attention is indeed that of morality. Religion is often confused with this morality, either inadvertently or intentionally by the abortion apologists, but the fact that those who believe in no God can favor or oppose abortion shows the fragility of the religious connection. Unless someone has lived a rather sheltered life, plain intellectual honesty would force him or her to admit this nonconnection. Nonreligious anti-abortionists, in fact, have become outspoken in their disaffiliation with any theistic pro-life position. During the June, 1978 convention of the National Right to Life Committee in St. Louis, there were placards bearing the unabashed statement "Atheists for Life." It would be totally unrealistic to label abortion as primarily a religious issue or exclusively the province of one religion, be it Catholicism or some brand of Christian fundamentalism. To emphasize any religious element in the abortion debate overlooks the basic moral convictions which religion has traditionally reinforced. This distortion may make a few propaganda points by arousing religious animosity, but truth has been slighted in the process.

The emphasis of this book is on moral judgments and how they are influenced through effective communication. Moral judgments are those rational determinations which are regulated by human interaction and thus have human consequences. In contrast with judgments pertaining to aesthetics and prudence, morality deals not with decisions of beauty and wise action, but with correct rules of interpersonal behavior. Moral judgment or moral decision-making should be understood as possessing a rational core. It is this reliance upon rationality that destines the moral enterprise to ultimate success. Contrary to popular opinion about the human mind, people prefer being rational to being irrational. We prefer that small but reliable voice of reason. Given enough time and enough insight and prodding, we will mend our ways to conform to the dictates of logic.

As will also be seen later, when we discuss in detail the most mature stages or modes of moral growth, the natural evolution of moral thinking within the individual appears to move ultimately to a religious view of the universe and of our place in it. The question, why should one be moral, can be answered only by a religious outlook; as we noted earlier, religion constitutes the cosmic background to the terrestrial human foreground of the moral life. One of the major contributions of the Gestalt perspective is that background and foreground are inherently and inseparably related. To have one without the other in any meaningful way is like the Zen practitioner's attempt to clap with only one hand.

The themes of justice and a respect for human life are elaborated over and over again by religion. In addition, and perhaps more importantly, religion brings basic moral structures within the essential range of human audibility. In fact, it is able to turn up the volume 100 percent if necessary. Although I realize that metaphors like this eventually break down and should not be carried too far, it is still possible to say that religion is an amplifier or hearing aid for those moral concerns which might not be heard otherwise. In short, it provides the conscience with good acoustics. It holds up an ideal of principled morality and helps give morality its justification.

Religion assimilates morality and while existentially integrated with it is also superordinate to it. Obviously, religion can do more for morality than morality can do for religion. A religious outlook advances moral growth. It provides people with hope and encourages them to solve their moral problems. It gives them breathing space to discern the true nature of the human condition. Contrary to the Marxian belief that it is the opiate of the people, religion requires more than simply coping—it compels us to change. By emphasizing autonomous moral decision-making, religion always intrudes upon the great moral issues confronting humankind and is (or should be) at the heart of every social movement concerning fundamental human rights.

An essential ingredient of the Judeo-Christian religious tradition is that morality is not futile but carries an important meaning. Reinhold Niebuhr said it well: ". . . any scheme of values is finally determined by the ultimate answer which is given to the ultimate question about the meaning of life."[24] Every moral code, including that part of the code dealing with abortion, depends upon an ultimate belief about ourselves and our place in the universe.

STRUCTURES OF THOUGHT

We strive for moral maturity. It is our developmental epitaph, be it glory or condemnation. Certain environmental factors, created and controlled through the educational function of social movements, can strengthen or weaken this striving. My intention is to show how this might be accomplished. Before I attempt to suggest a workable methodology, however, I must first describe a reliable substructure of theory. As has been said many times before, there is nothing so practical as a good theory.

At the outset, there is one key term that must be defined: the cognitive. The meaning of this term represents the limits of our theory—its potential strength and weakness. In essence, it concerns the strictly intellectual activity associated with reasoning or making judgments about the physical and social worlds. The cognitive judges and defines a situation. It might be better understood through comparison and contrast with two other psychological terms: the affective and conative. The affective concerns feelings or emotions; the conative concerns willing or action and is considered neutral with regard to the moral realm. Taken together these terms trisect the spectrum of mental functioning found useful in understanding human motivation. Since the Piagetian-Kohlbergian research has concentrated upon the cognitive and provides the basis for our own theoretical formulations, the cognitive will be the ordering and umbrella term for our conception of moral development.

GROWTH AND DIFFERENTIATION

Development is the biological concept from which everything we say about human mental functioning (and persuasion) is derived. It implies, above all else, a striving of the organism for greater organization or complexity. The developmental thrust is toward ever more effective adaptations marked by higher levels of balance between the organism and its environment. Piaget perceived by analogy that the human mind, as it attempts to make sense out of the physical and moral worlds, operates like any biological organism; it assimilates everything it can from its environment and accommodates to everything it cannot change. In this developmental process nature and culture always tend to move in the direction of more effective functioning. Striving for greater states of equilibrium, the organism (including the human mental function) is able to integrate and differentiate its parts. For the Piagetian structuralist, "human intelligence is simply a subset of biological functioning."[25]

Webster's Third New International Dictionary supplies the following intransitive form of the verb *to develop*:

...... 1a: to go through a process of natural growth, differentiation, or evolution by successive changes from a less perfect to a more perfect or more highly organized state: advance from a simpler form or state of existence to one more complex either in structure or function <a blossom ~s from a bud> <the fever ~s normally> <the embryo ~s into a well-formed animal> ......

A secondary definition is also revealing:

...... 2a: to become gradually visible or manifest <as the photographic negative ~s> <his interest ~ed as he watched her> b: to become apparent: come to light <it ~s that neither one paid the bill> <they waited to see what would ~ next> ......

By permission. From *Webster's Third New International Dictionary* © 1981 by G. & C. Merriam Company, Publishers of the Merriam-Webster ® Dictionaries.

The meanings contained in these definitions touch upon the basic ingredients of any developmental theory of mental functioning and are implied in the very nature of moral discourse.

Applied to our immediate topic of moral development, in the first definition (1a), development refers to a growth in outlook or perspective involving interpersonal relations and the conflicts they engender. Judgments are made about the rightness or wrongness, the good or evil of certain actions. At the heart of this moral developmental process is human reason or the cognitive ability. In the second definition (2a), development refers to the slow unfolding of the principle of justice which governs moral action choices. Early in the upward developmental spiral, the individual is oriented toward the *self*, but as growth occurs he or she gradually becomes oriented toward the *other*.

DEVELOPMENT

Self (egocentrism)   Low   High   Other (sociocentrism)

Figure 3.

DEVELOPMENT

External (constraint)   Low   High   Internal (cooperation)

Figure 4.

DEVELOPMENT

Heteronomous (dependent)   Low   High   Autonomous (independent)

Figure 5.

More technical terminology would describe a movement from *ego-centrism* to *sociocentrism*. Egocentrism is present in varying but diminishing degree until complete sociocentrism is reached and vice versa. The simple diagram in Figure 3 shows this. The sociocentric (high) end of the continuum includes value-centered concerns for the common good. Some might consider these concerns to reflect an existential outlook.

Reasoning which attempts to resolve moral conflicts undergoes a metamorphosis. Over the moral life-span of every individual this metamorphosis follows a course of development from lower to higher forms. The following series of diagrams will help describe this process from various angles. To begin with, moral reasoning can be said to start from *external* motivations that are induced by the *constraint* of pain and pleasure, etc., and then to move toward *internal* motivations that are induced by the desire for *cooperation*. (See Figure 4). Piaget speaks of these two reasoning extremes as *heteronomous* and *autonomous*. The former implies a *dependent* kind of motivation arising, as expected, from outside the decision-maker, while the latter repre-

DEVELOPMENT

Unilateral (consequence) Low   High Interdependent (intention)

Figure 6.

DEVELOPMENT

Concrete (specific) Low   High Abstract (general)

Figure 7.

DEVELOPMENT

Immature (irresponsible) Low   High Mature (responsible)

Figure 8.

sents an *independent* kind of motivation arising, again as expected, from inside the individual and constituting a belief in one's own accountability for moral action. (See Figure 5). But while heteronomy and autonomy do not describe the individual's total mental orientation, there does appear to be a natural movement from outer- to inner-directed behavior or from *unilateral* to *interdependent* concerns. There is a shift from a reliance upon outcome or *consequence* in assessing moral behavior to a reliance upon *intention*. (See Figure 6.) And from reasoning that is *concrete* and *specific*, the movement is toward reasoning that is *abstract* and *general*. (See Figure 7.) Finally, when we move more deeply into our analysis from surface to center, we will see more clearly why the overarching progression is from reasoning that is *immature* and *irresponsible* to reasoning that is *mature* and *responsible*. (See Figure 8.)

Thinking about mental development in general forces one to isolate a function like moral reasoning and trace its progression to maturity. From a growth perspective, persuasion and its motivational component can be demonstrated to occur at least partly through competence or the desire to master a mental or physical task. This means that within a developmental perspective, to perform an action well becomes its own reward; it is not necessarily the exclusive result of external stimulation. To advance developmentally is to achieve a more competent and, hence, satisfactory level of activity. In Piagetian-Kohlbergian terms, structures presented by the exigencies of the human environment and those within the human mind would be in better equilibrium.

Development represents a pulling along a fixed motivational course in which each new bend or upward spiral represents a greater degree of reasoning power, and the goal of full maturity is approached as iron approaches a magnet. This magnetic attraction, as it were, follows a motivational path of least resistance. Because the next stage up always seems to work better in resolving moral conflicts, it is apprehended and the previous stage is abandoned. In relation to classical learning theory, and in significant contrast to it, a developmental paradigm provides a channeling effect in which the parameters for any stimulus-response motivation are controlled. Piaget's developmental theory is clearly more applicable to the rhetoric of social movements than theories of persuasion based on rigid stimulus-response models.

Another important feature of Piagetian-Kohlbergian developmental theory is that it is dominated by a preference for neither the innate nor the environmental. It operates through a process of interaction between the structuring tendencies of the human mind and the countless structures of the physical and social worlds. Human thought is, therefore, looked upon as a structuring process. The human organism is active rather than passive. Its inherent freedom (or lack of it) lies in structuring a perceived world. As we will see later, those who would communicate a coherent system of moral values within a social movement can best do so by helping audiences to structure their own natural perceptions of the social world.

One of the ingredients necessary for moral development is human experience. By definition, nurture takes place through experience; it is embodied in all the opportunities for growth afforded by the environment. Culture represents part of the human environment and serves as a nexus for growth opportunities. Yet the experiential advantages of any given culture differ throughout the world. What remains universal, and requisite to our theory, is the developmental pattern that transcends culture. It is this universal pattern that Kohlberg has constructed from and verified with his many cross-cultural studies. He claims to have made the first attempt in history to conduct cross-cultural work in morality. His success awaits the verdict of additional scholarship.

☐

Kohlberg thinks of moral development as a process involving certain criteria. These are: (1) change in the general shape, pattern, or organization of response; (2) qualitative difference in response; (3) irreversibility (once there, always there); (4) universal stepwise invariant sequence (no steps are missed); (5) hierarchy of functioning; and (6) differentiation and integration. [KK69b-(98-9)] His theory does not take account of frequency and intensity of response, or associationistic learning possibilities; and, significantly, it does not emphasize either the content of the response (what one believes) or its correctness. Being a purely psychological theory, it attempts to determine how one believes or the way one thinks and not necessarily how well one thinks morally. The latter question, of course, is left to the discipline of philosophy. Kohlberg's theory presents a road map for ideal moral development. It is fundamentally form-oriented.

A person with common sense will also realize that growth in nature is not inevitable and that there are bound to be developmental tendencies which in some instances are normal and in other instances markedly abnormal. In the moral sphere, developmental disabilities do occur, and the environment often deflects, in whole or in part, the normal course of moral growth. Fortunately, as Kohlberg has shown in some of his work, and as social-movement activists the world over readily assume, moral disabilities, like physical ones, can usually respond to a wise and aggressive therapy. People can be reformed. And a healthy moral development in one area can be generalized to other areas. The question always left unanswered is: if human life can be respected by some people in some situations, why can't it be respected by all people in all situations?

The idea of developmental transformations in thinking about the object and subject worlds is certainly not new and hardly revolutionary. What may be at least open to question, however, is whether those who oppose abortion may be predisposed to grasping the developmental perspective easily. It would appear that for anti-abortionists, form, organization, or pattern should have inherent meaning; they should be able to perceive the constancy of humanity through all the transformations of intrauterine growth. An understanding of moral development is only one step removed from this and seems to be a warrantable extension of an empirically validated idea. I have found through experience, however, that although a basic understanding of development seems to come naturally, what is new, and perhaps even revolutionary, is the possibility of shaping this common-sense idea into an educational methodology.

Embedded within the concept of moral development is a theory of persuasion that can be applied to both the oral and written discourse of social movements. What was said in the preface bears repeating: it is the hope and purpose of this book to disclose as clearly as possible the nature of such a theory. Without a developmental perspective, rhetorical theory falls far short of explaining what really happens in the educational process of a social movement. In an open and pluralistic society, the goals of collective action are achieved primarily through persuasion. While vitriol, legal coercion, and the threat of force through social disruption always remain options, my experience has reinforced my acceptance of the truth of the old saw, "a mind convinced against its will is of the same opinion still." Until now, academicians investigating the phenomenon of mass persuasion have relied upon assumptions and methods of analysis that were traditionally applied to single-speaker, single-audience communications. However, what is useful in understanding the microcosm of persuasion is not wholly adequate to a proper understanding of the macrocosm. What has been largely overlooked is the special way moral problems are handled by the human mind. That way is distinctly and decidedly developmental.

To teach justice is to teach moral development. The concept of development is therefore critical to any realistic assessment of the abortion debate. And it is critical for two reasons: first, the idea of development provides an ultimate rationale for analyzing all pertinent moral arguments (whether correct or incorrect); and second, it establishes a plausible theory of human motivation. Thus developmental theory is applicable to the rhetoric of all social movements that arise from challenges to universal human rights. The rhetoric of the abolitionist crusade, for example, can readily be explained by recourse to a similar developmental paradigm. In this analysis, however, we will confine our observations solely to the issue of abortion.

Let us now sum up what has been said so far. Our theory of moral persuasion requires no internal drive states and does not need the reinforcement from the external environment that is so characteristic of most current theories. Neither nature nor nurture dominates. How one apprehends the moral world, as well as how one apprehends the physical world, is a gradual process which moves toward ever-more-precise equilibrium. The task of the educator or persuader, which will be explained in greater detail later, is to further this equilibrating process. His or her task is aided by the inherent human appreciation of the rational. We assume throughout these pages that the voice of reason, no matter how small, if permitted to grow and if appealed to effectively, will eventually bring succor and enable us to solve our moral problems (or at least to outlive them).

All of this would be so much academic esoterica if it were not for the fact that we are all affected by the rhetoric of social movements. The reality of more than a million abortions a year in America (and many more times that number worldwide) should be a sobering fact to those on both sides of the controversy. Those who welcome or reject this fact, and perhaps even those who may be indifferent, should at least be aroused enough to try to understand concepts that may provide a more satisfactory explanation of how fundamental social change is effectuated and how its course, if need be, is altered.

Stage and Sequence

A theory of stages breaks the concept of development into discrete units. Bearing in mind that people are both consistent and inconsistent in their thinking (and often at the same time), one focuses upon certain discontinuities, instead of focusing upon the more obvious continuities of thought. In moral terms these distinct elements may be likened to a sequence of philosophies for adjudicating disputes, or a series of coping mechanisms for dealing with social reality. They are universal categories or total ways of thinking. As Piaget would say, each stage is a "psychological whole" used to delineate thought or bring a moral question into a special focus. These clustered wholes represent a restructuring of thought on moral issues. Like a series of small stones that when dropped sequentially into water can generate concentric waves moving outward, with each new wave encompassing more physical space than the last produced, so too each new moral stage is destined to encompass a wider field of social experience.

The concepts developed by Lawrence Kohlberg have taken root in American religious education, particularly within institutions associated with the Roman Catholic church.[26] "Whenever there are conflicts between people and their claims," Kohlberg writes, "such conflicts are best resolved by a process of moral discussion and reasoning. This process can go on at various levels which we call moral stages." [KKSH75e-246] As a specialist in moral development, he sought to expand the Piagetian construct through a series of impressive scholarly essays. The developmental approach contained therein is empirically based and is now being extended by associates throughout the world. An important body of literature in the area of personal moral development thus continues to grow. Its application to areas outside strictly classroom settings is just beginning and bodes a bright future for the general theory. This volume, in fact another response to Kohlberg's views, attempts to link his developmental perspective to the broad educational and rhetorical dimensions of social movements.[27]

With Piaget as an inspiration, Kohlberg worked out a developmental theory using hypothetical moral dilemmas. While in graduate school at the University of Chicago in the early fifties, he began posing a series of questions involving contradictory moral-action choices to a select group of over 70 American boys. These questions enabled the participants to deal with the action choices on more of a personal level, rather than simply talking about them in a detached sense.[28] His findings, based on examinations conducted at yearly intervals, have produced a typology of moral thought processes, or a method for understanding how humans think about moral problems. This typology now consists of six basic stages and a seventh which, as yet, has not been clearly formulated. The stages were eventually derived from ten hypothetical moral dilemmas that permitted several possible but mutually exclusive solutions. Some of the dilemmas employed in the continuing study were taken from medieval religious texts used in teaching morality.

Stages are related to what Kohlberg calls "aspects" or "issues" or "values." [K71a-400] In his own words they are "categories of responses to moral situations, regardless of the content of those responses" and "appear to be the basic cognitive pieces which are used in real, deliberative structuring of problematic situations of moral conflict." [BK73d-362] They are punishment and guilt, property, affectional relations, authority and governance, law, life, liberty, distributive justice, truth, and sex roles. A correlation of these aspects can help show how one moral argument is related to another. Guilt as a motive, for instance, accompanies any value placed on life and depends upon the peculiar way life is actually valued at each stage. [KE75f-623] During the course of our discussion, we will talk about the value of life as it pertains to abortion. Other aspects will be introduced, as we go along, for additional clarity.

☐

The multitude of preferences exhibited by human beings includes ways of moral thinking.[29] In the Kohlbergian theory, each stage represents a new and more adequate solution to a moral problem. Yet, since each is only a partial solution, something always seems to be missing—and quite appropriately, a better synthesis emerges. Since the stages are part of a continuous change in quality of thought, each stage is both stable and unstable at the same time. Although qualitatively different from either the previous or ensuing stages, each stage is still in a temporary, if not precarious, state of equilibrium; it is always trying to complete itself. If one can see (understand) a higher stage, it appears more desirable to the moral reasoner than the previous stage, and objectively it actually is. Moral reasoning one step up resolves more problems, and also problems that are more difficult.[30] In a series of studies, Kohlberg found that children prefer the next higher stage if they can see (understand) it. [K71j-307] From these primary data one could claim that seeing and preferring are almost tautological, like claiming that seeing is believing or that what gains attention determines action. Although each lower stage may not be illogical, it is not entirely logical either. Stages that are more logical are more satisfying. The human mind, by nature, gravitates toward more complete comprehension.

Stages are structures that move. They are cognitive reorganizations or transformations of outlook of either the physical or the social (moral) world. As we noted earlier, universal ideas concerning the physical world exist because there is a universal physical structure. There are space, time, causality, etc. And by the same token there are universal ideas concerning the moral (social) world or the world of interpersonal relations. There is a sense of welfare, justice, etc. Likewise, just as physical concepts imply a universal structure of physical experience, so too moral concepts imply a universal structure of social

experience. If physics is a descriptive science, then ethics is its normative counterpart, with mathematical equations and interpersonal rules
applicable to each respectively. As Kohlberg cogently states ". . . it is
no more surprising to find that cognitive moral principles determine
choice of conflicting social actions than it is to find that cognitive
scientific principles determine choice of conflicting actions on physical
objects." [K69a-397]

The idea of stages or discontinuities in development seems to be
rather extensively acknowledged.[31] From time immemorial, culture
and religion have recognized that changes in the human organism
both physical and mental, with the latter including responsible moral
action, are tied in some way to maturational levels. Almost all of them
have recognized at least two major stages in the human developmental journey. One is the age period from 5 to 7 (usually the onset of
compulsory schooling) and the other is the period of early adolescence (usually the end of compulsory schooling). These stages are
likewise recognized in the Judeo-Christian tradition. In sacramental
Christianity, for example, the sacraments of confession and communion are conferred in the period from 5 to 7, the so-called age of
reason, and the sacrament of confirmation at the onset of puberty.
Judaism recognizes the latter with the Bar and Bat Mitzva.

THE DREAM PHENOMENON   Perhaps the best way to present
the basic idea of a stage sequence is to begin by referring to what all
who read these pages have experienced: the dream phenomenon. A
knowledge of the dream process is significant to our analysis because
the evolution of dreaming in each person shows how distinctions are
made between subject and object, internal and external reality, real
and unreal objects, psychic (thought) and physical (matter), and most
importantly, self and other. Progressive discrimination, as we will
learn, is the essence of stage theory. Fortunately, the dream phenomenon has been studied extensively by both Piaget and Kohlberg,
and their observations and conclusions have been carefully reported.
A brief review of their research will help explain the nature and
universality of stages of mental growth.

Piaget: In his research on the dream, Piaget asked some children a
series of three questions concerning (1) the origin of the dream, (2)
the place of the dream, and (3) the organ of the dream. The answers
he received were classified by age into three distinct stages.

Stage 1 (ages 5–6). The dream originates externally and remains there. The child at this stage will claim that the dream comes from outside, takes place in the room, and is accomplished with the eyes. It is highly likely that the child here confuses dream with reality.

Stage 2 (ages 7–8). The dream arises internally but becomes external. The child thinks that the dream is in the head but that it takes place in front of him or her. There is still confusion between dreams and reality, but the child begins to compensate or neutralize the differences.

Stage 3 (ages 9–10). The dream begins inside and remains there. The child at this stage finally realizes that the dream is a product of thought, and is able to disentangle dream from reality.

Kohlberg: Kohlberg found that a six-stage sequence was involved in dreams. Using data collected from American middle-class children and from Atayal children, members of a Malaysian tribe living in Taiwan, he further elaborated Piaget's earlier findings. Expressed in polarities, the stages Kohlberg discovered were real-unreal, visible-invisible, external (origin)-internal (origin), external (location)-internal (location), material-nonmaterial, and other caused-self caused. As the stages develop, the child begins to realize that (1) the dream is not really in the room; (2) others cannot see it; (3) it comes from inside; (4) it goes on inside; (5) it is a thought; and (6) it is self caused. These realizations occur over a period of three years (from 4 years, 6 months to 7 years, 10 months) and are universal. As each stage is reached, a clearer conceptualization of the dream takes place. [K66b]

This brief summary of Piaget's and Kohlberg's dream studies does little justice to the richness of their research. It is especially important to read Piaget's account firsthand to appreciate fully the nature of the data. Both scholars attempted to explain the mechanism of movement from one dream stage to another, but this need not concern us here. Reading what they discovered about dreams is a pleasant and, at times, dramatic way to understand the main characteristics of stage sequence.

Classical stage theory can be best understood by first briefly comparing and contrasting it with two other conceptual approaches to development. These are the differential and ipsative. The former is characterized by the work of Erik Erikson, which emphasizes a series of bipolar behavioral attributes within a stage sequence. Unlike classical stage theory, however, the differential sequence is not necessarily invariant. The basic developmental idea encompassed by his best-known work, *Childhood and Society*, deals with universal maturational tasks all humans must undertake.[32] Every individual strives to cope (and must successfully) with each task before moving to the next one. In contrast to the typical stage and differential approaches, Erikson's work does not seek a group average. Rather, it confines its developmental analysis to what its name suggests, the individual self. The ipsative approach attempts to answer the question, why did this person develop the way he did? What developmental pattern can be derived from this individual and others? In terms of the abortion debate, for example, a concrete application of this approach would involve the discovery and investigation of whatever developmental experiences may have prompted Justice Blackmun to rule as he did in *Roe* v. *Wade*. In a sense, all three developmental theories can be applied to the abortion debate.[33]

ERIKSON'S LIFE CYCLE   The Eriksonian sequence is content-oriented, in that the central concerns are *what* one thinks rather than *how* one thinks, the form that is central to the Kohlbergian sequence. Erikson's positive-negative polarities reflect the challenge each person faces when confronting certain potentially life-enhancing situations. As originally formulated they are:

> (8) Ego Integrity vs. Despair
> (7) Generativity vs. Stagnation
> (6) Intimacy vs. Isolation
> (5) Identity vs. Role Confusion
> (4) Industry vs. Inferiority
> (3) Initiative vs. Guilt
> (2) Autonomy vs. Shame, Doubt
> (1) Basic Trust vs. Mistrust

Before the individual can move to stage (2), he or she must first resolve the maturational conflict of stage (1) and incorporate the positive polarity within his or her mental outlook.

Erikson's maturational-life-cycle theory lacks the cognitive core of Kohlberg's moral-development theory and is not as empirically rigorous. The reason for this is that content, in contrast to form, has no distinguishable order. Although a certain average or normal order is present, in reality any rigid sequence will ultimately break down. Sexual intimacy may in fact precede the pursuit of a vocation and the assimilation of parental attitudes into one's own value system. What interests Erikson is whatever preoccupies the individual emotionally at a given period of the life cycle. His perspective is, of course, also a Freudian one. In contrast to Kohlberg and Piaget, whose theories emphasize an interaction between nature and nurture, both Freud and Erikson place greater emphasis on nature and consider nurture as a facilitator and inhibitor of primary forces that are intrinsic to the organism. [KM72b-451f.]

This brief overview of the Eriksonian life cycle helps bring into sharper focus and perhaps even justifies a most important criticism of the Kohlbergian formulation. The latter, in its emphasis on progressive moral development, does not take into account the possibilities of pitfalls in a malfunctioning system. If human beings move inevitably in the direction of finer and finer moral tuning, why do misuses of moral reasoning occur? We all know that they *do* occur. The justification for abortion-on-demand is just such a malfunction. The pages to come will consider the complexities of healthy, sound moral development.

Other criticisms of the Kohlbergian thesis can be found throughout the scientific literature. (See Appendix, Section B for a synopsis and list of references.) Two critics should be mentioned here, however, because their work bears upon the question of abortion. The work of Gilligan and Belenky, either singly or jointly authored, criticizes the hypothetical nature of Kohlberg's dilemmas and advocates the use of "real-life" situations of conflict to help illuminate the process of moral growth. Their interest in more naturalistic research was fulfilled through studies involving problem pregnancies whereby both clinical and developmental perspectives could be linked. Their co-authored effort attempted to investigate the relationship between judgment and action in a real-life situation involving conflict and choice. They wished to determine "how a clinical crisis can initiate a developmental transition."[34]

In addition to their efforts to make moral-development research more realistic, Gilligan also called attention to Kohlberg's apparent male bias in his original research design. Her thesis, while actually being more a corrective than a criticism of Kohlberg (she accepts his basic developmental paradigm), emphasizes a distinctively female form of moral decision-making. Using the abortion decision as a content area, she claims that the research findings she reported "suggest that women impose a distinctive construction on moral problems, seeing moral dilemmas in terms of conflicting responsibilities."[35]

While both scholars make a strong case for more realistic moral-development research, and while one of them calls attention to the distinctly female aspects of moral choice, their conclusions should be tempered with the realization that the interview samples used were apparently biased in favor of those first counseled in a pro-abortion setting. An important question is what would likely have been the responses of some of the women had they been first counseled at centers strongly opposed to abortion but advocating alternatives? Who were the initial counselors anyway? (A carefully drawn profile would have been helpful.) But apart from the serious methodological question concerning vague guidelines for sample selection, I am also troubled by Gilligan's insistence that "the essence of the moral decision is the exercise of choice and the willingness to accept responsibility for that choice."[36]

I would certainly agree that one should have choice before one can have responsibility. Yet, I find it impossible to believe that the choice of abortion in most cases can be a truly responsible decision. This point of view fails to acknowledge the pregnant woman's responsibility as a parent to care for her offspring, which means not only nurturing it but protecting it from harm. It seems more logical to think that the true choice comes in determining whether or not one should first become pregnant. That initial choice, it would appear, overwhelmingly determines the direction of future responsibility. In short, who is to be held responsible for the consequences of sexual behavior?

There appear to be two contrary psychological forces at work in the abortion debate: one pulls toward genuine moral growth and development and the other toward moral decay and dissolution. The struggle is really between a moralizing process that is authentic and one that is not. Moralizing that favors abortion is really an anti-development. A parallel is to be found in the relationship between the symbolic and the diabolic, a relationship with deep religious significance. The symbolic, meaning to throw together, is a centripetal or centralizing force, while the diabolic, meaning to throw apart, is centrifugal or disrupting. Religiously speaking, one strives for harmony and cosmos; the other begets disharmony and chaos. One leads to life and the other leads to death. (See Figure 9.)

Moral stages are filtering devices that help determine one's perception of social reality and help give meaning and impact to action

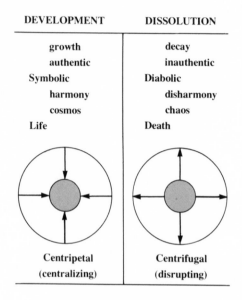

DEVELOPMENT	DISSOLUTION
growth	decay
authentic	inauthentic
Symbolic	Diabolic
harmony	disharmony
cosmos	chaos
Life	Death

Centripetal	Centrifugal
(centralizing)	(disrupting)

Figure 9.

choices, a series of variable lenses providing different degrees of vision. Through them each moral thinker apprehends the principle of justice as it emerges during the course of moral development. Some of the lenses are microscopic or telephoto and can take in only the immediate moral settings; others are macroscopic or wide angle and can view moral problems from a broad vantage point. Development, as we noted earlier, means movement toward something, namely, a clearer vision of one's moral options. Each succeeding moral lens, therefore, takes in more of our interpersonal surroundings.

Kohlberg summarizes the idea of a moral progression beautifully. Two passages, in particular, are worth quoting at length.

The six stages, which are logically ordered so that the higher ones are *necessarily* more advanced than the lower ones, comprise an analytical model that is open-ended only at the top. A principle of conscience (stage 6), freely selected, can *become or replace* a social contract (stage 5), which in turn can become or replace a law (stage 4), a role expectation (stage 3), an instrumentality (stage 2) and a guide for inflicting or withholding punishment (stage 1). Thus, every level is at least potentially infused with a principle of conscience and can act as an incubator of conscience (italics in the original). [KW72d-12]

Consider how each level of judgment leads into the next higher one. A young child growing up is punished or rebuked (stage 1) but soon realizes that these punishments coincide with his own best interests (stage 2). Unpunished activities are not only more pleasurable, but they anticipate role expectations encountered at home and in school (stage 3). Conformity to such role expectations over a period of time enables the child to understand the role he plays in a larger constellation of roles organized by legal authorities (stage 4). The child uses his awareness of lawfulness as the basis for his own contracts and interpersonal commitments (stage 5). After repeated formation of such voluntary commitments, he is able to abstract and apply those principles of conscience (stage 6) that render mutual relationships valuable and satisfying. [KW72d-(12–14)]

A paradigmatic rendering of the Kohlberg stage idea is located at the end of Part I.

From our developmental model, it is possible to conclude that higher stages are more adaptable than lower ones. This is true because higher-stage thinkers usually have a greater variety of naturally acquired social experience to stimulate them. Movement through the sequence implies a keener sense of moral discrimination or an improved ability to differentiate. Conversely, these lens filters also become baffles or screens of the lower stages and act as blocks to or defenses against perception of the next-higher stage and the type of moral thinking attached thereto.

Once the idea of structure or stage is understood, the question arises, can there be a regression? The answer is yes, but only in a functional sense. Bearing in mind that function concerns how a structure is *used* and does not characterize the structure itself or the way in which it is *formed*, true regression in a purely structural sense, by definition, never occurs except in rare cases, like senility and schizophrenia. The psychoanalytic expression, "regression in the service of the ego," is another way of pointing to the manner in which a stage is used. In this sense, both progression and regression are functional and not structural.

Functionally, both progress and regress may be difficult to identify and interpret. An apparent regression might actually represent a step forward in that a developmental pattern must break up before it can consolidate at some higher plateau. If a stage is a type of freezing that thaws before refreezing at some more advanced stage, is the thaw prior to the refreezing or prior to complete liquefaction? A better question might be: is the sun that Franklin observed rising or setting? Only a trained observer could really know.

In structural transformation, what the untrained observer sees is the evidence of a breaking-up and not what is to be created anew. A better synthesis, whose coming is now only dimly perceived, may actually be aborning to usher in a new day. Indeed, this may be the case with regard to the world movements involving respect for born and unborn human life. Relaxed abortion laws, for example, by calling attention to the problems of stressful pregnancies, may be a temporary thawing out before advancement to a more secure level of moral functioning where social justice is more authentically observed. Social excesses, devoid of foresight, are often signals that something is seriously amiss but can still be corrected.

In light of what has been said so far about the idea of stages, once again we must return to the problem of distinguishing form and content. Kohlberg's developmental theory maintains that a stage is a way of thinking (a form) used to support either side of an action choice (a content). Abortion, for or against, is such an area of action choice, and the reasoning pattern used to advocate or deny it is a form. To a strict developmentalist, whether or not abortion is accepted as a course of action is independent of the moral reasoning employed. Kohlberg asserts emphatically "We are not looking for a 'right answer' but rather for the level of moral judgment used in reaching a decision." [KW72d-12] But while this separation of form and content may be a workable hypothesis or analytic tool, any rigid distinction seems to me to be inappropriate to the abortion question. It would be wise to remember Kohlberg's own admission that "Although structure is one thing and content another, there is a probabilistic tendency for specific stage-structures to generate specific attitudes." [KE75f-628] In one of his essays, he shows how normal stage growth brings eventual opposition to capital punishment. As we shall see presently, I contend that the same also holds true for induced abortion. I contend that the higher one develops, i.e., the more completely, the greater the likelihood that one will oppose abortion. What must be kept carefully in mind, however, is that while behavior may never indicate stage, stages can to a degree actually predict behavior.

Throughout our analysis, we must also confront repeatedly the relationship between logical and emotional facets of moral thought.

As we have said, it is probably less troublesome emotionally for humans to talk about their physical worlds than about their moral worlds. In reality, cognitive stages interpret and channel emotion which is really neutral. Cognition orchestrates the emotional side of moral reasoning. [K71b-(230–31); K71d-353] Developmentalists hold that "There exists no pure cognition without affect, just as affect cannot arise in a vacuum without being channeled by cognitive structuration."[37] The full emotional impact of human relationships can often, in a moral sense, disrupt cognition. This often happens in the trauma of the abortion debate.

Emotions can block moral development. As ancient rhetoric would say, they make crooked the ruler of judgment,[38] or as Kohlberg would say, moral stages can be disrupted by emotion (will, desire, etc.). Yet, something should be said about the positive side of emotion; if channeled wisely it can also facilitate moral growth, even though it becomes less a determining factor as we move up the scale of development. Emotion may not be as reliable as reason in making moral decisions, but it helps to give impetus to reason.

☐

The Piagetian-Kohlbergian research data support the following generalizations about moral stages:

1. Higher moral stages imply lower ones, but not the opposite. This means that the development forms a hierarchy with the flow all in one direction. The lower-stage components integrate at a higher level or become available to higher levels.

2. The structure of each stage is its logical component. This means that whatever emotions are present in moral thinking are channeled by the reasoning process, that emotions in moral-developmental theory lack a clearly defined structure, and that emotions should be regulated by an intelligent view of reality.

3. Each moral stage extends the individual's ability to solve problems. This means that more advanced stages equip the individual with a greater selection of judgmental tools.

4. Moral stages are not wired in but depend on innate organizing tendencies. This means that the moral growth pattern does not reflect an automatic maturational response that is present in miniature form at the very beginning; it must unfold gradually through continuing interaction with the social environment.

5. Moral stages are different but not necessarily better. This means that the reasons supplied by the moral decision-maker, even at the higher and more functional levels, do not categorize him or her as a moral giant or degenerate, a moral saint or sinner, since one never loses the ability to reason at a lower level.

6. A single stage cuts across all moral situations. This means that each stage represents a consistent moral evaluation which can be extended or generalized to every moral predicament.

7. Moral stages reflect neither maturation nor learning alone. This means that a stage is not something innate or something environmental, but a combination of the two. (Maturation means the advent of a new stage regardless of experience or mental reorganization, while experience alone can produce only an integration and not movement to a new stage.) Stages are an equilibrated pattern of interaction between the organism and the environment, between nature and nurture. Within this developmental process, quality and competence govern the ability to perform. (Quantity and performance itself refer to how well one performs and are nondevelopmental.)

8. Reversibility moves toward universalizability. This means that only the final moral stage is completely reversible. It includes the universality of the categorical imperative (what can be wished for all) and the Golden Rule (do unto others, etc.).

9. Moral stages are cross-cultural, though the end points may differ. This means that preliterate societies do not develop the most advanced stages or the developmental speed of literate societies. Environmental factors accelerate or retard the rate of moral growth but not the quality (form) or sequence of growth.

10. Moral stages are invariant. This means, with due regard to overlapping, that stages develop one at a time and in the same order.

11. Moral stages exhibit increased differentiation and integration. This means that each stage produces a fuller elaboration of the principle of justice, i.e., better organization extends justice to more content areas. The elaboration of these areas functions with increased unity at higher stages and becomes more streamlined, i.e., the parts increase, but mesh more easily.

12. Moral stages are connecting experiences. This means that the stages represent different ways of organizing mental material. Stages are rules for processing information and not the information itself. Effective communication not only generates material but helps to process it.

In addition to being viewed as stages (patterns, structures, organizations, systems), these mental emergents can also be viewed as conditions, positions, or segments of thought, or even as sequential episodes arising from the interaction of the structures of the mind and the structures of social reality. One must be careful with the labels one uses, however. Labels, like medicines, can produce unintended results or side effects which can impede or confuse human understanding. It could be argued that the Kohlbergian labels of stage and level may be pedagogically unsound in that they predispose the individual to put other people in boxes. To say that one is at a certain stage or level can be patronizing, even when not intended to be so. Surely, the labels chosen should not be convenient devices for name calling, belittling, ridiculing, or putting someone down. The search for appropriate labels has not been exhausted and, just ahead, I will suggest two characterizations which may prove helpful.

THE SYNCHRONIC THEORY

To avoid the pitfalls I have enumerated I propose a change of perspective, a change from a diachronic to a synchronic or from a dynamic to a more usable static view.[39] Remove the motion from Kohlberg's structural theory and one has a series of still pictures of moral reasoning, i.e., moral thinking categories. The set diagram in Figure 10 helps us to visualize this conversion. Each large circle represents a sector or domain for processing information about moral issues. The portion common to all three is the core of justice that pervades the developmental sequence. Such a diagram, borrowed from mathematics, treats each of the three categories (levels) of moral thinking as equal to any of the others. By contrast, the standard diachronic model would be a series of parallel lines advancing upward to show dynamic growth. Such a diagram is pictured in Figure 11. Although, technically, every part of a set diagram is equivalent to any other, such an equivalence is not really faithful to the concept of moral growth. Accordingly, Figure 12 is presented to visualize increasing differentiation and integration while still preserving our synchronic idea. Each concentric circle represents a different quality of moral thinking. Justice is again the motivating factor that pervades the series.

N.B. From here to the end of the book, the reader is asked to apply the proper meaning to the following two pairs of terms which are vital

SYNCHRONIC (static)

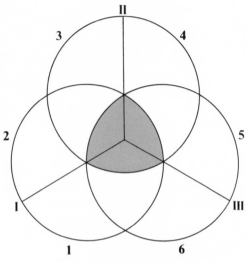

Figure 10.

DIACHRONIC (dynamic)

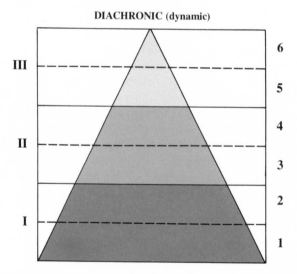

Figure 11.

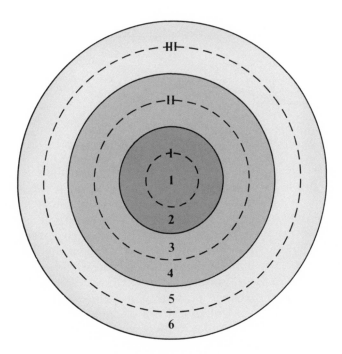

Figure 12.

to my exposition: (1) level and stage, and (2) phase and mode. The first pair are diachronic or dynamic terms used in the traditional Kohlbergian sense, while the second are synchronic or static terms used by me in a rhetorical sense for analytic purposes. By the time the reader finishes Part I, the differences should become apparent.

Something must again be said about normal and abnormal development. Kohlbergian theory is largely silent about the fact that healthy moral growth often runs parallel to its opposite. Just as cancer cells mimic healthy ones, so too injustice often masquerades as justice. Attitudes in favor of abortion, like those in favor of capital punishment, do not mesh or track completely with Kohlberg's stage sequence; they are out of synch with the normal unfolding of moral awareness. As will be seen, only the anti-abortion position is synchronized totally with the Kohlbergian series. Each stage may respond differently to justifications for abortion, but the fact is inescapable that

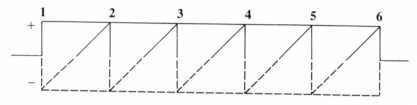

Figure 13.

only one action choice, i.e., not to abort, is developmentally sound and in phase. Just as two windshield wipers can be out of phase, the decision to favor abortion is out of phase and developmentally unsound.

An important question left unanswered by Kohlberg's theory is the whole idea of negative moral choices. What are their consequences? How should moral failure be evaluated? What about sin and depravity? Consonant with biblical description, if wheat and weeds (tares) grow together in some grainfields, might not moral and immoral reasoning exist in the same person? A more accurate and realistic approach to the process of moral growth might be admitting the possibility of an inverse set of moral stages or a negative hierarchy of choice mirroring the positive. If such a possibility were to exist (and I have a strong feeling it actually does), the phenomenon could be visualized as in Figure 13. Perhaps sensitive moral issues like abortion exhibit an ongoing, though largely hidden, dialectic somewhat like the stages in Erikson's life cycle. A positive advance to each successive stage cannot be made until the negative response to that stage has been satisfactorily overcome. This possibility, I think, needs careful investigation.

As an open developmental system, Kohlberg's original stage sequence is partly teleological and deontological. What this means is that the end of moral growth or moral reasoning can be found in its beginning and that the entire process involves duty or moral obligation.[40] The growth trajectory, which is basic to all developmental theories, appears to unfold according to some plan; the first stage reaches toward the final stage. Mathematically, this goal orientation could not really be predicted since all that can be hoped for is a movement toward the stage that follows immediately. The developmental process, unless hindered, moves toward ethical maturity, with the individual at each stage ignorant of all the others except that which comes next. Kohlberg's developmental system is based on the idea that one stage of moral reasoning establishes the groundwork and is inherently necessary for the emergence of the next stage.[41] His theory is premised on the assumption that nature interacts with nurture to bring ever-increasing moral maturity.

The Kohlbergian theory can be applied to the abortion controversy only if it is modified to conform to the way in which moral issues are really argued in the public forum. An individual's position on abortion by itself can yield no clear indication of how that individual will respond to other moral issues. Single comments on abortion can hardly reveal a modal stage of moral reasoning. The stage at which an individual is functioning can obviously not be assessed unless several content areas are examined and evaluated simultaneously.[42] What we are faced with, then, is a built-in constraint to the Kohlbergian perspective. It is an impractical tool for communicators if more knowledge is needed for its proper use than can be obtained from a given audience discussing any single issue like abortion.

PHASE Terminology sometimes reveals hidden or unacknowledged assumptions. Kohlberg's terminology, for example, is socially oriented. His labels for the major plateaus (what he calls levels and we call phases) are: preconventional, conventional, and postconventional—a terminology clearly oriented to the social. Accepted social norms dominate moralizing at the conventional level, while they exert less influence, or none at all, at the pre- and postconventional levels.

Phases are characterized by degrees of equilibrium between rights and duties. At Phase I rights are highly personal, with little attention paid to duties. At Phase II these rights have become social, and more attention is paid to duties. Finally, at Phase III, rights and duties become rational and achieve a balance so that, for example, if I have a right to my own life I also have a duty to respect other lives and defend them, if necessary. As noted previously, where the developmental model fails to track with the reasoning that is typical at that stage, the model is said to be out of phase.

Each phase represents an aggregate view of the moral world. Abortion and other moral problems are viewed in certain typical or characteristic ways. In Phase I the view is dominated by self-interest, in Phase II by social interest, and in Phase III by a rational or universal

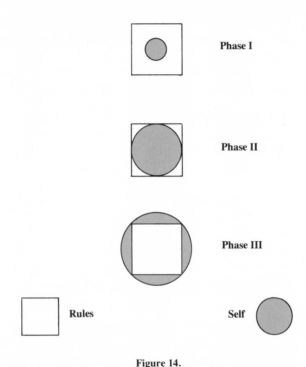

Phase I

Phase II

Phase III

Rules

Self

Figure 14.

outlook which is existential, or outside of both self and society. Movement through the phases is a search for an ever-more-autonomous
morality. The personal arbitrariness of Phase I and the social relativity of Phase II produce a certain dissatisfaction which leads to the
rational moral creativity of Phase III.

Each phase represents a major change in the way moral problems
are handled. At Phase I the externalized moralizing relies upon the
concrete, while at Phase III the moralizing becomes internalized and
abstract. The reflex thinking of Phase I gives way eventually to the
careful reflection of Phase III. Stability and self-sufficiency thus become the end points of the phases.

Another way of looking at the phases is as rule clusters with the self
defined in relation to them. Figure 14 visualizes these relationships.
At Phase I the cluster of conventional rules and moral expectations is

viewed as external to the self; at Phase II the self indentifies with the rules and expectations; and at Phase III the self becomes differenti- ated from them, though not superior to them. [GKCS76b-22] Each phase offers a different perception of one's relationship to society and to its rules and expectations. Each perception originates from a better vantage point and represents a qualitative change in the way rules are conceptualized.

The phases can also be viewed as indexes of mature moral thinking. Phase I exemplifies the moral child, who makes decisions in terms of power relationships; Phase II, the moral adolescent, whose morality is dominated by peer-group influence; Phase III, the moral adult, who becomes a fully autonomous moral agent who reasons logically about moral issues.[43] Each phase represents a greater degree of sophistica- tion and is not necessarily a measure of good or evil. A good moral child, for example, is better than an evil adult but no better or worse than a good adult. Each phase represents the best moralizing available to the individual.

Ideal conduct at each phase of moral reasoning is regulated by the degree of concern for intentions. There is a continuum of intention running through the phases, from no concern at Phase I to a pre- ponderance at Phase III. To the Phase I thinker the bad is construed not as being selfish or deceitful but as producing either sorrow or joy. At the other extreme of Phase III, the bad is defined in terms of ultimate justice, which must be pursued regardless of pain or plea- sure.

What is especially important to the student of persuasive ccm- munication is that each phase is fashioned by a different moral senti- ment and represents a different type of motivation for moral action. Phase I, for example, relies on fear, since pain and pleasure, penalty and reward, dominate the individual's moral landscape. The Phase II moral enterprise is regulated by shame, with favor or disfavor attached to a given action and the urge to conform a motivational given. Phase III is characterized motivationally by guilt or self- condemnation, a result of the autonomous nature of the moral deci- sion-making. In contrast to the externality of fear and shame, the motivation becomes internalized and the moral conscience more fully formed.

An interesting and perhaps compelling way to view this tripartite motivation is from the perspective of Christian liturgy. In *The Book of*

Common Prayer the priest at the baptismal service in the Episcopal Church (U.S.A.) prays that the child be strengthened to defeat "the devil, the world, and the flesh."[44] Although liturgically presented in anti-climactic order, the three phases of moral reasoning are clearly evident. Phase I is represented by the irrational temptation of the flesh (personal), Phase II by the world (social), and Phase III by the devil (rational).

The abortion debate is a grand exposition of praise and blame in which the noble and ignoble elements in human conduct are assigned to the moral justifications advanced by each side. Heroes and villains play an indispensable part in the clash of argument. They are called forth in the attempt to assume a strong moral position. Their vices and virtues feed the moral imagination and assist each person's decision about the right or wrong of abortion.

No explication of the persuasive moral sentiments can ever be complete without some understanding of the motivational meaning of praise and blame. Virtue and vice, the behavioral opposites reflecting good and evil, are centrally significant to mass persuasion. They constitute the stuff of what heroes and villains do to warrant approval or disapproval. In assigning praise and blame within a Phase I context there is a concern for being rewarded or punished. At Phase II the praise and blame are assigned to conforming or nonconforming behavior; at Phase III, to encouraging or inhibiting, creating or destroying, a perceived moral state of affairs. The final phase does not obligate anyone to praise or blame; its judgments are self-contained and detached from conventional motivations. For the most part, however, society needs rules for labeling virtues and vices since social control and utility profit thereby.

Let us describe the phases in more detail:

Phase I—Personal Phase I thinking justifies moral conduct on the basis of self-interest. Satisfying personal needs is more important here than in the other two phases. The prohibition or encouragement of a particular class of human action makes the meaning of good and evil highly personal. Since there is no concern about intention, virtues and vices are insignificant. Right is determined by physical or social power, or the power to punish or bring pleasure. Characteristic of this phase is behavior arising from obedience.

In contrast to the other phases, the chief organizing principle of

Phase I is simple hedonism. A dyadic calculus of self-interest and self-satisfaction dominates the morality, and cultural labels of good and bad, right and wrong are interpreted in terms of both immediate and long-range physical and/or psychological consequences. There is no sense of social obligation (Phase II) or rational obligation (Phase III). What others may think has no value, since the individual is now a social outsider. Likewise, there can be no deference to abstract rule.

The morality of Phase I and the persuasive appeals attached thereto are tied to concrete needs, happenings, or circumstances of special concern to the individual without reference to the larger concerns of society or to universal standards of moral conduct. And since the primary motivation of this phase arises out of fear, it is easy to generate a secondary motivation arising from a promise of reward. At Phase I each person avoids pain and seeks pleasure.

Phase II—Social At Phase II, on the other hand, the individual believes not only in obeying, but also in actively keeping or maintaining the law. It is more encompassing than Phase I, but its prescriptiveness often leads to constant self-contradiction in defining what is right. The Phase II moral thought process reflects an inability to live in a world without rules. Laws and guidelines are its hallmark, and it lives in lockstep with society's institutions. It is typically noncritical in its approach to regulations. It justifies and supports the status quo.

For the first time, group identification determines the general shape of the moral domain. Starting with the family and ending with the national household, one's loyalties are circumscribed by what is perceived as the immediate society. Like ripples on the placid surface of a pond (to employ a metaphor used earlier), each concentric ring of social awareness draws the individual away from the further moral stagnation of self-concern. The attainment of what is expected by others becomes satisfying. Changed rules now demand an institutional allegiance which for most will provide the necessary ingredients for a peak moral experience. All that is required for self-sacrifice is the acknowledged gratitude of the group. Most people never progress beyond this phase.

In supporting and justifying the social order, Phase II thinking represents a radical shift in moral focus. From extreme egocentrism in Phase I to a reliance upon what others think, the group emerges as centrally important. Consequences to the group are now placed before self-interest. There is a distinct pleasure derived from living in harmony with others. The group is unconsciously recognized as the source of valid behavior, and the individual depends upon it for rewards of esteem and approval. There is devotion to group needs rather than to personal needs. The context of moral action is interlaced with law, taboo, and social preoccupations.

Conventional social wisdom dominates Phase II moralizing. Popular opinion ascribes virtue and vice and assigns praise and blame to interpersonal behavior. Behavior is largely conformist, with the peer group becoming—often simultaneously—family, group, or nation. Good is defined in terms of the prevailing social environment, so that Democrats are favored over Republicans (or vice versa), Americans over foreigners, and parents over offspring, etc. Phase II is fundamentally social in outlook. Rights are defined as whatever the mood of society expects and are supported whenever encountered or experienced by the individual. Kohlberg calls this phase modal for most cultures, i.e., it occurs most frequently.

Phase III—Rational　Phase III decision-making represents what is universal in moral conduct. For the first time human interaction is seen as the product of values and principles that have validity beyond personal or social concerns. A characteristic of this phase is the attempt to define a code of behavior and apply it to pressing moral problems. Phase III goes beyond the moral thinking of the previous phase which, as we noted, was culture-bound or relative to certain groups. Problems now are solved in a stable, self-consistent way.

In the moral problem-solving arena of Phase III, the decision-maker becomes essentially autonomous, or self-regulating. At this phase an attempt is made to reconcile the discrepancies between the previous two phases, and laws are created instead of merely maintained. Recognizing the possible conflict between what is good for the individual (Phase I) and what is good for society (Phase II), the moralizing of Phase III introduces the idea of reciprocal rights and duties. In Kohlberg's words, choice at Phase III "is based on the principles that supersede convention, just as previously the claims of society or convention were seen as the grounds for adjudicating differences between individuals." [K80a-61] The self is made to conform to standards of conduct shared by all.

Phase III defines justifiable actions or behavior for anyone in any situation. Other moralizing is necessarily incomplete, since the moral situations have too narrow a focus. The content of each moral decision must transcend personal and social needs to qualify for Phase III status. "A person cannot engage in principled moral action if he is not aware of moral principles." [K73f-10] Only what has universal application can be morally satisfying. Phase III is derived philosophically; it is the thinking person's phase.

MODE   As we focus our analysis ever more sharply, we move from phase to mode. Again, it bears repeating that our conception of mode is akin to the Kohlbergian conception of stage in that the same language can be used to describe either designation. However, a mode is used to describe moral thinking within a single content area at a given point in time, whereas a stage covers an array of content areas as they converge over a period of time to yield a temporary equilibrium point in the moral-developmental life-span of the individual. The macroanalysis of Kohlberg gives way to the microanalysis of the present study. For a telescope we substitute a microscope (or magnifying glass).

Unlike the Kohlbergian scheme, the modes as we conceive them have no genesis or chronology. They are alternative or substituting thought processes that overlap, run parallel, or coexist in the same person. Immature modes continue alongside mature ones. They are employed as needed by the moral decision-maker and are reflective of differences rather than of positions that are higher or lower. For pedagogical purposes, however, we will treat them in a sequential fashion. When the analysis is complete, the reader will see the inadequacies of each mode, how disequilibrium is reached, and how the next mode compensates. We will be moving in our analysis from externally to internally motivated thinking, from dependence to independence, from concrete to abstract thinking. In short, we will see how, in connection with the abortion question, moral thinking is slowly extended beyond one's immediate motivational situation and how each mode provides the reasoner with a more adequate moral perception. Each mode is a truth, but the next mode is a greater truth.

Considered sequentially, the modes represent different moral emphases which extend a person's view of the moral domain. Each mode is a moral vision encompassing more territory and providing a more adequate perception of what it means to be moral. This increasingly wider vision liberates the moral reasoner from the strictures of the previous mode and progressively broadens the moral sphere. Each mode represents an exclusive emphasis which is determinative or diagnostic of that mode. Taken individually, each mode becomes a special type of moral characterization—a marker of discontinuity.

The modes of moral reasoning are more finely tuned versions of each phase. They are hierarchies of value, with each mode transcending and subsuming the one before it. The modes move toward an ideal of justice which pictures a world where human life has an inherent priority over all other considerations. Like way stations for an emerging concept of justice, each mode becomes increasingly independent of the factual properties of the life in question. In applying this modal way of reasoning to the topic of abortion, the questions to be asked are: Will the pregnancy or its termination bring pain or pleasure, approval or disapproval, a twinge or a salving of conscience? It might also be helpful to remember that most arguments in the abortion debate involve bits and pieces of moral thought, and that from a practical standpoint each mode usually represents a mixture rather than a pure type.

Key elements in the idea of moral modes are differentiation and integration, as well as consistency, reversibility, and universality. The first two represent a progressive disentanglement of moral values from other types of values—the value of human life, for example, from its relation to personal happiness, property, or freedom. With this progressive disentanglement the value residue of respect for human life becomes increasingly stronger until the entire value system responds to each moral conflict completely and with total ease. The latter three elements represent moral judgments that are arrived at in the most ideal human fashion independently of culture and time.

We repeat that the Kohlbergian position on progressive moral growth is supported by extensive cross-cultural data. Investigators over the years have discovered the same sequence of moral development in such diverse cultures as Mexico, Turkey, Taiwan, and India [K80b-23], as well as in Great Britain and the United States. Cultural divergence has no effect on sequence except in terms of speed and distance, or how fast the stages are negotiated and the ultimate stage attained. There is some evidence that semiliterate cultures as a whole pass through the stages of moral reasoning at a slower pace and do not reach the most advanced stages.

☐

Before taking up each mode in detail it would be well to consider briefly an important aspect of the guiding metaphor of our theory. The perceptive reader will detect in the organicism of our critical approach a correlative idea of systemic interdependency.

Biology, society, and, by extension, rhetoric can be described by means of organized wholes. Modern scientific reason has passed beyond the simple connection of cause and effect or the direct relationship between two entities. What now dominates some of the most productive scientific thinking is the concept of interdependent systems, or the relationship of parts to whole. These relationships, which are multiphasic in nature, characterize organized units. If the unit is dependent on an environment it is said to be dynamic or open to the future. Such dynamic systems can be found in the study of life, society, and rhetoric.

The rhetoric of a social movement is a superordinate system composing a unity beyond the sum of its parts. As the human body with its critical cardio-pulmonary-neurological triumvirate is supported by a single animating principle, so too the rhetoric of social movements is organized by a single principle of construction. The modes of moral discourse are incomplete wholes connected to each other through the superordinate principle of justice. This principle is a coordinating nexus or binding thesis. Self-regulation arises through the way in which justice is perceived by the individual. And rhetoric, by aiding the individual's perception, enhances the self-regulatory process. Thus the development of conscience can be viewed as cybernetic.

We have just finished what for many readers will undoubtedly be the most complicated part of the book. It behooves us, therefore, to refresh our memories with a brief summary.

TABLE. DEFINITION OF MORAL STAGES

I. PRECONVENTIONAL LEVEL

At this level the child is responsive to cultural rules and labels of good and bad, right or wrong, but interprets these labels in terms of either the physical or the hedonistic consequences of action (punishment, reward, exchange of favors), or in terms of the physical power of those who enunciate the rules and labels. The level is divided into the following two stages:

STAGE 1: *The punishment and obedience orientation.* The physical consequences of action determine its goodness or badness regardless of the human meaning or value of these consequences. Avoidance of punishment and unquestioning deference to power are valued in their own right, not in terms of respect for an underlying moral order supported by punishment and authority (the latter being stage 4).

STAGE 2: *The instrumental relativist orientation.* Right action consists of that which instrumentally satisfies one's own needs and occasionally the needs of others. Human relations are viewed in terms like those of the market place. Elements of fairness, of reciprocity, and of equal sharing are present, but they are always interpreted in a physical pragmatic way. Reciprocity is a matter of "you scratch my back and I'll scratch yours," not of loyalty, gratitude, or justice.

II. CONVENTIONAL LEVEL

At this level, maintaining the expectations of the individual's family, group, or nation is perceived as valuable in its own right, regardless of immediate and obvious consequences. The attitude is not only one of *conformity* to personal expectations and social order, but of loyalty to it, of actively *maintaining*, supporting, and justifying the order, and of identifying with the persons or group involved in it. At this level, there are the following two stages:

STAGE 3: *The interpersonal concordance or "good boy—nice girl" orientation.* Good behavior is that which pleases or helps others and is approved by them. There is much conformity to stereotypical images of what is majority or "natural" behavior. Behavior is frequently judged by intention—"he means

We discussed at length the development of conscience as a necessary ingredient for the understanding of moral discourse. This discussion included two major topics: (1) treatment of the relationship between morality and religion, and (2) a description of structures of thought. Under the first topic we concluded that, although they are well" becomes important for the first time. One earns approval by being "nice."

STAGE 4:   *The "law and order" orientation.* There is orientation toward authority, fixed rules, and the maintenance of the social order. Right behavior consists of doing one's duty, showing respect for authority, and maintaining the given social order for its own sake.

III. POSTCONVENTIONAL, AUTONOMOUS, OR PRINCIPLED LEVEL

At this level, there is a clear effort to define moral values and principles which have validity and application apart from the authority of the groups or persons holding these principles, and apart from the individual's own identification with these groups. This level again has two stages:

STAGE 5:   *The social-contract legalistic orientation,* generally with utilitarian overtones. Right action tends to be defined in terms of general individual rights, and standards which have been critically examined and agreed upon by the whole society. There is a clear awareness of the relativism of personal values and opinions and a corresponding emphasis upon procedural rules for reaching consensus. Aside from what is constitutionally and democratically agreed upon, the right is a matter of personal "values" and "opinion." The result is an emphasis upon the "legal point of view," but with an emphasis upon the possibility of changing law in terms of rational considerations of social utility (rather than freezing it in terms of stage 4 "law and order"). Outside the legal realm, free agreement and contract is the binding element of obligation. This is the "official" morality of the American government and constitution.

STAGE 6:   *The universal ethical principle orientation.* Right is defined by the decision of conscience in accord with self-chosen *ethical principles* appealing to logical comprehensiveness, universality, and consistency. These principles are abstract and ethical (the Golden Rule, the categorical imperative); they are not concrete moral rules like the Ten Commandments. At heart, these are universal principles of *justice,* of the *reciprocity* and *equality* of human *rights,* and of respect for the dignity of human beings as *individual persons.* [K71b-(164–65)]

independent entities, morality and religion have a mutually supportive relationship. In evaluating this relationship, we inspected the phenomenon of objects and subjects, the theory of the Natural Law, and the virtue of justice in the assessment of moral judgment. Regarding these three subtopics, we further concluded that before the major arguments surrounding the abortion controversy can be analyzed, those arguments that primarily involve conflicts concerning interpersonal relations must be isolated. We then considered how a natural-law philosophy supports a psychology of moral growth and provides a common ground for those on either side of the debate. Finally, we argued for the centrality and unifying function of justice in analyzing the reasoning component of moral discourse.

Under the second topic, structures of thought, we adopted the premise that for moral development to occur, certain structures of the mind must coincide with similar structures of the social world. Pursuant to this premise, we delved into the foundational concept of growth and differentiation before narrowing our focus to consider the idea of stage and sequence. We looked at the former from the standpoint of biological functioning and showed that moral reasoning, through a process of attaining higher stages of equilibrium, was a form of adaptation to one's social environment. With the latter, we focused upon the need to view the flow of moral reasoning as a series of discontinuities of thought which follow an established pattern. We then attempted to clarify this idea with an analysis of the dream phenomenon and of Erikson's life cycle.

At this point there was an abrupt shifting of gears with the introduction of a new perspective, the analysis of moral thinking synchronically. Up to this point we had been discussing only the diachronic perspective. The reader was asked to keep the notion of progressive movement in mind and, at the same time, to consider the periods involved as descriptive categories for inspecting moral discourse. Level and stage became phase and mode. We viewed a phase as a distinctly large-scale picture of the moral domain and divided this picture into three spheres—personal, social, and rational. Each sphere was said to depict motivation differently, starting with what concerns our immediate interest, advancing to what others think of us, and ending finally with what we think of ourselves. Modes were described as timeless thought constructs which broke the ethical domain into smaller discrete units, with each characterized by a dominant social perspective.

With this label change serving as an important transition to what is to follow, we turn now to an application of our theory.

PART II
The Modes of
Moral Discourse

Education is the point at which we decide whether we love the world enough to assume responsibility for it and by the same token save it from that ruin which, except for renewal, except for the coming of the new and young, would be inevitable.

ARENDT

[N]one of the funds provided by this joint resolution shall be used to perform abortions except where the life of the mother would be endangered if the fetus were carried to term; or except for such medical procedures necessary for the victims of rape or incest when such rape or incest has been reported promptly to a law enforcement agency or public health service.[1]

So reads the last enacted version, applicable for fiscal year 1980, of the famous rider to the appropriations bill for the Department of Health, Education and Welfare (now called Health and Human Services) that is known as the Hyde amendment. Since the amendment typifies the way in which moral perspectives are often subjected to the reasoning process, it is well to encounter it here as a prelude to our analysis of the modes of moral discourse.

For the most part, as previously noted, moral perspectives appear not as pure and well-developed forms that are clearly isolated, but rather as mixtures found in fragments or bits and pieces of several moral arguments. Imbedded in the Hyde language and the legislative debate that surrounded it are the two ways of moralizing that we have labeled Phase I and Phase III, the personal and the rational. While the major appeal of the language is ostensibly to a concern for principle, the more fundamental appeal might well be to what Kohlberg calls instrumental relativism.

On the surface, the Hyde amendment emphasizes a citizen's right to refuse to participate in an immoral act. The moral question is thus reduced to one of unconditionality. For many anti-abortionists, indiscriminate taxation for abortion imposes an unwarranted guilt by forcing action counter to conscience. Yet in another sense, and, we will argue, a more fundamental sense, there is a not-so-subtle appeal to predominantly selfish concerns: the moral arguer decides to reject public funding for abortion not out of conscience but out of a belief that the rejection will ultimately mean lower taxes. (It might just as easily be argued that those who support public funding for abortion—conservatives or otherwise—do so because ultimately abortion would mean lower child-welfare costs.) Insofar as the decision in favor of the Hyde amendment reflects a habitually conservative approach to spending measures, the moral reasoning can hardly be classified as arising from a matter of conscience. It rather arises from simple selfishness. To test the authenticity or consistency of the funding rejector's or acceptor's moral reasoning, one would have to see how each might respond to funding acceptable nonviolent, positive alternatives to abortion.

Interestingly, the disguised ambivalence of the moral thinking of those who support the Hyde amendment has a parallel in some Kohlbergian-type research regarding protest activities of college students. In the late 1960s, moral-judgment interviews were administered to over 200 Berkeley students who were contemplating, but not yet participating in, an act of civil disobedience (sitting in at the university administration building). The interviews disclosed that the issue of free speech was so clear-cut to the morally principled students that 80 percent of them eventually sat in. Surprisingly, the next-largest contingent to sit in was composed of those who might be characterized as instrumentally hedonistic. Sixty percent of them participated in the nonviolent demonstration. One might fairly speculate that to these students a nonviolent demonstration was fun. From longitudinal studies, Kohlberg's objective assessment supports such speculation. This research points out that a student who engages in this kind of moral thinking "cannot tell an autonomous morality of justice from one of egoistic relativism, exchange, and revenge." [K71j-307]

Let us turn now to a detailed discussion of each mode of moral discourse.

MODE 1. PUNISHMENT

Nietzsche once remarked that all morality begins in fear. The same thought was expressed more poignantly by Santayana, who graced it with the observation that the world responds first to the cry of life and then to reason. Both comments, of course, are reactions to the simple biological truth that the human organism's pre-emptive activity is to avoid self-damage. By definition, behavior that is moral avoids what is lethal or hurtful.

As the initial expression of Phase I thinking, morality at Mode 1 is a reaction to external stimuli. What may happen to the individual, whether actual or potential, determines interpersonal behavior. At Mode 1, the prospect of being punished is the most compelling reason for engaging or not engaging in a moral activity. As a result, reciprocity becomes a routine mechanical equivalence made evident in the Old Testament injunction of an eye for an eye and a tooth for a tooth.

Avoidance of punishment is the most primitive form of reciprocity. Judgments of right and wrong are wholly determined by the physical and concrete. Negative consequences become decisive in justifying human behavior. With regard to abortion the reasoning is straightforward: Don't get an abortion because it is against God's law and you will be damned to hell forever, or don't get an abortion because if you are caught you might be put in jail. Equally imposing is the admonition: Get an abortion and avoid nine months of pregnant servitude and a lifetime of underachievement, or several months of infant care and the heartache of releasing for adoption.

Mode 1 sets the moral enterprise in motion. According to the empirical evidence of those who study such matters, at one time in the developmental trajectory of every human, all moral decisions were made initially on the basis of avoiding possible personal injury. (While an even more primitive mode could be described as Mode "O" in that for some individuals, particularly the very young, good and bad are simply whatever is liked or disliked, for our purposes morality first emerges as a power game or is reduced initially to the avoidance of punitive consequences.) [K79d-72] Action is justified in terms of eliminating the disagreeable or of deferring to some unquestioned power. Persons or standards are given no weight in determining what is to be done. The exclusive emphasis is on the pain of reprisal.

As described in the literature of moral development, Mode 1 reflects an unquestioning deference to superior power or prestige. The moral reasoner cannot see the human meaning of his or her behavior; moral decisions relate only to the self. Bad is equated with getting into trouble—the ultimate wrong—while good is equated with avoiding such trouble. A more extreme form of egocentrism is hard to imagine. Except solely in terms of the self, the ideas of justice and love are unavailable to the Mode 1 moralizer.

A sense of concern for others and for a universal standard of justice, which in some degree is characteristic of the other modes of moral reasoning, is not available to the Mode 1 reasoner. The overwhelming egocentric preoccupation with avoiding negative consequences at all costs, places the physical or material in the forefront of what is judged to be good or bad. Moral actions have no inherent value beyond what is felt. And the feeling level of Mode 1 is directed not to possible benefit, for even such a simple calculus is beyond the purview of Mode 1 moral reasoning, but to an uncomplicated obedience. There is no moralizing directed toward actively obtaining positive consequences, for such an objective would be too sophisticated for the Mode 1 reasoner.

At Mode 1 any notion of justice is entirely egocentric, and the individual's physical and/or psychic well-being become overriding. The value accruing to a human life derives from whether or not that life, or, in the case of abortion, the procedure used to end it, threatens physical or mental harm. Based on such reasoning, the unborn child's continued existence becomes arbitrarily dependent on what will happen to the mother.

Both children and adults engage in Mode 1 reasoning. Children do it exclusively—at early periods of their moral development they can't reason any other way—whereas adults, unless they are permanently locked in Mode 1, choose to do so whenever it is convenient for them. The adult, however, unlike the child, is usually able to see that the legal punishment exacted by society supports some kind of underlying moral order and hence amounts to a different kind of moral justification. If conscience is the ability to tell right from wrong, the

Mode 1 reasoner exhibits a severely restricted ability to form a conscience. Even the nuances of right and wrong are really too complex for Mode 1 thinking. Peremptory obedience compels one to disregard the morality of the actual command; what becomes more important is who issued it.

Spiritual retribution is a form of Mode 1 thinking. The minister, priest, or rabbi conveying to the moral transgressor a vision of divine hellfire or of some milder equivalent is tapping the Mode 1 fear of punishment. God is pictured as the vengeful punisher of those who trespass His law through abortion. To suggest that one need not fear such retribution because the scriptural mandate is not boldly stated is a counterappeal which taps the same basic motivation. Every cleric or religious denomination that endorses abortion is simply using this mode of moral reasoning. If abortion is all right with God's emissaries, it must be all right with God. The message is clear: Do not fear God's wrath, for God in His infinite wisdom gave us the freedom to weigh our options and make the most compassionate choice—a choice that includes abortion.

The developmental basis of Mode 1 is that no person can respond to more sophisticated moral reasoning until there is first a feeling of safety. Any threat to survival is therefore a pertinent motivation. In terms of abortion, society must weigh the physical and emotional consequences. Will the pregnant woman really kill herself if she is denied an abortion? What are the proven sequelae? Is the risk of a back-alley abortion greater than the risk of carrying a child to term? These and other similar questions constitute a type of moralizing that is distinctly Mode 1.

Appeals are made to Mode 1 motivation every time the abortion debate is reduced to compliance with authority. Subconsciously, nature is the authority most feared. A substantial part of the argumentation of both sides amounts to a lining up of nature's retributions either on the side of so-called safe and legal abortions or through the aftereffects of unsafe and illegal ones. Nature's punishment is blind and automatic, be it from contraceptive failure or from pregnancies too closely spaced.

☐

Kohlberg and his associates formulated a classic moral dilemma in the story of Heinz: *

Story III. In Europe, a woman was near death from a special kind of cancer. There was one drug that the doctors thought might save her. It was a form of radium that a druggist in the same town had recently discovered. The drug was expensive to make, but the druggist was charging ten times what the drug cost him to make. He paid $200 for the radium and charged $2,000 for a small dose of the drug.

The sick woman's husband, Heinz, went to everyone he knew to borrow the money, but he could only get together about $1,000 which is half of what it cost. He told the druggist that his wife was dying, and asked him to sell it cheaper or let him pay later. But the druggist said, "No, I discovered the drug and I'm going to make money from it." So Heinz got desperate and broke into the man's store to steal the drug for his wife.

Thus Heinz, when reasoning in Mode 1, is faced with two threatening possibilities. If he steals the drug to save his wife, he could get caught and sent to jail; if he does not his wife will likely die. Confronted by an apparent no-win situation, Heinz is compelled to respond out of fear, the fear of suffering painful consequences. There is no internalized sense of right or wrong. The decision to act is determined by the desire to avoid trouble. Fear of punishment becomes the sole motivation, and everything of value is generated from it.

Consider another hypothetical situation that exemplifies Mode 1 moralizing.

The Case of Melissa

At the beginning of her sophomore year in high school, Melissa discovered she was pregnant. She kept her pregnancy a secret as long as she could, but finally had to tell her parents, who strongly urged her to have an abortion. Without consulting her they made an appointment with the local abortionist.

Melissa seriously considered having the abortion *because*

1. She couldn't bear to lose her boyfriend, who insisted upon it.

---

*From "Moral Judgment Interview," *Standard Scoring Manual*, Form A (January 30, 1973), p. 1, and *Moral Stage Scoring Manual*, Part II: Tables (June, 1975), p. 4. Courtesy of the Center for Moral Education at Harvard University.

2. She would have to drop out of school and be educationally handicapped for the rest of her life.

3. She learned that having a baby at such a young age would probably injure her physically.

or, Melissa seriously considered having the abortion *until*

1. She learned from her best friend that since it was to be her first child, she would risk permanent physical damage if she did so.

2. A doctor warned her of the dangers of possible sterility, cervical incompetence, hemorrhaging, etc.

3. She remembered hearing of someone who had an abortion at a local clinic and died from a massive infection.

In all the above examples, Melissa's responses for or against abortion are attempts to dodge some form of pain. Hence the Mode 1 method of moral reasoning is being used.

Now, consider the Mode 1 moral reasoning actually used in the oral testimony of witnesses participating in a U.S. congressional hearing. The true-to-life examples which follow are selected from among hundreds in the oral testimony of witnesses called before the Subcommittee on Constitutional Amendments of the Committee on the Judiciary of the United States Senate, Ninety-Third Congress, Second Session, and the Ninety-Fourth Congress, First Session, chaired by Senator Birch Bayh (D-Ind.). The experts cited during the period from March 6, 1974, to July 8, 1975, represent views either favoring or opposing a constitutional amendment banning abortion. Information at the beginning of each entry lists the last name of the expert and where the testimony appeared in the published transcript (part and page). The entries are placed in a time sequence and will be referred to hereafter as the HLA (Human Life Amendment) testimony.

HLA Testimony

Buckley I-81
From a medical perspective, abortion is—contrary to the proponents of legalization—still a high-risk medical procedure. The risk of dangerous infection, of uterine perforation, of subsequent sterility, miscarriage, and birth defects, is substantial. The proponents of abortion work a tragic injustice in not bringing such facts to light, Mr. Chairman, and I would urge the committee to give this matter its most serious attention.

Abzug I-103
Each year before the Supreme Court decision was handed down, physicians

had to treat about 350,000 women suffering from complications arising from illegal abortions. Each year, it has also been estimated, some 400 to 1,000 women died as a result of illegal, out-of-hospital abortions. Sometimes months of intensive care would be required to save a woman's life.

Tietze II-2

I hope to present evidence from several countries which will show that legal abortion during the first 12 weeks of pregnancy, in healthy women and without concurrent sterilization, is associated with mortality rates between 1 and 4 deaths per 100,000 abortions, compared with a rate of maternal mortality from complications of pregnancy and childbirth, excluding abortion, of 18 deaths per 100,000 live births in the United States in 1970, the last year for which these statistics are available.

Hellegers II-108

If we are to do one million legal abortions in the United States, and 500,000 of these are on the unmarried, if the 4 percent sterility is true, then we are causing 20,000 sterility problems per year. And that is something of a health problem, because it is irreversible.

It is not like infection which one can control by penicillin, or blood loss, which one can replace. These are irreversible changes.

Levi II-570

I have watched a 21-year-old die of an infection incurred during a criminal abortion. I, as a physician, could not reconcile her death with my oath to preserve lives.

I have seen a mother of four die, leaving her children without her love and guidance, because she could not afford another child. Her act of love for her children led to her death from a self-induced abortion.

I have seen a desperate 27-year-old threaten suicide if she was not given an abortion. This was in 1967, and being forbidden to help her, we denied her the abortion. She committed suicide.

Goltz III-110

Legal abortion results in an overall complication rate to women which is horrendous: 35 percent of all women aborted in Germany suffer long-term ill effects. In Japan the figure is 29 percent. In Canada, 39 percent among teenagers. In Czechoslovakia, 20 to 30 percent. In Australia, two studies show figures of 20 percent and 70 percent, the latter in a public hospital.

Lancione IV-668

When the day comes—and it will—that she realizes what was aborted, how will she be affected? Like the woman who phoned us who had an abortion 40 years ago and is only now feeling the abject depression and remorse and in need of psychiatric help?

Emerging from the congressional testimony cited above is Santayana's cry of life. Both sides reason morally from a biological imperative, capitalizing on the tragic sequelae of abortion—legal and illegal—and of childbirth. The physical and psychiatric penalties of induced abortion contain a clear moral meaning: Don't get an abortion because it hurts. And for a public becoming increasingly sensitized by the media to the threat of cancer and other diseases environmentally caused, the Mode 1 motivations for or against abortion are not likely to fall on deaf ears. The moral reasoning calls for a full-term pregnancy or an abortion without complication, discomfort, or pain.

A larger view, one not yet touched upon in our analysis of Mode 1 moralizing, must include the problem of interpersonal relations. Beginning with the externalized motivation of Mode 1, there is a real concern about the impact a pregnancy might have on one's sexual partner, whether spouse or lover (and upon one's parents or one's peers). Actually, our concern here is not with the reciprocity of relationship but rather with the way in which one person in a relationship can coerce or compel a certain moral decision. The pregnant woman is often pressured into an abortion by the fear of losing the affection of a spouse or lover. The threat of this alienation is painful. One could argue, in fact, that some fear of a deteriorating relationship is at the heart of nearly all requests for abortion.[2]

Before passing to the next moral mode in our discussion, we must consider one final observation about language. Consideration of the relative harm of a full-term pregnancy as opposed to a legal or illegal abortion is couched in a terminology of pain. Such words as "bondage," "force," or "slavery" and especially "compulsory" as applied to a quite normal pregnancy are often juxtaposed with such words as "clean," "safe," or "therapeutic" to describe a legally induced abortion. These words, because they imply harm and coercion or their opposites, are freighted with the meanings of Mode 1 moralizing.

MODE 2. PLEASURE

Although the Mode 1 approach to moral reasoning proves adequate and quite helpful in dealing with certain moralizing situations, it falls far short in dealing with many others. As the initial expression of Phase I which, as we noted earlier, is oriented to the personal and for the most part is naïvely egoistic, Mode 1 thinking reacts in a totally negative fashion. Any positive reaction is beyond its moralizing capability and constitutes its most important over-all limitation. Mode 1, for example, is more concerned with not being caught than with making out, more concerned with avoiding a threat than with pursuing an advantage. In the language of Harvard behaviorist B.F. Skinner, one would say that Mode 1 reacts to negative reinforcement.

Mode 2 moralizing, on the other hand, while still intensely egoistic, is able to react to positive reinforcement. The Mode 2 moralizer soon discovers that some rules can be violated with impunity and that they can also be considered instrumental to one's desires. Thus while still oriented to consequences, Mode 2 transcends the purely negative to include whatever actually enhances the organism. Moral actions are still judged by the material and physical, but the results now include the positive. Instead of simply avoiding pain, the moralizer recognizes the advantages of seeking pleasure. And because of this he or she now begins, in the words of a once-popular song, to accentuate the positive and eliminate the negative. In short, a personal cost-benefit calculus obtains, and our moralizer becomes a pleasure seeker.*

In Mode 2 thinking, the unborn child becomes an object of future pleasure and is valued for his or her usefulness in satisfying the needs of the parents (or grandparents). The value of intrauterine life becomes instrumental in promoting one's own or another's happiness. Babies are valued not in themselves but for what they can do. In anti-abortion eyes they are seen as smiling, cooing bundles of joy, and sometimes as evidence of one's reproductive prowess. They can be kissed, cuddled, and played with. In rejecting abortion, therefore, the parents look forward to the pleasures they expect to derive from the child—the joys of motherhood and fatherhood.

By contrast, pro-abortion moralizing at Mode 2 pictures the new baby as expensive (it costs thousands of dollars to support a child through college) and, at times, naggingly inconvenient. What about the trip to Europe that will have to be postponed, the new carpet for the living room or linoleum for the kitchen that must be forgone? While these, of course, may seem to be mainly middle-class preoccupations, they are not meant necessarily to depict trifling, selfish people. More crassly, however, what about those sagging breasts and

---

* The reader should not confuse this Mode 2 calculus with the full-blown cost-benefit analysis of Mode 5. The latter is an example of utilitarianism.

unsightly stretch marks as reasons for abortion? To some men, a pregnant wife or lover may no longer look fetching in a bikini bathing suit at poolside. A pregnancy might even curtail a healthy or at least regular sex life. As the male folklore suggests, there is always more and better sex without pregnancy. We have all heard these reasons for wanting or not wanting an abortion urged by innuendo or elaborated in compelling ways. The reader should be able to add many others.[3]

□

Before Mode 2 thinking can occur, a transformation must take place in the way people are viewed in the moral equation. In Mode 1 people or events imposing sanctions were considered all-powerful. Now, a different view obtains. This new perspective among children, for example, is truly significant. Kisses really don't heal hurts, and Mom and Dad really aren't Wonder Woman and Superman respectively. In Mode 2 thinking, people are considered as less than perfect. They begin to assume life size. They are human. And once considered human, people can be looked upon as occupying the same life-space. Since we are all in this together, the moral reasoning goes, why can't we be useful to each other?

If there is one word which describes Mode 2 moralizing, that word is "pragmatism." Beyond the physical threats of the previous mode, Mode 2 has another dimension to manipulate in the decision-making process. Not only is pain minimized but pleasure is maximized. Risks are taken to satisfy immediate practical needs, much as one might take a chance in parking conveniently but illegally. In weighing such options, the moral reasoning is more rational than in Mode 1 and represents a definite growth toward freedom. Satisfaction is now added to frustration in shaping the decision-making calculus.

The process of earning and saving up bargaining points, including the general scheme of political exchange of favors and indebtedness, is part of a Mode 2 morality. With the help of cross-cultural research, a number of interesting variations can be distinguished. To the hypothesized question: Should a man steal food for his starving wife, a Taiwanese village boy would likely respond, "Yes, because otherwise he will have to pay for her funeral and that costs a lot"; his Malaysian counterpart would answer, "Yes, because he needs her to cook his food." Less dramatically, John decides not to tell on his brother because he might want him to do something for him sometime. I'll do this for you, if you do that for me.

A few years ago there appeared on prime-time television a dramatic presentation filled especially with Mode 2 moralizing. The drama was about prison life, and because of the main character's great interest in running, it was titled *The Jericho Mile*. Along with an absorbing plot, there was what appeared to me to be some realistic convict dialogue. In fact, the dialogue reinforced my belief (a belief supported by Kohlbergian research) that interpersonal behavior in prison makes frequent use of a Mode 2 exchange of favors whenever convicts help each other do "easy time." At one point in the presentation, sugar for an illegal still was exchanged for shortening the waiting time for a conjugal visit. Some of the dialogue surrounding this transaction comes to mind readily: "No big thing. You got it. What's it cost" (paraphrase)?

Although the moral reasoning is more rational at Mode 2, in that bargaining requires a certain amount of cleverness and the labeling of good and bad is no longer totally blind, it is still basically egotistical and self-serving. The conscience does allow for giving, but only as a basis for getting something in return. Sharing and a sense of fairness are present, but they are interpreted pragmatically. Moral behavior is that which satisfies the individual. There is an exchange of favors, but it is based on a "fair" return. A morality of the marketplace prevails, and human relations are viewed as business transactions with the seller always looking for a successful investment. Pleasure becomes another block of stock in the moral entrepreneurial enterprise.

Since they make no real difference, true loyalty and gratitude are absent at Mode 2. The image of the faithful wife or husband is only cosmetic. One is concerned about the needs and motives of others, but only insofar as they are personally useful. Others are looked upon as equals, but only in the sense of equal bargaining partners who can instrumentally satisfy one's needs. This, of course, implies reciprocity and a wider view of the moral landscape, but it is only rudimentary. The real emphasis is upon "what have you done for me lately?" or, simply, "what's in it for me?" And since the prevailing attitude is "I'm number one," sex among other things can be used as a bargaining chip. In the TV version of the popular novel *From Here to Eternity*, the officer's wife says to her enlisted-man lover, "If you become an officer, I'll make it worth your while" (paraphrase).

An exchange at Mode 2 may be one of favor or disfavor, including revenge. Yet the fact that there is an actual exchange is a distinct advance over the previous mode. Even though some other person becomes a mere object of pain or pleasure, at least the moral actor becomes minimally aware of the "significant other." This is a decided improvement and reflects an expanded moral capacity. The other is recognized for the first time as a competing moral agent.

In Mode 2, justice and love are still egocentric, but the egocentrism now has the added feature of pleasure-seeking activity. The individual pursues pleasant consequences. He or she becomes engrossed in getting his or her share and prefers need fulfillment to simply avoiding punishment. A type of sibling justice prevails: "Roger had a candy bar; why can't I have one?" Those who play this moral game exact the keen-edged rules of the children's playground. For the first time there are trade-offs reflecting a rational self-interest.

From a religious standpoint, Mode 2 moralizers cannot understand the maxim, "It is better to give than to receive." Instead they substitute the maxim, "Be good to God and God will be good to me." The individual considers the Almighty as something to be manipulated like any other person. God becomes part of a bargain, and any love directed heavenward has strings attached. "I'll be good, God, but I'm expecting something from you in return." The individual obeys God's law so that God will grant temporal and eternal favors. Religion therefore becomes a focus for Mode 2 morality and is treated instrumentally.

Building upon the motivational power of pain which directs the moral decision-making of the previous mode, Mode 2 is motivationally driven by pleasure. Judgments of right and wrong are now governed by whatever is perceived to be gratifying. Moral decisions are suffused with instrumentality. People become instrumental to the needs of others. A primitive reciprocity is achieved by offering to do something for another if there is something offered in return. It is everyone for him- or herself. "You scratch my back and I'll scratch yours" is the catch phrase which describes this mode.

The Heinz dilemma at Mode 2 represents a moral transaction at risk. On one hand, to say yes and steal the drug means that if Heinz gets caught, he can always give it back and would probably get only a small jail term. And for this he would have his wife around when he got out. On the other hand, to say no and not steal the drug would mean that since there is no absolute guarantee the drug would really work, not being in jail, he would be free to give personal attention to a wife who might die in either case. In any event, the important restriction with Mode 2 is that Heinz would be willing to steal for his wife but probably not for a stranger or even a neighbor; the latter behavior would require a more advanced stage of moral decision-making.

Now let us look at our hypothetical example in light of Mode 2 moralizing.

The Case of Melissa

Melissa, basically a lonely girl and now three months pregnant, finds that her relationship with her steady boyfriend of several years (the father of her child) is very unstable and deteriorating rapidly. They finally break up.

Melissa decides to have an abortion *because*

1. She doesn't want to damage her chances with a new boyfriend.
2. She wants to pursue her childhood desire to become a champion figure skater.
3. She doesn't want to turn down an upcoming opportunity to visit her relatives in Europe.

or, Melissa decides to keep her baby *because*

1. A baby would be a solution to her chronic loneliness.
2. A baby would remind her of the love she once had.
3. A baby would help attract attention and exhibit concern toward her.

Although the hypothetical example used here and in the previous mode may seem one-sided in picturing only the woman's moral quandary, abortion, obviously, can also be a problem for the male who is directly involved as well. In terms of Mode 2, some of the moralizing of the father might include favoring abortion because a baby would crimp his playboy lifestyle or opposing it because he wanted a male heir to continue the family name. Although the male perspective could be greatly elaborated, we will emphasize the moral dimension as seen from the woman's perspective.

Mode 2 moralizing probably appears too crass to most advocates for them to use it extensively in the abortion debate. There was a marked scarcity of Mode 2 appeals in the oral testimony during the congressional hearings on the Hyde amendment. While still potent, Mode 2 does not appear to be a dominant mode of thinking, at least in a face-to-face argument. For evidence of its use one would have to look elsewhere. For example, in Russia, where a population decline has been a matter of concern to government officials, it was reported that pictures of smiling babies grace the walls of obstetric facilities to en-courage births.[4] Also, in some Western democracies, the same policy of population expansion is implemented by tax concessions to families willing to produce children. Again, social policy encourages the max-imizing of pleasure by calling attention to and facilitating the acquisi-tion of some of the joys inherent in parenthood.

HLA Testimony

Katz II-323

But once deterioration became very apparent and we saw her lose all aware-ness of us, all awareness of her own human functions at all, and the inability to control them herself or to perform them herself at times, this was too tragic, since the facilities were available to prevent its recurrence, and we just felt that it would be impossible for us to go through this again, because we could not go through it the same way. We would know, even if we did not go through amniocentesis, surely we would have the child tested at birth and we would know from day one that we were going to lose the child. And you just cannot keep giving, giving, giving, without extreme, I think, mental anguish and pain, and I think after a while it begins to be just pain and not happiness any longer, because you cannot enjoy the child's infancy.

Johnson II-548

I would like to make it clear that I do not propose a test of morality here, nor substantiate immorality. I feel morality is not the issue for consideration, for it is my firm belief that in every situation where fertilization occurs, the mother should be happy and the baby should be healthy; and with the help of trained concerned medical guidance, she, the mother, should participate in that choice.

Roudebush III-180

A 17-year-old college freshman on a scholarship, overwhelmed by her new liberties, has too much beer at her first all-night party, and finds three weeks later that she is pregnant. She comes from a family where sex was not dis-cussed, from a school with taboos against any kind of instruction in family planning, from a community just getting underway with birth control clinics that will treat minors. What now are her alternatives? Society afforded poor ones before the Supreme Court decision legalized abortion. Let's look at them. There is marriage—if she could be sure which boy was responsible and coerce him. Percentage of success for those marriages is very low. She might go to

another city, have the child and put it out for adoption. This would mean giving up her scholarship, giving up college, maybe forever.
Shoup III-189
Most people support the right to free choice of abortion because they love children and are concerned for the welfare of potential children and those already born. This concern is a highly moral and practical one. Often, if a woman is forced to have a child before she is ready to care for it, she may never know the joy of having a wanted child.

Despite all its shortsightedness, Mode 2 transcends the limitations of Mode 1 in that there is a positive conception of the good and a more adequate view of interpersonal relations. The individual takes on a more optimistic view of the universe. One looks for good to come out of actions and no longer acts exclusively to avoid predicted bad consequences. In short, hope emerges in anticipation of reward.

With the addition of this second mode to the moralizing process, self-interest reaches its greatest intensity. At Mode 2, "One good (or bad) turn deserves another" and "what's in it for me?" become powerful obsessions. There is a willingness to bargain, but the bargaining is devoid of any real social concern. There is nothing but the most superficial understanding of the trading partner, who is nothing more than a commodity in a morals game trade-off. Mode 2 represents the triumph of pragmatism and an unimpeded search for pleasure.

One final word. The motives described in Mode 2 may seem ignoble, but they are not meant to be. While most individuals in prison operate at this and the previous mode [KKSH75e-255], selfishness is a fact of moral life and, at times, becomes characteristic of all our thinking.

MODE 3. PEER PRESSURE

At Mode 3 the standards of the community identify what is good or evil and a striving for the good opinion of others becomes the dominant concern. Whatever is perceived to be in society's best interest or the nice or appropriate thing to do is acted upon as morally right. Opinion polls purporting to show the wish and conscience of the community are thought to reflect the good. Collective judgment is extolled as the unquestioned and unerring voice of the people, the consensus of what is proper behavior. And because few want to be left out of the consensus, behavior often becomes trendy and subject to the vagaries of the fickle crowd. *Vox populi, vox Dei,* the voice of the people is the voice of God.

Mode 3 moralizing, which begins Phase II, represents the power of social convention manifested primarily in the desire to be liked by others. If fear was the controlling emotion of Phase I, a feeling of shame is its counterpart in the next phase. There is a radically new kind of moral thought at Mode 3. John refrains from tattling on his brother Tom not because, as in the previous mode, Tom might be able to reciprocate later, but because Tom trusts his brother and John wishes to be worthy of that trust. Note, however, that the moral reasoning at Mode 3 can be operationally indeterminate. By the same desire to do what is expected, John could tell his father about Tom because John's father can also be trusted. While the form of the responses may be the same, contradictory outcomes are possible. The crucial point is, however, that at Mode 3 feelings are enslaved by what others may think.

From the intense self-centeredness of Modes 1 and 2, there finally emerges at Mode 3 a genuine concern for others. The individual begins to gain moral knowledge from the inside, and compassion and sympathy emerge. Conscience becomes "other-oriented." Judgments of right and wrong are now determined by approval and disapproval. Moral identity is tied to others. Social status becomes deified. Model husbands, wives, and children who live in model communities people this conventional world. Mode 3 moralizing taps a functioning Dick and Jane book with Pleasant Street brought back to life. There are no discouraging words. All is a cliché of sweetness and light, or so it seems. Familial relations (including, by extension, the national family) are marked by a reciprocity based on gratitude for favors given and by a constant striving for achievement and a constant effort to maintain mutual expectations. If winning the approval of others means turning the other cheek, then so be it. At Mode 3 an incipient religious or philosophical social ethic begins to emerge.

Two important shifts occur in Mode 3 moralizing. The first is that pleasure becomes less concrete or physical; instead, it expands to show concern about protecting and enhancing one's reputation. We like to be well thought of so we begin to create an image of the respectable person. We do this by helping and pleasing others, by showing loyalty and by expressing gratitude. Our being nice generates social acceptance, satisfies the ego, and forces us to conform to social expectations. We go out of our way to cultivate good interpersonal relations. The second shift, in a sense, develops out of the first. Because of our concern for what others think, we now become aware of intention for the first time and judge the behavior of others accordingly. We give credit to another's actions, even when those actions may have been inept. Recognizing the fact that "He (or she) meant well" marks the beginning of a shift away from determining good by consequences only. The result is to give the moralizer more judgmental freedom.

The advantage of Mode 3 moralizing is that in behaving to please others and in conforming to the majority will, the moralizer soon begins to see what is right from another point of view. At Mode 2 this was impossible because the moralizer was locked into his or her own selfishness. Now, with the loosening of personal interest, the moral categories become social, and moral decisions are influenced by the expectations and feelings of others and the desire to win their approval. Mode 3 persons learn that others exist and that being kind to others is socially enhancing. For the first time in the moralizing process others count, and the question can be asked: What should a respected person do?

The concern for what others think can be seen in the fact that illegal abortions have never really been eliminated even in the most permissive societies. Independent observers would generally agree that they occur in Japan at a rather substantial rate and that they have never been eliminated in any of the countries of Eastern or Western Europe.[5] That they occur in the United States is well known. A policy of unrestricted abortion is no guarantee that illegal abortions will not occur. No liberalization scheme has yet been devised to bypass the natural moralizing tendencies of Mode 3. Many women who obtain illegal abortions, more than likely, do not want someone to know, be it an unsuspecting husband or parents or even neighbors or social acquaintances. The abortee is often concerned with what others think.

□

The approval so earnestly sought at Mode 3 begins parochially with those closest to us and expands to include ever-larger groups. But here is where certain limitations also begin. People belong to many groups that are often in competition. To whom should one be loyal?

If right is defined by the groups to which one belongs, and if one's behavior is motivated by group loyalty, the question can be asked, how are disagreements resolved? Mode 3, because of competing loyalties, can provide only an imperfect answer to these questions. A more complete answer is provided by some other modes we will be discussing.

As a guide to moral conduct, the arbitrary thinking of Mode 3 fails to achieve a satisfactory equilibrium. Role-taking becomes a matter of identifying with a stereotypical good boy or nice girl and of being guided by a bag of virtues consisting of honesty, loyalty, cheerfulness, and all the other ingredients of the Boy and/or Girl Scout Law. Any decent fellow would help another person out, or will do something because Joe or Jane Doe thinks it's OK, and, after all, Joe and Jane are pillars of the community—moral rocks of Gibraltar. Left unaddressed is the problem of what happens when two virtues compete with each other.

Pre-eminently conventional is the moralizing produced by the educational arm of Planned Parenthood-World Population. In fact, judging from what I have seen, most of it does not rise above the social conformity of Mode 3. Several years ago, for example, a PP-WP commemorative stamp was issued by the U.S. Postal Service which pictured a mother, father, and two children, a boy and a girl. Here was the ideal family size, and here also was a message to all newlyweds. Identify with that which is good for society. Keep down the birthrate. And, although not stated explicitly, if an unborn child happens to stand in the way of the new social enlightenment, abort it. Without even discussing the controversial question of the so-called contraceptive mentality, one could argue plausibly that, given the legality of abortion and a contraceptive failure, making a two-child family appear attractive would also tend to make abortion more attractive.

The limitations of Mode 3 moralizing can be seen graphically in the issue of capital punishment. If we were to relegate ourselves to the position of the murderer, we would oppose it. But, if we were to assume the plight of the murderer's victim, whose death might have been prevented by the deterrent effect of such a penalty, we would favor it. In like manner, a satisfactory resolution of the abortion question is also limited at Mode 3. Abortion becomes an abuse of the national (or international) household if a future Mother Teresa is killed *in utero*, but the nation benefits if the victim happens to be a future Madame Defarge. Here, as with capital punishment, there is nothing beyond a consensus to help resolve the conflict. Since at Mode 3 favor and disfavor are socially ordained, killing a possible Madame Defarge would have the same moral necessity as permitting a Mother Teresa to live.

☐

The appeals of both pro- and anti-abortion rhetoric are strongest at Mode 3 as the emotional rhetoric reaches out to a clearer delineation of "the other." If the moral reasoning could stop at this mode, the judgmental outcome might well be deadlocked. A woman squats in a pool of blood, the victim of a self-induced abortion. A baby aborted through the excruciatingly painful salting-out process looks out at the world as if to judge it. Both photographs, used extensively in the debate, are heartrending and magnify the contradictory tensions at work in the abortion controversy. Sympathy abounds at Mode 3. A tearful Gerber baby on a pro-life bumper sticker says it all, "Never to laugh or love, nor taste the summertime."

Almost exempt from rational discourse is the Mode 3 moralizing involved with problems of rape and incest. In the entire debate on abortion, no other combination of tragic circumstance seems to sustain the same intense and prolonged emotion as that associated with these reproductive traumas. Merely to mention them appears to short-circuit the thinking process. Most anti-abortionists consider rape and incest the most difficult problems to handle.

The moral reasoning associated with rape and incest is interlarded with loathing and disgust. Both print and broadcast media, in bringing these questions to public attention, provide just enough detail to stimulate the imagination. The average person recoils at the thought of babies resulting from such activities. Under ordinary circumstances the traumas of rape and incest cannot be discussed rationally. And this is doubly true when a pregnancy is involved.

As with the rape and incest problems, so also the sympathy generated for unfortunate children speaks to the human concern all must have for a well-developed morality. Mode 3 reasoning answers such a need. In the abortion debate concern is shown for potentially defective offspring. Birth anomalies such as spina bifida, Down's syndrome, and the emotionally jolting D-trisomy are often singled out by those favoring abortion. Also, in this connection, there was a major outpouring of sympathy in the mid-sixties for victims of Thalidomide and earlier for the plight of Sherri Finkbine of Arizona, who received considerable media coverage when she decided to go to Sweden for an abortion. Rubella, which, if contracted by the mother early in pregnancy, can cause moderate-to-severe deformities in the developing offspring, is another perennial sympathy raiser. When all these gestational anomalies are placed within a context of moral reasoning, they operate at Mode 3.

□

In general, some of the most poignant moral reasoning about abortion enters the debate as Mode 3. And examples abound on both sides of the argument. We know, of course, that ideal husbands and wives produce only wanted children, for shame is attached to parenting which displays unwantedness. Children the world over are to be loved and cared for with the best of available resources. The best product is a quality product, and population control is advised, if necessary, to maintain this high quality. Too many people just won't fit into a policy of high quality, and, besides, fewer people will make it easier to protect the environment. If individual and demographic needs require abortion as a social policy, that policy becomes even more compelling.

Along with a Mode 3 pitch for quality, one of the most sensitive and revealing moral arguments used in the abortion debate concerns wantedness and unwantedness. Of course, there isn't much of a rebuttal to the notion that it's always nice to be valued beyond what one can contribute to the interpersonal bond or to be simply desired for one's own sake. The popular mind, swept up in the fervor of some utopian vision, attaches no end of emotional problems to unwantedness, including anything from poor job performance to suicide. Anyone promoting wantedness, therefore, is considered a nice person who is sensitive to the needs of others.

Those who oppose abortion reject it out of hand as a remedy for unwantedness. They claim that the problem really belongs with those who do the unwanting and not with the unborn child. This response points up a limitation in pro-abortion thinking. The anti-abortion position, however, exposes itself to the same Mode 3 limitations when it stresses the great need for babies to adopt. Children should not be aborted, as the reasoning goes, because there is a real demand for them. They are wanted by parents denied their own offspring by nature (or by preference).

Advancing and defending society also have an anti-abortion thrust. Indicative of Mode 3 moralizing is the argument that a new human being is not a static product, but one that is inherently dynamic. Humans should be viewed as a valuable natural resource. Most babies are born with two hands and an intelligence to help solve humanity's problems and make life more enjoyable. The promise of the unborn is so great that some underpopulated countries like Canada, in fact, have actually provided certain financial incentives to stimulate an expanding population and work force. Anti-abortion sentiment which emphasizes military needs also reflects Mode 3. Military recruits are required to defend borders in time of war, and, in the case of a nation with global interests, to pursue those interests abroad successfully.

□

At Mode 3 the natural thing to do is what the majority is doing. One's behavior becomes stereotypical of those behaviors thought to be engaged in by everyone else. Such stereotyping, according to one commentator, is "the keyhole" that shapes a Mode 3 concept of persons; and "the *content* of the stereotypes varies according to the culture, subculture, or significant group" (italics in the original).[6] The frequent citation of public-opinion polls and the official positions taken by certain religious bodies are cases in point. Also, a behavior's acceptability in the past gives it the ancestral sanction. If so many believe in abortion, can it really be evil? This, of course, is the classic bandwagon propaganda technique that caters to the gullible through the urge to conform. Its genesis can be traced to the typical Mode 3 process of identification in which one identifies with those most admired. Each side in the debate has a list of Nobel Laureates which it uses when playing the authority game seriously.

Citing polls has another effect if public opinion appears to be evenly divided. It makes social expectations seem ambiguous so that perplexed individuals become ripe for a clever appeal to what "nice" people are doing. Illustrative of this are the occasional media reports of glamorous and successful women who have had abortions. The apologists for abortion took full advantage of this Mode 3 moralizing characteristic during an abortion referendum in Michigan. Prior to the statewide voting, there appeared in a Detroit newspaper supplement an article that highlighted the pictures of some internationally prominent women who admitted to having had abortions. For the Mode 3 moralizer only one conclusion could be drawn: how can abortion be so evil when so many nice people are doing it?

The urge to conform is tested repeatedly in the turmoil of ideological dispute. And few for very long can withstand the pressure to walk in step with the rest of society. Particularly when a social movement is very young and the issue involved both controversial and deep-seated, the protester/activist is a frequent target of Mode 3 moralizing. Both before and after *Roe* v. *Wade*, for example, a stand against abortion represents a challenge to conformity. Among those who oppose abortion and wish to say so publicly, by way of picketing or handing out literature on street corners, the taint of religious fanaticism is to be expected. Their behavior is nonconformist.

Obviously, to brand someone as a religious fanatic in today's secular society is a way of saying that his or her behavior is abnormal and that he or she does not satisfy accepted social norms. Since every person who exhibits the moralizing tendencies of Mode 3 has the desire to please and be approved by others, it takes a certain amount of courage not to be affected by the charge of fanaticism. And for the conservative middle-aged protester who has never before carried a sign or helped form a picket line, the need for courage may be considerable. The image of the little old lady in tennis shoes is hardly representative of the American cultural norm.

Some of the strongest invective leveled by each side in the abortion debate involves Mode 3 moralizing. No one wants to be considered "inhuman" or "insensitive." Yet these epithets are both mildly and vehemently applied. (Both sides, for example, point to the greed and callousness of those who run abortion clinics and blame their existence on the other side of the dispute.) And after a particularly gruesome back-alley abortion is recounted, the power of epithet increases enormously. The anti-abortionists, likewise, do not hesitate to call abortionists anything from intrauterine child abusers to baby killers. For those with thin skins, such accusations are enough to take the enthusiasm out of participation in a social movement. The loss of self-respect that participation could bring may be the reason some social movements are so difficult to get started and even more difficult to sustain over a long period.

A more subtle form of Mode 3 invective is the labeling of views as outmoded or antiquated. Each side accuses the other of this, and for those who already feel they are part of a beleaguered minority, the verbal blow falls doubly hard. But even subtler and more emotionally crippling is the suggestion that you are out of step with the rest of society. Anti-abortionists are portrayed as kooks, misfits, or zealots who should not be taken seriously. Pro-abortionists are thought to be possessed of the devil and should be taken seriously. One way or the other, the message to bystanders is, "don't identify with them; it might weaken or even ruin your reputation."

The shame factor is clearly visible in the Heinz dilemma. The Mode 3 case for saying "Yes" to stealing the drug would more than likely include the fact that if you do, no one will think poorly of you. On the contrary, you will be considered a real humanitarian. And, what is more, if you don't steal it, your family, and especially your wife's parents, will think you insensitive or even inhuman. The Mode 3 case for saying "No" to stealing the drug includes the same interpersonal sanctions but in reverse, and derived from a different group. The neighbors will consider you a criminal, and you will bring disgrace and dishonor to yourself and your family. Deciding either to steal or not to steal will make it difficult for Heinz to look everyone in the eye. He is caught in a no-win role conflict.

Mode 3 moralizing can be seen in the following hypothetical example.

THE CASE OF BILL AND FRANCINE

Bill and Francine are a midwestern farm couple. Reared on neighboring farms, they were childhood sweethearts who married shortly after both had graduated from the nearby consolidated township high school. Six months later Bill, who was very patriotic, volunteered for the army and was sent to Vietnam. When his enlistment expired he returned home and enrolled in the state university, where he majored in agriculture. After ten years of marriage and the births of a son and daughter, Francine discovers that because of a contraceptive failure she is once again pregnant. She and Bill, who have recently reconciled after a brief period of living apart, discuss the possibility of an abortion.

They decide to have an abortion *because*

1. They already have two children and want to do their share in fighting overpopulation.

2. A drug Francine has been taking to alleviate a severe skin problem might produce a child with birth defects.

3. They do not want a third child to prevent them from providing adequately for the other two.

or, they decide not to have an abortion *because*

1. Both sets of grandparents are devout Catholics who would be deeply offended.

2. People might speculate that the aborted baby was illegitimate, and such gossip would be a disgrace.

3. They want to win the approval of their farm neighbors, most of whom have large families.

To show the range and complexity of the abortion issue, we have exchanged the hypothetical case of a pregnant teenager for that of a young married couple. Had we continued with the former we might have pictured her deciding to get an abortion because a baby would have been an embarrassment to her parents or because she would have been rejected by her peers. In deciding not to get an abortion she might have reasoned that other girls were keeping their babies and, since she was now looking unmistakably pregnant, if she had an abortion her best friends would find out and disapprove.

HLA Testimony

Thompson I-(366–67)

. . . Severe stress between religious groups would result if either of these constitutional amendments come to the States for ratification. Because religious people hold deep and contrary views about their theology and abortion, the harmony of our religious institutions will be disrupted as persons on each side of this question marshal their arguments and prepare as citizens to influence each State legislature. The ecumenical movement will be tragically fractured.

. . . Finally, the effect on American communities will be divisive. Where church members have strongly differing views about abortion, the State-by-State ratification of these proposed amendments will erode the mutual respect and goodwill upon which our democracy is built.

Rees I-429

Now, I have been getting a lot of letters on this subject, so I decided to poll my district. I have a district of good, God-fearing middle class people. They are intelligent. Their educational level is high. Many of them are business and professional people.

I asked the question:

A recent United States Supreme Court decision legalizes abortions which are performed by qualified physicians during the early stages of pregnancy. This allows an abortion to be a decision made by a woman and her doctor, rather than regulated by the government. Do you favor the Court ruling?

Yes, 85.6 percent; no, 9 percent; and no opinion, 5 percent. My constituents are good people, and I think they believe very deeply in their religions, and they believe very deeply in their children and their homelife, and the quality of life in California and the United States.

Hogan I-455

Now, to those who argue that with abortion we are avoiding a generation of unwanted children, I might say that the year's long wait for the adoption of babies indicates that these children are wanted by many would-be parents.

Dellums I-543

I thought that the Supreme Court had appropriately decided this issue in January 1973. It disturbs me that a small minority of Americans are now urging Congress to amend the Constitution and remove a woman's basic human right to decide when to have her own children. It disturbs me that the leaders of a pluralistic society are asked to shape legislation around the religious views of a few.

Hartle II-327

It is said that those who may be deformed should be aborted so they do not have to lead an unhappy life and so as to not cause a great hardship on their families. I wholeheartedly disagree with this argument for several reasons. First of all, many unborn babies whose mothers are exposed to German measles are not born with birth defects, do not live unhappy, lonely, unproductive lives. Thirdly [*sic*], I know my parents would carry me to term again, if they had to do it all over again, and I am sure this is true for most other parents of disabled children.

Bernstein II-340

I am so busy living my life that I cannot seem to find time to write about it. If I ever do an autobiography I shall call it A Fairy Tale, because that is what it has always been. It is a fairy tale right now. Even before I was born, something remarkable happened to me. Let me tell you about it.

I was my mother's seventh child. My mother did not want a seventh child, so she decided to get rid of me before I was born. Then a marvelous thing happened. My aunt dissuaded her, and so I was permitted to be born. Think of it, my dear fellow. It was a miracle.

And as if to show my gratitude for my debut in the world, right away I began to show an aptitude for music. You see, I wasted no time. When I

was a year old, believe it or not, I could carry a tune, and at four I played
the overture to Poet and Peasant four hands with my sister.

This was from an article in Holiday magazine, and the musician was Artur
Rubenstein. The point is, just because a woman does not want a pregnancy at
a particular time, does not mean she will continue to not want it and produce
a battered child.

One of the more intriguing Mode 3 arguments exemplified in the
congressional hearings is the appeal to the spirit of Christian ecumenism. It is so contradictory to the general thrust of pro-abortion rhetoric that it merits further comment. The spirit of ecumenism is said to
be threatened by the uncompromising anti-abortion attitude of the
Roman Catholic church, which is accused of trying to impose its
morality on others. Years of careful tending have enabled the church-
es to weave a delicate tapestry of interfaith harmony. All of this will
supposedly come unraveled if the anti-abortion position of the Catholic church prevails. In terms of our Mode 3 analysis, nice people
suppress disharmony and nice people think that abortion is morally
acceptable. Nothing less than domestic tranquillity is at stake. Yet, no
careful observer of the abortion debate in America can fail to miss the
stressful undercurrent of hostility generated by pro-abortion rhetoric
toward the Catholic church.[7] Ecumenism, it would appear, should be
made of gentler stuff, or at least should not imply unity at any cost.

A concern for needs beyond the self begins to emerge at Mode 3;
the new focal point is a concern for others. Exchange of value for its
own sake, as in the previous mode, is subordinated to putting oneself
in another person's shoes. Human life is valued in terms of how that
life relates to other lives and to their mutual interdependencies. Kohlberg describes this mode simply and, I think, memorably:

In a second grade Follow-Through classroom a teacher explained to children why books and reading were important. She told them that "books are a
child's best friend." One boy became visibly upset, raised his hand and said,
"But books aren't a boy's best friend, a dog is a boy's best friend. Books don't
help you and care about you, dogs do." [K77b-29]

The point Kohlberg makes here is that at Mode 2 friends are objects
to be used instrumentally like books, while at Mode 3 they become
persons who can participate in affectional relationships. What this
further implies is that the value of human life is determined by the
empathy that is generated toward it. Institutions like the family, and,

by extension, the national "household," shape the interpersonal contours of the social fabric and, in Mode 3, provide a powerful motivational impulse.

Mode 3 is a great battleground in the abortion debate. Conflicting attitudes toward the proper expression of social concern help bring the issues into sharp focus. At stake are modalities of treatment for the poor, the deformed, the unwanted, victims of rape and incest, etc. Which way will society choose to go? Will it prepare new abortion facilities, or will it heed the passionate striving of each life, once started, to live—and the unconscious cry of every mother that the world is better off with her children?

Mode 3 provides a fertile soil for persuasion. This is because, as we have seen, a great variety of moral reasons grow out of our concern for others. Any prolonged and meaningful exposure to the intricacies of the abortion issue, coupled with an adequate understanding of the modes of moral discourse, should offer ample support for the claim that Phase II, of which Mode 3 is the initial installment, characterizes the moral thinking of most people. Further proof that America moralizes about abortion primarily at Phase II will be seen in our analysis of Mode 4.

MODE 4. LAW AND ORDER

Respect for law and order runs deeply. As a moralizing factor, the American ethos draws heavily upon it, just as the Hollywood western has immortalized it as an integral part of the American makeup. Men in white hats made pledges that were never taken lightly. In the Old West a man's word was his bond, and bargains struck by words alone were as good as any signed on paper. The pioneers made treaties with Indians which, though they were honored rather loosely, can be viewed as law-and-order instruments deemed essential to regulate the use of a common resource—land. There was a need in those days to draw boundaries and apportion spheres of influence. Alexis de Tocqueville noticed this moralizing characteristic of Americans in the reverence we accord the law, as well as the power we invest in our legal system.

Law-and-order moralizing creeps into our thinking at every turn. How many who read this will wait for a traffic light to change at a deserted intersection late at night or hesitate to park illegally even when the chances of getting caught are nil? The pull of Mode 4 moralizing can be felt in the shame mixed with fear one might feel in disobeying these simple ordinances. Misplaced as it may sometimes be, this reaction points to a respect for an underlying moral order and a desire to obey the law for its own sake. If one were to pursue the reaction far enough, one would encounter a concern for not disrupting social harmony. After all, if everybody risked noncompliance, there would be social chaos.

When the Mode 4 mind-set takes hold, the individual, while yet retaining some of his Mode 3 allegiances, begins to feel him- or herself a member of society. If Mode 3 was more concerned with the significant other or some third party, Mode 4 caters to the "generalized other" or society at large. This Mode 4 idea of society is more abstract than that of Mode 3. The increased abstraction can be seen in the new emphasis upon codification of acceptable behavior patterns rather than in the reliance on personal relationships. In Mode 4 thinking, rules determine proper behavior. They appear to have an intrinsic value. They seem right because they exist, and they begin to take on an existence all their own. They are needed to prevent social disruption. What the law does is give form to the approvals and disapprovals of the previous mode. Law then becomes of overriding concern, and its impersonal authority, at least in theory, transcends all personal loyalties. The Mode 4 individual believes that no group or person should be above the law.

In addition to an increased facility for abstraction, the thinking of Mode 4 moralizers becomes generally more sophisticated. They know that duties befall those who are given rights. Along with the idea of fixed rules, they readily acknowledge the fact that the very idea of a respect for an underlying social order, and of maintaining it for its own sake, implies a sense of duty. In Mode 4 thinking, one does not fear the disapproval of others so much as the possibility of harming them by disobeying some rule. The military, which is based upon a strong sense of duty, is a well-known example of this. Because infractions of discipline in wartime can clearly have disastrous consequences, failing to do one's duty (legally imposed) is considered the ultimate harm.

What we can justifiably call the law-and-order syndrome has a crucially important feature, that of maintenance. Mode 4 moralizers accept the system as it is and do not wish to change it. They try to preserve existing patterns of reward and punishment. They prefer conformity and are oriented to ties that bind (legally). They like governments that are legitimate and orderly, and gladly render to Caesar all the things that are Caesar's. If a sense of loyalty was characteristic of Mode 3, its Mode 4 correlate is a sense of duty. The duty is to obey and maintain lawfully constituted authority.

The emphasis upon shared values which is the essence of any social morality is passed on from Mode 3 to Mode 4. At Mode 4, however, the values are viewed in legal terms instead of in terms of what nice people are expected to do. Group loyalty and pleasing behavior give way to codification of those rules deemed necessary to a smoothly functioning society. At Mode 4, morality is no longer subject to the vagaries of simple approval and disapproval. The inevitable competition among groups leads to the establishment of fixed impersonal standards. And since competing interests are inadequately dealt with at Mode 3, the battle cry for Mode 4 is law and order.

In any evolutionary view of morals, group identification ultimately leads to system identification. The morality of Mode 3 soon proves inadequate to sustain social harmony in the light of competing interests. If one's allegiance to group A conflicts with allegiance to group B, some other group which transcends both soon becomes necessary. Perhaps the easiest way to see this is in the search for some kind of world authority to help regulate the behavior of sovereign states. Organizations like the UN are attempts to solve some of the inadequacies of sovereignty. As improved communications make the world smaller and increasingly interdependent, some type of regulation through convention seems almost inevitable. This regulation of group interest becomes mandatory in the face of diminishing natural resources.

The Mode 4 moralizer makes no distinction between law as social convention and law as eternal principle. As long as an individual law promotes harmony and prevents disharmony, the moralizer is satisfied it is a good law. "It's the law of the land" or "the law is the law" are maxims which have been absolutized without regard to whether or not there is any reference to an ultimate standard. Those who reason at Mode 4 are not really concerned about the source of law, be it a dictator, a democratically elected legislative body, or a supreme being. And although Mode 4 represents a much greater ability to abstract than the other modes we have discussed, the abstracting ability is limited in that it cannot separate into discrete categories law that is made (positive) and law that is discovered (natural). These distinctions must await the liberating abstractions of Phase III.

The extent and impact of Mode 4 moralizing can be seen in the standard fare of commercial television, one of the great modern socializing influences. On almost any night in prime time there will be at least one channel telecasting a law-and-order theme. Many of the dramatizations are built around glamorous occupations connected with bringing the guilty to justice. Others can be caricatures of Mode 4 morality like those seen in *All in the Family*'s Archie Bunker or Johnny Carson's Mr. Turbo. The law-and-order theme can be treated seriously or not so seriously. Without question, however, the visual broadcast media cater to it heavily.

It is not merely coincidence that America's favorite kind of moral decision-making is Mode 4. [RTK69c-(240–41); K75g-51] The preponderance of Mode 4 law-and-order themes in the nation's print and broadcast media is a solid indicator of how moral decisions are likely to be made by the average adult. And since a smoothly functioning society is a primary business of government, citizens believe that law should protect the equal rights of all and that disruption by civil disobedience is somehow unfair. Although these same citizens believe in redressing grievances, they have trouble reconciling even legal and peaceful demonstrations with accepted procedures for social change. If change does not subscribe to custom, it is automatically suspect. Preferring a Mode 4 orientation means that most people do not clearly understand the norms which undergird their political system.

☐

The first quasi-institutional response in America to the abortion phenomenon was clearly and significantly a Mode 4 response. In the late fifties the American Law Institute, a study group established by the American Bar Association, began promulgating a model penal code. The code called attention, among other things, to the apparent widespread disregard for the then-existing abortion laws by respected medical personnel who were performing them illegally. For a nation immersed as we have seen in the conventional moral reasoning which Mode 4 typifies, any discrepancy between rule and practice is shocking and provocative. Those legal scholars who drew up the model code must have found this particularly distressing, for even a simple layperson believes that justice is ill served when laws are flouted.

To anyone aware of the normal course of moral development, the reaction of the ABA study group to the presence of illegal abortions was predictably, and cynics might say hopelessly, conventional. Declare abortion legal for selected reasons such as pregnancy from rape or incest, potentially defective offspring, and psychiatric complications, and the judicial landscape has been contoured all over again. The nagging dissonance between precept and practice no longer exists, and once again law and order prevail. To plug "loopholes" or to make legal what was previously illegal serves a Mode 4 reasoner well. The law, so to speak, has been tidied up, and social disharmony held in abeyance. Like the closing circle of Thor, the legendary forces of chaos have temporarily been defeated.

The anti-abortionists react in a similar vein. They show a concern for the flagrant abuses of some abortion clinics, including Medicaid fraud, referral kickbacks, and substandard medical attention which has even led in a few instances to abortions being performed on women who were not pregnant. How do anti-abortionists treat this situation? Among other things, they pass restrictive zoning ordinances and make sure that abortion clinics undergo rigid inspections. Without recourse to a constitutional amendment guaranteeing a right-to-life, those who oppose abortion fall back upon the instrumentality of the law as a stop-gap measure en route to achieving their objective. Law-and-order reasoning is employed by such tactics as the Hyde amendment and by slowly chipping away at the *Roe* v. *Wade* decision through the appellate jurisdiction of the federal court system. These maneuvers all reflect a Mode 4 morality.

In America, the institutional focal point for Mode 4 reasoning is the Supreme Court. It is doubly significant, then, that the role of judge consistently ranks high in prestige on scales of occupations. Since the law tends to be viewed as sacred by most people, symbolically those who adjudicate become high priests. To intensify the illusion, the judges wear black robes and, in the case of the U.S. Supreme Court, the building where decisions are made actually looks like a Greek temple. What the judges decide therefore tends to lose its human origins and appears to emanate from the divine. In terms of our analysis, the high court assumes a grave responsibility in ruling wisely. With a decision like *Roe* v. *Wade*, not only were abortions made legal, they were encouraged. To eliminate the legal barriers to an action is, for many, to render it moral and thereby give it sanction.

As this book is written, a substantial number of state legislatures in America have passed resolutions calling upon Congress to set up a constitutional convention for the purpose of drafting an amendment to balance the federal budget. The national furor which this proposal has caused is indicative of the strength of the law-and-order sentiment that prevails in so much of our moral reasoning. At the heart of the controversy is a great fear that a convention so established could not be restricted to budgetary matters, but would expose the entire Constitution to the possibility of being rewritten. Such a possibility, it is alleged, might put in jeopardy the basic document from which so much of the nation's law-and-order morality flows.[8] In fact, even with a constitutional convention restricted to a single topic, many probably feel that constitutional change should be beyond the purview of the average citizen and left to some Olympian elite.

The most revered secular document in the United States is the federal Constitution. In the eyes of the average citizen (and of many legislators), the mystique surrounding it enhances the sacredness of law and the corresponding duty to uphold it at all costs. Fearing the takeover of such a constitutional convention by well-organized factions whose ideologies might threaten the peace and tranquillity of the republic, many congressmen, as some preliminary votes have already indicated, would vote without hesitation against the necessary enabling legislation. The rationale behind these negative votes would arise from Mode 4 reasoning, which extols the maintenance of the social order. To place the Constitution in jeopardy would shake the foundations of the federal system and leave the country up for grabs. While it would be naïve to imagine that the fear of social chaos is the only reason for recommending a negative vote, it would be equally naïve to conclude that it did not exist. To the extent that fear of disorder actually prompts voting behavior, it also reflects Mode 4 reasoning in action.

At different times in the abortion controversy both sides have used the same basic Mode 4 appeal. Prior to the *Roe* v. *Wade* decision, for example, anti-abortionists were arguing that any relaxation of state laws against abortion was unconstitutional since the Constitution supposedly protected the inalienable right-to-life of all citizens. Now that the U.S. Supreme Court has interpreted the Constitution in favor of abortion, the anti-abortionists threaten to reverse the decision with a constitutional amendment. Two avenues of constitutional change have been advocated: the traditional procedure through a specific amendment proposed by Congress, and one that, like the budget-balancing proposal mentioned earlier, would call a special constitutional convention, something never before attempted. In response to these proposals, the pro-abortionists contend, in typical law-and-order fashion, that one should not tamper with a Constitution probably amended enough already (26 times in nearly 200 years), that even amending the Constitution would violate the Constitution, and that a convention would risk anarchy. To counteract this Mode 4 moralizing, anti-abortionists reply that the agenda of a constitutional convention could be restricted (something also suggested by an American Bar Association study) and that an amendment would not radically change the basic document, only fine-tune it. And so the arguments go, with each side claiming to uphold the Constitution and to promote law and order.

☐

One of the clearest examples of Mode 4 reasoning can be seen in the references made by pro-abortionists to the problem of illegitimacy. Their rhetoric presents illegitimate children as serious violations of a social expectation, i.e., to be born according to law. To the pro-abortionist, these children represent a disordered society. Pregnant women on welfare break a social norm in begetting illegitimate children. They place an unfair burden on taxpayers in the form of increased welfare costs. If these violations are allowed to multiply, society will cease to function. Thus, a serious social problem can be averted through aborting out-of-wedlock pregnancies.

The Mode 4 reasoning of pro-abortionists also uses the law-and-order theme to introduce newer and greater evils into the debate. They claim that a constitutional amendment banning abortion would create chaos in American law. Using the protection of equal rights as a paradigm, they see the U.S. court system as inundated with litigation involving negligence and property law, murder, manslaughter, accident, assault, inheritance, and wrongful death, not to mention medical malpractice. An amendment would impose unacceptable burdens upon courts that already have crowded dockets and upon law-enforcement agencies that would have to expand, increase, and speed up investigations. These collateral consequences would add confusion, uncertainty, and needless complications. Topping off the newer and greater evils is a reduction to absurdity—funerals for embryos are suggested as a logical extension of the pro-life position.

The anti-abortionists respond with newer and greater evils of their own. They agree that the Constitution should not be treated casually through the amendment process, but claim that a right-to-life amendment, with the respect for life it would inspire, is a vital proposal that would strengthen and clarify the constitutional guarantee of fundamental rights. In a more pragmatic approach to the perceived Mode 4 evils of *Roe* v. *Wade*, anti-abortionists have attempted to expose the law-and-order inconsistencies of parents prevented from disciplining their children (a daughter needing parental consent for ear piercing but not for aborting), of pregnant women forced by circumstance to make choices without adequate knowledge (the speed and superficiality of pro-abortion counseling), and of a medical profession chastising its members for practicing traditional Hippocratic medicine. Anti-abortionists see in abortion not a victimless crime but a crimeless victim.

☐

Built into the idea of civilized law, particularly as expressed by American law, is the notion of extenuating circumstances. The belief that certain motives are ameliorating facts which can mitigate the severity of a punishment introduces the concept of intention. With the other modes we have discussed, this was impossible, since moral decisions were influenced by the external environment and not by the internal. Now, with Mode 4, the moralizer begins to look inside the guilty person in order to insure that justice reflects reality and is honorably carried out. In the abortion controversy, for example, most state laws before *Roe* v. *Wade* took into consideration the emotional state of the woman and the circumstances, real or imaginary, that may have prompted her to abort. If abortion is indeed murder, as some would say, a mere five years in prison, which was the maximum penalty in most states, would seem outrageously inappropriate to the crime. When these state laws were drawn up, however, provision was made for exceptions caused by circumstance, and penalties for abortions were reduced accordingly. This reflected not a weakness in the Mode 4 mentality so much as an acknowledgment that wise laws teach morality while adapting to the dilemmas of the human condition. We shall return to this observation later in the book.

A respect for life at Mode 4 falls into a categorical scheme of religious or moral duty. Without considering life as inherently sacred, the moralizer protects it through compliance with some overriding authority, whether divine or human. It may sometimes be difficult for the religiously oriented to accept or understand any moral abstraction beyond Mode 4. In fundamentalist thinking the Bible says it all, and God's law is absolute in covering every contingency. There is no separation between a divine injunction and the concept of a natural law created by God. In essence, with this perspective, the increased moral autonomy of Phase III is imperfectly understood when it is not rejected outright. There is no morality beyond what God has ordained. Why bother? It's all in the Bible, Koran, or Talmud. For fundamentalists moral reasoning remains forever conventional, and religion itself is never viewed as pointing human beings in the direction of more autonomy.

Those who adhere to some facets of strictly fundamentalist Christianity have a tendency to be more concerned with divine than with civic order. The Jehovah's Witnesses exemplify this tendency in their refusal to accept the draft, give the pledge to the flag, celebrate any secular holiday, or submit to blood transfusions. According to the Kohlbergian interpretation, these attitudes are generated not by an autonomous conscience but by a respect for divine authority. Jehovah's Witnesses do not engage in those activities because God has so ordained. A similar attitude is held regarding abortion. For many fundamentalist Christians (and such a term crosses all denominational boundaries) there is no reason to go beyond what the Bible dictates. What passes for a twinge of conscience is really a respect for authority—a relic of Mode 1 thinking. Perhaps, because of a weak, little-emphasized theology of nature, God has become a supercop.

Mode 4 solves certain problems created by Mode 3 but, in turn, creates other problems that are beyond its ability to solve. The loyalties of Mode 3 can degenerate into mere sentimentalism or favoritism which, if severe enough, can create problems for any society. History is full of notorious examples of political nepotism and cronyism that were not in society's best interest. Human nature being what it is, excessive loyalty can blind one to the corruption of one's friends. Furthermore, unless there is a wider and controlling social context,

Mode 3 groups will have difficulty surviving. There must be a compelling sense of order that can overcome the divisiveness of partisanship. A more realistic idea of a functioning society is delineated at Mode 4.

A glaring inadequacy of Mode 4 can be seen in its customary view of justice. So much stress is placed on law and order that justice seems unnecessary. If we have law and order, why worry about justice? It will take care of itself. Justice at Mode 4, therefore, is subsidiary to organized social relationships and is defined in terms of what produces harmony. This emphasis upon the nonchaotic implies an unquestioning maintenance of the status quo, which includes the basic rules of the social structure. In this moralizing scheme what can't really be dealt with are violations of individual or even social rights caused by the preservation of imperfect laws.

In the Heinz dilemma, stealing the drug would set a bad precedent which, if duplicated enough times, would cause social anarchy. If it is right to steal the drug in this one instance, where does a person stop? One bad turn generates another. On the other hand, if the drug is not stolen, Heinz would be in violation of his duty to his wife, which was expressed in his wedding vow—"in sickness and in health." He would lose his sense of honor.

The following hypothetical example characterizes Mode 4 moralizing.

THE CASE OF BILL AND FRANCINE

Bill and Francine have reared their family and now find extra time to devote to their local church. Recently, they participated in a study group that was to help determine their church's national policy on abortion.

They and other members of the study group favor abortion *because*

1. It is legal (after *Roe* v. *Wade*), and no one should tamper with the Constitution.

2. It is what God wants because it is an act of compassion.

3. It will cut down on illegitimacy.

or, they and others oppose abortion *because*

1. It is illegal (before *Roe* v. *Wade*), and abortionists should be prosecuted to the fullest extent of the law.

2. It is against the spirit and substance of biblical teaching.

3. It violates nature and, at times, disregards parental rights.

As the abortion question lingers in the public consciousness, American society is becoming painfully aware that one cannot establish good by decree. Some, in fact, would even agree with Aristotle that it is impossible for a voted resolution to be a universal rule. To these people the Preamble to the U.S. Constitution means that governments are established to secure or protect rights that already exist and not simply to make or create them. In contrast to this interpretation, however, Mode 4 moralizers have a tendency to believe that justice is made rather than recognized. They believe that law gives sanctity to human life and are not aware that some other law could take it away. They are content to obey and maintain any law until it is changed, but since their vision of the law is so restricted, the actual process of change awakens in them no curiosity.

HLA TESTIMONY

Abzug I-102

I oppose these amendments because I believe they might create insoluble conflicts within the Constitution. They could inflict upon us arbitrary legal definitions of physical processes for which there is no universally agreed upon medical definition. They would produce legal chaos. And they would not work.

Krol I-161

The other implication here is that as a rule legalized abortion eliminates illegal abortions. We can speculate about that, but rather than speculate we should use the available information from the experience of abortion in other countries. And the fact of the matter is that in other countries which had legalized abortions, Japan, for one, while the legalized abortions ran to a number in excess of 1 million, there were also illegal abortions. I would like to read this short quote: "In Japan in 1955, when abortions were available on request and as many as 1,170,000 legal abortions were performed, the Japanese Minister of Health estimated from 300,000 to 400,000 criminal abortions were performed as well."

Rees I-430

I think that with the split of feelings among the American people on this issue, good people on both sides, that this constitutional amendment would be divisive in this country. It would cause people to resort to breaking the law. And in terms of the definitions in these constitutional amendments, the felony-murder rule, and the estimate that 1 million illegal abortions were committed before the Supreme Court decision, I would hate to say what would happen in the judicial system of this country.

Hogan I-448
An argument often raised to support legal abortion is that restrictive laws are broken. This argument is inconsistent and is not based on logic or jurisprudence. Virtually all of our laws are broken, and that is hardly a legitimate reason for repealing them.

Tyler II-175
These resolutions will certainly eliminate the legal practice of abortion. But even as powerful a legal force as a constitutional amendment will not end the practice of abortion itself. In 1955, the expert group at the Arden House conference on abortion estimated that there were no fewer than 200,000 abortions performed illegally each year. Now, 19 years later, the number of American women in their reproductive years has increased by more than 10½ million, and these women have an independence of attitude and action that could not have been anticipated in 1955.

Tribe III-347
And so, as I read the text of these amendments, the upshot is that they would not achieve their intended result. They would confuse the law, leaving it rather obscure. They might have some unpredictable consequences, but it would take an extremely strained reading of these amendments to use them as I think they were intended to be used.

There is an ancient dictum, traceable at least as far back as the Greeks, that the majority of people derive their morality from the law of the land. Codified social custom, in effect, encourages the average citizen to behave in morally acceptable ways. In Mode 4 terms the typical initial reaction to a new and challenging behavior pattern is to ask the question: Is there a law against it? That the law has an important teaching function was assumed in the mid-fifties with the desegregation ruling in *Brown* v. *Board of Education*. Its most recent expression can be found in *Roe* v. *Wade*.

Abortion made its first persuasive inroads via the nation's preoccupation with law and order. Indeed, if it had been part of a long-range rhetorical strategy, the ALI's Model Penal Code could not have been better suited to America's dominant mode of moral reasoning. The average American, we have contended, is vulnerable to appeals for maintaining social harmony. This observation is consistent with the theory of moral development and the empirical evidence accumulated in support of its postulates. America's moral thinking is centered at Phase II with a distinct preference for Mode 4. By accident, design, or even inevitability, the rhetoric of the initial thrust for abortion was nothing less than a masterpiece of audience adaptation. It might well have been one of the most significant early victories in the entire debate.

MODE 5. UTILITY AND CONTRACT

Whereas Phase II thinkers are content with conforming to the demands of society and maintaining existing structures, Phase III changes all that dramatically. Mode 5 introduces a critical or skeptical orientation to morality; logic prevails over individual and social concerns, and emotions are more readily separated from thinking. Emphasis is placed upon arriving at moral decisions primarily in light of consequences to others. The emphasis shifts from the unquestioning defense of law exhibited by Mode 4 to a concern for creating new laws to meet community needs. Convention is seen as a poor substitute for an enlightened social policy based upon flexible notions of reciprocity.

If a representative democracy is able to have an official though unspoken morality, that morality would almost have to be Mode 5. This is the language of the most hallowed instruments of the U.S. government, the Constitution and the Declaration of Independence. It is the language of the Bill of Rights and the due-process and equal-protection clauses of the Fourteenth Amendment. It is the language of duty as defined by the social contract whereby the individual agrees to obey impartial laws grounded in utilitarianism, or the best balance of good over evil. Mode 5 considers "a hypothetical State of Nature in which men rationally and nondestructively pursue self-interest and have rights." [GKCS76b-35] Laws are created and standards of conduct are agreed to by the whole society. The "public interest" is a Mode 5 catch phrase.

In transcending conventional morality, Mode 5 decision-making takes two basic forms: (1) utility or welfare maximization, and (2) focus on human rights and the social contract. The first amounts to a full-blown utilitarianism, while the second includes a constitutional government's insistence upon the concept of due process. Crystallized in the opening lines of the Constitution's Preamble to "promote the general welfare" is the one essential and favored instrument for achieving a maximum social utility: the creation of legislation. Due process, on the other hand, involves judicial strictures against arbitrary incursions upon individual rights. This is crystallized in the Constitution's Fourteenth Amendment: "Nor shall any state deprive any person of life, liberty, or property, without due process of law; nor deny to any person within its jurisdiction the equal protection of the laws." Both utility and the social contract define justice at Mode 5, but the rewards can be obtained only after full due process has been realized.

Utilitarian calculations are probably the most forceful and persuasive manifestation of Mode 5 moral reasoning. Implied in this utilitarianism is a cost-benefit analysis producing the greatest good for the greatest number.* Pro-abortionists, for example, emphasize the costs of caring for defective offspring and imply that the money would bring greater utilitarian benefits if spent on medical problems having a more favorable prognosis. Abortion, it is said, will serve women by eliminating a prime cause of their problems, and the utilitarian calculus adds this to benefits accruing to other affected parties (husbands and children, grandparents and employers, etc.). Because unborn children are denied personhood, they are not included in the calculus. If they were, the outcome would be vastly different. Then an inherent weakness of utilitarianism would emerge: How can the various utilities, in fact, be fairly weighted? How can one specify the good? What calculus can measure one person's happiness against another person's life? Until these ambiguities are resolved even mass slaughter can be justified as a utilitarian option, the "final solution" not just for Jews, or other minorities, but for unborn children as well.

□

The Mode 5 credo rejects the group mind in favor of logic. *Roe* v. *Wade* does make a feeble attempt in this direction through the formula that state interest increases as a pregnancy progresses to parturition (trimester by trimester), but since any arbitrary sequence neglects nature's fundamental continuity, the formula is not grounded in the basic structure of the physical world. The gratuitous expression, "You don't have to have an abortion if you don't want one," is likewise a caricature of Mode 5 thinking. While rights at Mode 5 may be individual standards agreed to by society, doing or not doing one's thing fails to deal with the fundamental issue of individual human rights.

---

*Again, this should not be confused with the personal cost-benefit calculus of Mode 2.

Mode 5 thinking is the focal point for the emergence of the concept of universal human rights. As Kohlberg carefully notes, such a conception requires a sense of "justice or liberty and equality prior to property rights." [K71b-201] Yet, for this to happen, a scheme of rights and duties must be placed within the context of natural law. Rights and duties derive from our nature as social beings, and as we noted in connection with Mode 4, the power of the state is thereby limited to protecting or "securing" these rights. At Mode 4 the law was considered fixed, but at Mode 5 it is looked upon as a human invention to meet human needs. Positive law is justified because it helps human beings. As Jesus reminded the Pharisees: "The Sabbath is made for man and not man for the Sabbath."

In a world marked by conflicts between competing self-interests or between rational self-interest and legal sanction, there soon arises a critical awareness of the need for nonarbitrary procedures to assure justice to each party. Due process is the phrase used to describe the distinctive American constitutional response to this problem. It is the natural outgrowth of entering into a social contract, a response to the problem of legal relativism. A desirable reciprocity works best when the contract is drawn flexibly and allows compromise between free and equal parties. Mode 5 moral reasoning permits all this to take place.

The denial of Mode 5 due process in the case of abortion rests upon an interpretation of the meaning of privacy. A well-known pro-abortion slogan expresses this meaning graphically: A woman should be permitted to control her own body. While privacy is never mentioned in the Constitution directly, it is thought to be derived from the individual's freedom to be left alone. Since a man's home is his castle, he has the right to enjoy it without leave of anyone else. Anti-abortionists contend that a woman's womb is the castle of an unborn child whose privacy has been denied through abortion. This interpretation, however, seems never to have been entertained by the U.S. Supreme Court. The *Roe* v. *Wade* decision has declared that a fetus does not have a right to be left alone.

Historically, the privacy doctrine points to the quasi-legal connection between abortion and contraception. In the latter case, the *Griswold* decision gave privacy its greatest triumph. Some anti-abortionists like to draw a connection between the increased use of contraceptives and the abortion mentality. This possible connection is furthered by the pro-abortionists themselves who have insisted that to outlaw abortion one would have to outlaw contraception, since certain widely used contraceptives, like the IUD, may well be abortifacient. While the physical and moral relationship between the two is not clearly understood, it is possible that both behaviors are caused by some common third factor. That abortion and contraception are related, although perhaps not causally, therefore seems likely.

The case of abortion presents a clear challenge to the idea of the social contract. Parties to the contract (i.e., the woman and her unborn child) are in unequal bargaining positions, with one party being entirely excluded. The weaker of the two parties needs a guardian or interlocutor, but even this was prevented by the 1973 decision in *Roe v. Wade*. The tragedy of this decision is compounded because it blessed with due process what many consider to be the taking of a human life. Due process is satisfied whenever a pregnant woman requests an abortion. And because the fetus has been tacitly declared a "nonperson," it does not enjoy equal protection of the law—another socio-contractual concept.

□

As stated earlier, America's Constitution is written primarily in Mode 5 language. It is the language of universal human rights, protected by the doctrine of the social contract and due process and enhanced by the expansion of community welfare. Unfortunately, according to Kohlberg, few citizens today can really understand such moral language, since the focus of their moral reasoning is Mode 4. However, there is cause for some guarded optimism as to the future. Kohlberg and his associates report that today a larger proportion of adults are engaging in Mode 5 moral reasoning. One longitudinal study "indicates that about twice as many young male adults (ages 26–34)" are moralizing at Mode 5 than were their fathers. [KE75f-619] If true, this is a healthy sign. With a change in mode of functioning there will be a greater sensitivity to moral problems. It cannot be stressed enough that one important reason why alternatives to abortion have not been adequately supported in the nation's legislatures is that they represent an imaginative rule-making capability which is distinctly Mode 5, while in Kohlbergian terms, the majority of American citizens, including their elected representatives, appear to be fixated at Mode 4.

The one core problem Mode 5 cannot resolve is the determination of when it is morally right, or even obligatory, to violate the law. Utility and due process are both inadequate approaches to this problem: the former because there is no principle which can resolve conflicts between competing welfares, and the latter because due process is too arbitrary and contextually grounded to be anything more than a weak substitute for principle. [K71c-62] Kohlberg puts the matter succinctly by asserting that a Mode 5 definition of universal human rights "cannot clearly define personal duties corresponding to these rights in the absence of legal agreement and the social contract." [K77e-191] Thus there is no Mode 5 principle which can resolve the conflict between pregnant women and their unborn children. Nor is there a principle within Mode 5 which can reject the notion that it is all right to abort because the U.S. Supreme Court has so declared. These are both serious shortcomings.

HLA Testimony

Hogan I-(510–11)
I think what we are talking about in our whole system of jurisprudence, and what my constitutional amendment addresses itself to is due process. Our whole system of jurisprudence is involved with the balancing of one person's rights against another person's rights. Now, where the right of the child is sacrificed for the convenience of the mother, or for her economic situation, or because her psychological well-being would be adversely affected by having a baby, I say that is not a sufficient justification for interfering with the basic right of the other human being involved, the child. But, where you have a situation where the mother's life will be lost if the child is not aborted, then you are balancing one human life against another human life, and I fully accept that because we have accorded due process to that unborn child.

Bayh II-573
Let me think out loud just a moment, and then throw this question out to any of you or all of you. This argument, at the risk of oversimplification, has oft times been described as a conflict of seemingly divergent rights, on one side the right of the child to be born, on the other side the right of the mother or the woman to make this decision. So I think it can be argued that we do have a due process question here. I have seen pictures in some infinite detail about the development of a child at various stages in the womb of the mother.

Pilpel IV-235
One thing is clear. If the fetus were a person entitled to due process and equal protection from the moment of conception, every pregnant woman would

constantly be acting at her peril. Presumably, the State could enjoin a safety regimen on every pregnant woman and hold her accountable, civilly and criminally, for any injury that the fetus suffered which she might have avoided. This would be such a profound invasion of the right of privacy of every fertile, and certainly every pregnant woman, that even the worst totalitarian systems of surveillance would seem mild by comparison.

In keeping with the new emphasis upon logical processes, moral reasoning at Mode 5 conceives of law not as an unassailable pre-existing system, but as something made by human beings and subject to human imperfections. This more relaxed and realistic attitude holds that while the law is not sacred even when protecting areas of personal freedom, it still should be obeyed for the common good. The narrow parochial interests of Phase II simply will not suffice. Whereas Mode 4 has difficulty coping with diversity beyond its system boundary, Mode 5 believes that diverse cultural systems can help humanity in appropriate ways. The Mode 5 criterion for a good law is that it serve humanity; if not, it should be subject to change. What is more, any Mode 5 law must be arrived at through proper procedures, and these especially include the consent of the governed. The content of law will be good if the method of law-making is sound. Due process and equal protection figure prominently in Mode 5 thinking. Law by decree, no matter how beneficent, is unacceptable.

One notable characteristic of the abortion debate, and perhaps its saving feature, is that both sides are at least capable of arguing in Mode 5 terms. They know the value of consensus or they wouldn't be trying to obtain it. They search, however feebly, for compromise and are willing to conform, however reluctantly, to the majority will. Both sides, for example, acknowledge the existence of an arbitrary element or starting point from which an eventual agreement may be reached. Both sides also support such alternatives to abortion as helping women who choose to keep their babies. The search may be inadequate and the goal beyond reach, but both sides so far have been willing to work mainly through the social structure, adapting set procedures to rid society of what each side considers to be a peculiar form of injustice. This modicum of cautious tolerance is to the credit of those who participate in the debate. They have agreed, it would appear, to work within the system, which is the only workable morality for a pluralistic society.

MODE 6. UNIVERSAL PRINCIPLE

Mode 6 moralizers subscribe to pan-human values, or those which are valid for everyone, everywhere and every time. They prefer laws which are universal, logically comprehensive, and consistent. The proposed moral action must be good in itself and in accord with some superordinate abstract principle. Justice and equality and respect for a person's inherent dignity and individuality are hallmarks of Mode 6 functioning. A human being is used only as an end, never as an instrument or means. The law is as binding on mothers and abortionists as it is on anyone else. Mode 6 is the stuff of which moral heroes and heroines are made. It is the end of moral dialectic; it integrates everything that comes before it.

Moral maturity and responsibility epitomize Mode 6. Self-chosen standards of right and wrong based upon the individual conscience as a directing agent in human affairs are the guideposts. Mode 6 stresses internal control over one's conduct. Guilt or self-condemnation is the motivational force; failure to act in accord with one's conscience becomes a painful experience. Compromise is ruled out because laws are subordinate to the principle of justice. If necessary, the Mode 6 person is willing to stand alone.

Immanuel Kant's categorical imperative is a prime example of moral thinking at Mode 6. Act in such a way that you would be willing to have everyone act in a similar way when placed in the same situation. Lincoln recognized this principle instinctively: "As I would not be a slave, so I would not be a master." If you would not wish to be aborted, then do not abort or advocate the abortion of anyone. The reciprocity is exact, the balance struck. Rights and duties are correlated. Expressed in the language of the Golden Rule, the categorical imperative is universalized positively as "Do unto others as you would have them do unto you," or negatively as "That which is displeasing to you, do not do unto others." If this moralizing were adopted universally, all conflicts would be resolvable. There would still be the conflicts that represent different points of view, but these would be amicably and creatively resolved. Lasting peace would reign in every person and among all humankind.

Role-taking finds its ideal expression at Mode 6. The person who engages in moral discourse at Mode 6 is able to project what consequences the contemplated action will have on those likely to be affected. Each claim is carefully considered. The final moral judgment is made with complete role reversibility. Full rights are accorded to each person so that the role-taking becomes reciprocal and therefore self-corrective. The expression "There but for the grace of God go I" is a recognition that roles can be reversed and that it is the better part of discretion to treat everyone as an equal. Complete role exchange is the purest form of justice.

All earlier modes impede complete role reversal. As we observed, for example, at Mode 5 the killing of 6 million Jews could be justified on the basis of a utilitarian pursuit of the general welfare. An atomic bomb can be dropped on two Japanese cities to save a million lives and end a war sooner, a Vietnamese village can be destroyed in order to save it, and a baby can be aborted for the good of the family or simply to justify some vague collective good or to protect someone's privacy. None of these things could happen at Mode 6. A distorted Mode 5 thinking directed the destiny of the Enola Gay and those who commanded the destruction of My Lai; and it governs many of those physicians who wield the curette. Mode 5 would not preclude those actions; Mode 6 would.

Although complete role reversal at Mode 6 is the ultimate ideal, the reality of the moral dialectic in everyday life reveals a subtle and significant inadequacy. The ideal of reciprocity can falter when one's concept of self-worth is so debased that it also debases one's relationships. A perfect but distorted reciprocity can be seen in the motto of international terrorist warfare—"No quarter asked and none given"—and in Gary Gilmore's desire to be executed. In the latter example, the convicted Utah killer considered both his own and his victim's lives to be worthless. Indeed, some might consider it ironic that when society obliges a killer's quest for capital punishment, it becomes essentially a collaborator in a murder-suicide. There can be no healthy role reversal when self-esteem becomes self-abuse.

Nonreversibility in human relations does not always mean a simple black-and-white case of injustice. In some instances it may signify a concept of human relations that is mutually degrading and despairing. Hence the prostitute's eagerness or lack of concern at being used as an object. She reasons that although she is used she also gets paid for it. Thus, to even things up, both the payer and the payee are mutually exploited. And more appropriate in terms of the abortion debate is the case of the parent who, having been abused as a child and thereupon feeling unwanted, decides to get an abortion in order to prevent another supposedly unwanted child from suffering. In despair, a distorted role reversal can suggest that the unwanted child might be better off not being born. When this happens role reversal is no longer self-corrective. To act reciprocally, moral decision-makers must act out of their own dignity.

☐

One of the sensitive unresolved issues within the American pro-life movement concerns the question of states' rights versus human rights. At first appearance, this may seem like a simple academic exercise. Yet, upon closer inspection, it is clear that what is really in evidence is a crisis in Mode 6 moral thinking. A deference to states' rights in attempting to solve the abortion problem runs contrary to principled thinking. Human rights, as characterized by Mode 6, should always take precedence over states' rights. Letting the representatives of the people decide is akin to letting the woman decide. Only an outright prohibition of abortion can satisfy the strict demands of Mode 6.

Since *Roe* v. *Wade*, dozens of anti-abortion sit-ins have occurred with the immediate purpose of saving lives. As one large Midwest newspaper observed: "The pro-life language has created a raw moral imperative to engage in illegal acts 'to save the lives of our brothers and sisters.'"[9] It is this kind of moral reasoning that places nonviolent direct action squarely at Mode 6. There is another, related idea that is crucial to our analysis: If one has an inherent right-to-life, then one has a corresponding duty to safeguard it in others. [K73e-641] This idea expresses the principle of nonviolent direct action. It is a restatement of Gandhi's satyagraha.

Almost from the very beginning of its status as a major social issue, the abortion question has been a catalyst for peaceful and not-so-peaceful demonstrations. Sloganeers on both sides have carried placards in strategic public places in order to attract media attention. With the *Roe* v. *Wade* decision, pro-abortion protests have quite noticeably declined (at least up until 1980), and their anti-abortion equivalents have increased while assuming an even more compelling form as abortion-clinic sit-ins. One way or another, these nonviolent protests are almost exclusively Mode 6 phenomena. They can be thought of as nonverbal statements of principle or as principled statements concerning some basic right. The ideological clash is between a woman's right-to-choose and an unborn child's right-to-life. These "right-to" slogans and their accompanying physical activities are powerful methods of moralizing. As of this writing, their increase in size and number seems likely.

The strategy behind the abortion-clinic sit-in is potent in its simplicity: to prick the conscience of an indifferent public through a highly visible media event and, more importantly in both long and short runs, to save lives. The confrontation between property and life is partly symbolic. A greater good justifies invoking the ancient law of trespass and necessity. In fact, to a large extent, it is this last emphasis which sets anti-abortion sit-ins apart from both the civil rights and anti-war sit-ins. The main thrust of these latter protests seemed to be conversion of the violent.

☐

A principle recognizes the primacy of justice over all other considerations. Whereas Mode 5 reasoning could not condone civil disobedience as an expression of a moral attitude, Mode 6 recognizes it as a warranted and necessary form of protest if it prevents a legally condoned injustice. Mode 5 people, as we learned, think not in terms of breaking laws, but of changing them. They are willing to redress grievances only through accepted means. Mode 6 people, on the other hand, would be willing to break them. The desegregation and anti-war sit-ins of the 1960s are prime examples of this. Peacefully calling attention to injustice has been part of the democratic and Judeo-Christian tradition, at least since the time Amos cried out against the oppression of the weak.

Perhaps the best way to understand a principle is to contrast it with a rule. To begin with, no mere prescription for behavior can be a true principle. Rules are prescriptions or means to ends and not the ends themselves. Principles are more abstract than rules and are not culture-bound. The Judeo-Christian decalogue, for example, is composed not of principles but of rules dealing with particular behaviors. "Thou shalt not steal" is a rule dealing with a specific behavior in a specific cultural environment. There may be exceptions to rules but never to principles. Any exceptions would disqualify the statement from Mode 6. A principle is a meta-ethical rule for evaluating other rules. As such, it is universal, consistent, and integrated.

The right-to-life slogan as a manifestation of justice also reflects a moral principle used for resolving competing claims. In addition to representing an ideology, it enunciates a "truth" found in the Declaration of Independence, that all human beings have the same inalienable right-to-life. In reflecting the principle of justice, the right-to-life should be universally and consistently applied in order to merit that reversibility not found possible with any of the other modes of moral reasoning. With an ideological slogan such as a woman's right-to-choose, personal freedom becomes more important than life itself. Rights and duties are then in disequilibrium. Choice is an insufficient ordering principle for human action. The right-to-choose is not a guide for behavior and is not reflective of Mode 6 thinking.

As we have just noted, a principle is a universal method of choosing which people may adopt in any situation. It is not the act of choice itself, but a guide for making choices. To choose or not to choose is never a reason for action: it includes no definition of what is right. Only justice meets this definition satisfactorily; only justice can be considered a truly principled reason for choosing correct behavior. Justice is principled moral thinking; choice is not.

Justice or equality is the only basis for resolving competing claims. With it everyone's claim is impartially regarded; without it only the strong prevail. No matter how small or insignificant a person may be, justice demands that fundamental rights be guaranteed. Human beings have an equal worth as ends in themselves. To abort them is to use them instrumentally and to deny them an inherent right to exist. Justice demands a universal respect for persons or it is empty of moral content. Mode 6 is the culmination of a sense of justice whereby justice becomes completely disentangled from the dominant concerns of the other modes. It is the recognition of a covenant each has with his or her fellow human beings. Only the perfect dilemma of one life for another, as in self-defense, can abrogate it.

HLA TESTIMONY

Lancione IV-670

If one believes in the brotherhood of man under the Fatherhood of God, mutual respect, care and love for one another as a way of life, a mentality of "what happens to you happens to me" and one of wishing for others what one would wish for oneself, one cannot sit back and seeing needless destruction, do nothing.

Except for Mode 6, at every mode of moral discourse, the principle of justice remains impure. Mode 1 entangles it with punishment, Mode 2 with exchange of favors, Mode 3 with social approval and disapproval, Mode 4 with law and order, and Mode 5 with utility and the social contract. Finally, at Mode 6 justice is disentangled from every other competing interest or cultural concern. Put in terms of the abortion debate, each life becomes inherently worthwhile; its worth transcends every other advantage or relationship. Human life becomes inviolate or intrinsically sacred. Valuing life, which is equivalent to respecting the individual, becomes a universal principle at the apex of the moral reasoning process. Any diminution of human life exposes society to a glaring moral weakness.

It should be remembered, however, that any legal prohibition of abortion must not be confused or equated with the totality of what Mode 6 implies. While Mode 5 moral reasoning can invoke the protection of due process and the provisions of the social contract, Mode 6 is not so restricted. It is obvious that because of the challenge of *Roe v. Wade*, justice regarding abortion can be achieved in America only by means of an HLA amendment to the U.S. Constitution. But it should be stressed that in situations involving biomedical ethics, right conduct can be pursued in society without recourse to law. At the other end of the life spectrum, for example, one could choose to deal with the problem of so-called brain death by simply not legislating in this area. In other words, for very practical reasons society may not wish to intervene. Let the doctors decide case by case. Even with the best of intentions, by first defining "brain death" narrowly, legislatures have perhaps set a precedent to define it very broadly at some later date. Not all moral situations are justiciable. Social justice in some areas can be pursued without recourse to legal sanction. After all, the moral system in China has held together for thousands of years without detailed legal descriptions of justice. As we noted previously, morality transcends the law.

While sometimes attaining a degree of social prominence, Mode 6 thinkers are rare (Kohlberg claims that they represent only 5 percent of the adult population) [K80a-60] and have sometimes lived a rather precarious existence. Almost since the beginning of civilized people's historic record, their destiny has usually been a death from unnatural causes. Socrates and Christ are two prime examples. And in our own time and place the names of Gandhi and Martin Luther King, Jr., stand out noticeably. All were condemned by segments of their culture for acting in accord with principle. The unadorned historical reality is that to operate at Mode 6 at an elevation of great social visibility is to invite hatred which, given the right circumstance, can turn to disaster. Humanity has traditionally dealt harshly with authentic Mode 6 behavior.

MODE 7. COSMIC AWARENESS

The question never asked by the modes of moral discourse is why be moral, or, apart from the Golden Rule, what is morality? It is never asked because it is basically a religious question, and the problems of moral decision-making are customarily resolved logically or rationally. Each mode asks the question, but no clear answer is possible until one can think in terms of principles that transcend space and time. Mode 7 enables us to do this, to find the ultimate meaning in life.

At Mode 6 justice survives tenuously in an unjust world. Our realization of moral inadequacy compels us to adopt a new focal point by broadening our vision. From finite considerations we turn to the infinite. We believe in a power beyond ourselves, in a God who represents the foundation of our moral existence. This is a new dimension of faith or belief in an independent reality. This wider vision gives us peace of mind through the realization that we are part of an infinite whole. Purely human concerns give way to the ultimate questions of life and death. We now possess the strength and courage to act on the principles of justice in an unjust world.

From the vantage point of the Mode 6 structure of a universal ethical principle there emerges a cosmic awareness. This awareness may be considered a hypothetical Mode 7, since unlike the other modes we have discussed, there is no hard empirical evidence to support it. There is more than a modicum of truth, however, in the observation that Mode 7 is a necessary outgrowth of Mode 6. Each mode is an incomplete expression of moral reality, and each logically demands another. Each mode presages a more integrated view of one's ethical responsibilities. Each mode brings new strength and a clearer vision of what we can become. It is out of this almost inexorable progression that Mode 7 emerges to represent an even grander view—an infinite perspective necessary for human health.

The rationale behind the existence of a Mode 7 is that no system can justify itself by itself. This reasoning is found in Gödel's Incompleteness Theorem, which stipulates that proof for a given system must be located at some higher level of conceptualization. If each stage of moral judgment displays a harmony in which unanswered questions are resolved, any unresolved questions must be dealt with at a more advanced stage. I have attempted to visualize this in Figure 12 (see page 49).

An infinite perspective is built into this key visualization of my developmental thesis. The concentric circles radiate outward to resolve new unanswered questions. Beyond the largest circle with its hypothetical boundary for Mode 6 is the largely uncharted domain of cosmic awareness. Part of this cosmic awareness can be seen in our striving to be in harmony with nature—a striving which, in turn, may lead to a more sensitive conscience. As explained by the theologian Paul Tillich, one modern philosophical interpretation of conscience links it with perfect ethical taste when educated properly. "Conscience works better and more accurately," he explains, "the more the taste for the universe and its harmony is developed." Carried to its logical conclusion, and echoing the philosophy of Albert Schweitzer, a moral developmentalism would seem to demand some kind of reverence for all life, not only human life. A genuine cosmic awareness thinks not only beyond space and time, but even beyond an exclusive concern for only the human family.

Our hypothesized Mode 7 can be likened to a shift in emphasis from foreground to background. Although both are inseparable because they are located in relation to each other, there is a shift in the perception of the Gestalt. The modes of moral discourse construct an ever-clearer foreground picture of what it is to be moral, enabling us finally to ponder what is essentially of ultimate concern. What are human beings, and why are we here? Only a religious outlook can provide an answer to these questions.

The cosmic outlook of Mode 7 gives people the confidence to solve their problems by forcing them to look for a reality beyond themselves. As a religious outlook, Mode 7 pushes to the back of the mind what makes one empty and fearful. To the despair of our age it represents a spiritual reply which is the rational counterpart of atheism. [K73a-(202-3)] As Kohlberg explains, Mode 7 is essential in "the sense of being a part of the whole of life and the adoption of a cosmic as opposed to a universal humanistic" perspective. [K73g-501] In terms of the abortion debate, the counterfeit of true Mode 7 thinking is the nihilism and self-destructiveness of the abortion mentality. Abortion is part of a great lethal complex with links to other forms of destruction, including war and capital punishment.[10] The constructive vision of Mode 7 promotes life and growth.

Modern anthropology conceives of Homo sapiens as a species immersed in time and open to the future. Our openness is a theme of great significance because it is essentially developmental in outlook. We become what we already are. The core of just moral decision-making is within us from the beginning; we need only to be helped in expressing it. In the final analysis, it is the teacher/persuader who must be relied upon to perform that function.

Part II ends the central theme of our discussion. It was written to investigate the power of the moral-developmental model in analyzing a pressing social problem. It was not written to present a clinical assessment of the moral reasoning of those who may be contemplating abortion. Since it considers how a moral stance is argued in the public forum, lengthy case histories were purposely excluded. It remains to be discussed how these insights can be applied to fashion a workable approach to movement rhetoric.

PART III
The Alliance of
Thought and Action

No man can reveal to you aught but that which already lies half asleep in the dawning of your knowledge.

GIBRAN

GOALS

Public education about the realities of abortion is more than the dissemination of scientific data—much more, in fact, than the discussion of when human life begins. If there is an overriding educational goal, it would be difficult to find a more significant one than the stimulation of the natural development of moral judgment. [K71g-9] In a more specific sense, it could also be said that the ultimate educational goal of those who are engaged in the abortion controversy is to help their neighbors recognize a simple moral truth—that human life is worthy of utmost respect at all stages of its biological development. By taking an active part in the unfolding of the public dialogue, the moral educator attempts to get audiences to reach higher—to strive for a broader view of our responsibility toward each other. And it is hoped that this process, once begun, will create a nation of self-reliant moral decision-makers.

To be sure, any persuasive campaign or movement is by definition one of goal directedness. This observation is based on the assumption that human beings can direct change consciously; it is the essence of what we said at the end of Part I about open systems. Embryonic growth and segmentation, metamorphosis and maturation have their analogical counterparts in the modes of moral discourse. Through interaction with a social environment the modes help modify our perception of justice.

But as the system of justice expands, a helpful environment can become harmful and cause developmental delay. This allows us to speak of system dysfunction and, ultimately, to study the role of rhetoric as a constituent of healthy social change. Developmental stress and strain, as suggested by Robert Merton, provide the social philosopher with an analytic approach to system dynamics. Rhetoricians, as social philosophers, share this provision.

Facilitating moral growth should be the goal of any humane society. And since growth is largely a personal discovery, helping audiences in the process of discovery implies an educational program that is tailored to the special learning characteristics of each individual. To nourish the learner's natural tendency to grow morally, the educator engages in a guided discovery. He or she teases moral growth out of society, literally coaxing people to be moral by optimizing those conditions necessary for extended moral growth. And insofar as more mature modes of moral decision-making reflect moral growth, the educator engages in the practical art of helping others to prefer moral decisions that are at more advanced levels. " . . . [k]nowledge of the good is always within but needs to be drawn out." [K70c-159]

Those who are steeped in the developmental philosophy of moral reasoning must at some time face up to the relationship between thought and action. Until quite recently, this part of Kohlberg's and Piaget's theory has been neglected (the latter de-emphasizing emotion and both emphasizing reasoning), but it is of uppermost concern to anyone engaged in conflict resolution. It is here that rhetoricians begin to part company with strict developmental education. For me, whose formal education has been in the rhetorical tradition, the distinction seems to be as follows. Developmental moral education is concerned with stimulating over-all growth, i.e., through the entire moral domain. On the other hand, developmental rhetoric is more concerned with promoting a single response, or with stimulating growth in a specific area. Rhetoric requires a special type of effort. It attempts to achieve a specific conflict resolution involving a broad public-policy issue like abortion. Though keenly aware of the importance of stimulating audiences to higher stages of general moral growth, the rhetorician would simply prefer to have audiences understand given modes of moral discourse. The rhetorician's goals are limited and immediate; he or she must be concerned mainly with action and commitment. In short, the narrower the developmental focus, the greater the need for some type of rhetorical response. Only the rhetorician can decisively bridge the judgment-behavior dichotomy or, in the consciousness-raising idiom of liberation theology, fuse thought and action.[1]

Education cannot be detached from social reality. Moral education transcends the artificial disjunction of form and content and is best imparted within a context of behavior. Initiating a successful problem-solving process in an area of great moral concern like abortion requires a direct personal involvement. Moral educators must be socializers and advocates. Because of the critical nature of the moral problems facing society, they must teach value content and behavior. Kohlberg is correct in now modifying his theory by admitting, and even stressing, a concern about content for its own sake. His work with alternative schools shows this. [K80b-47; K80d-459] Generating or reinstituting worthwhile moral values, or defending them when they are under attack, promotes a society's best interest. Surely this type of education for action need not be authoritarian but can be accomplished through accepted democratic procedures. If not, then democracy itself seems threatened and may well become meaningless.

The goal of rhetoric is a social order in which humans reciprocate to mutual satisfaction in modes of increasing moral equilibrium. The result is the moral maturity to which every individual is drawn by nature. Rhetoricians, as instigators to goodness, engage in a modified teleological enterprise whose aspiration is nothing less than to draw cosmos out of chaos. The ultimate struggle is between order and disorder, between alienation and solidarity, between social disruption and a sense of community. In short, we are condemned to persuade.

□

Social movements arise because the normal settings for teaching moral development have somehow failed. Family, school, and church are felt to be inadequate to the task of inculcating basic moral values or, at best, are thought to be unreliable. Societies falter when these traditional channels for enlarging moral perspectives become otiose. The field of value teaching is simply too vast to entrust to any single institution. Because each is necessary but not sufficient, social movements try to take up the slack. In an open, pluralistic society, social movements are expected phenomena which can signal a regeneration of moral growth. The rhetoric of a social movement is a form of compensatory education for missing developmental experiences. As nature may abhor a vacuum, so too a social movement abhors the absence of clear social guidelines for unrestricted moral change. Moralizing experiences are usually on the wane when social movements are on the rise. Each moralizing institution (and above all religion) operates within a very limited range to provide the moral learner with growth experiences. It is as a means to provide these missing experiences that social movements can always continue to justify their existence.

At this point, it bears repeating that modes of moral discourse do not represent a person's moral worth, nor do they reflect a person's stage of moral development. The labels we selected to identify and describe them can in no way be converted to boxes or pigeonholes for conveniently categorizing people; just as maps are not territory, stages are not people. Realistically, the abortion question represents a very limited decision-making area and is not at all sufficient for labeling purposes. Even if such labeling were actually our intent, we would obviously need a much larger inventory of content areas. And, besides, the dedicated rhetorician should be concerned not so much with where development begins, but where it ends. Just as IQ measurement should not lead to treating those with lower scores as having less worth, measurement that evaluates moral reasoning should not lead to scorn for those operating at less mature modes. A label is a kind of negative evaluation that is not in the spirit of the developmental perspective. Negative judgments are "put-downs;" they are destructive of honest conflict resolution. They weaken a sense of mutual respect and make effective negotiation and leadership difficult. What is most relevant to the communicator is not how fast one may respond to the proddings of cognitive conflict, but how correctly. Modes or styles of thought should not become tools of victimization. Kohlberg roundly condemns such victimization in some of his strongest language.

It should be clear by this point that the stages represent "ways of moral thinking," not kinds of personality. Yet the extent to which the moral stage descriptions have been used as "diagnostic"—i.e., pejorative—labels on people is dismaying. It cannot be over-emphasized that stages are types of thinking or functioning, not types of persons. [GKCS76b-41]

For the mature communicator, the only significant question must be: Is the moral decision in phase with right reason?

□

The theory advanced in this book describes the course of moral development for all humans. In a series of interactional emergents we call modes, it shows how the notion of justice differentiates and expands to include more interpersonal territory. It is not ethically neutral, however; it ultimately settles issues one way or the other. The contradictory paired-action choices we plugged in have this important characteristic: at the highest reaches of moral thinking, one fits and the other does not. And when human life is at stake, as with abortion, this characteristic makes all the difference in the world.

There is a probable relationship between moral mode and moral action at Phase III. While a strict developmentalism may not distinguish between action choices at Phases I and II, once the moral learner embraces Phase III, he or she is channeled into a certain behavior or compelled to act in a certain way. A very important hiatus exists, therefore, between Phase III and the two previous phases. The more immature thinking of Phases I and II can produce both good and bad moral decisions. At Phase III, however, the mature use of moral reasoning, with its characteristic logic, can point to only one outcome. Wilcox notes, for example, that although choice may not determine one's mode of reasoning and one may function morally at any mode, still in the classic Heinz dilemma, at Mode 5 pro answers (i.e., to steal the drug) were the rule and con answers the exception.[2] It could be argued even further that form and content, reason and choice, actually converge at Mode 6. How else could one explain Gandhi's claim that abortion is wrong[3] or, better yet, the determined opposition of Mother Teresa of Calcutta, who spoke out so strongly against abortion in her acceptance speech for the Nobel Peace Prize?

The unconscious distortion of certain realities of the physical world which I have discussed elsewhere in the case of the promotion of abortion[4] helps deflect the course of moral reasoning from its complete developmental trajectory. It is my view as stated earlier that the moral decision-making process that favors abortion exhibits a morality out of phase with normal development. To reject "the other" (unborn children) is a mockery of the very idea of human justice. And without the other there can be no reciprocity; no equilibrium can be reached in human interactions. The panoply of pro-abortion moral reasoning, by denying the other, can only mimic true moral growth. It is inauthentic on its face and represents a pathological moral condition. Pro-abortion reasoning is an abnormal description of the total moral growth process and cannot fit the entire Kohlbergian composite except as a mental aberration. Insofar as the single content area of abortion is concerned, we are dealing with a serious developmental problem.

☐

The more a movement educational program expands and the more it is borne by increasing numbers of willing messengers, the greater the likelihood that developmental retardation can be avoided and the possibility of normal growth still kept open. As this is written, society appears highly vulnerable to moral regress in the area of respect for and protection of human life. Like a lethal cancer, distorted moral reasoning has a tendency to metastasize to other proximate areas of social concern. Those who consume perceptively the average daily dose of print and broadcast media will easily understand. And the perceptive historian looking back upon this period of moral doubt cannot help but conclude that we humans are a death-fixated species. After abortion came renewed discussion of euthanasia and a more benign view of infanticide. The world indeed is a large clinic for those who would instigate moral growth.

In general, how can the instigator to goodness keep the developmental mechanism from jamming or, more specifically, keep the modal accessibility channels open? A response to these questions would seem to demand a twofold responsibility. First, one must determine the audience's approximate mode of moral functioning and, second, one must carefully distinguish normal from abnormal growth. In both instances, the teacher, like a physician, must be a keen diagnostician. And, although the accuracy of the diagnosis can be enhanced with sophisticated paper-and-pencil measurements like questionnaires, the teacher need only rely upon simple verbal behavior as an index of moral reasoning. Critical listening, of course, is mandatory.

CRITICAL LISTENING

If a single skill in the communicator's repertoire can be considered to be of pre-eminent importance, that skill is listening. Volumes have been written on it. In order to stimulate moral growth, the communicator must first understand the thought habits of those who express moral judgments. As we have noted throughout the book, moral decision-making can be categorized by the type of reasoning used. The modes of moral discourse are styles of thinking, and to comprehend them is to understand audiences more completely. Before communicators can effectively persuade, they must recognize the true nature of the thought process of those who are to be persuaded. Listening with extreme care, therefore, is a prerequisite to speaking with care. It shows a critical sensitivity to the needs of audiences.

To be sure, listening with care is more than a social grace; it is the skeleton key to understanding human motivation. And since our theory stipulates that the persuader's task is to impose structure on samples of verbal behavior, the persuader must be alert to every nuance of meaning. Education that is a guide to future human conduct must first reach the audience where it is. To be an active listener, one must take in not only what those to be persuaded are actually saying, but also, more importantly, what they are really trying to say. Successful persuasion demands, as it were, listening between the lines with a clinician's sensitive inner ear. Persuaders should listen carefully so that their audiences may eventually see more clearly. This is the minimum prerequisite for any moral education program. It is also the essence of good audience adaptation.

Persuaders who stimulate moral growth are really social counselors. By paying critical attention to what is said, they make visible to the moral reasoner what before has been invisible. Dynamic listening exposes patterns of thought frequently used but never clearly understood. The growth in moral awareness of those to be persuaded implies the transmission of new ways of thinking and judging made manifest by the persuader. This, of course, requires that individuals be encouraged to express themselves openly, completely, and sincerely. And it also requires that they be persuaded to think about the reasoning they are using so that they discover on their own whatever appears to be morally relevant and adequate. A strong case can be made that to gain moral insight requires less arguing and more critical listening.

☐

In a frequently quoted passage from one of his epistles, St. Paul said that the fate of humankind is to look "through a glass darkly." What we have come to know as the modes of moral discourse are filters in the mind or lenses of varying power which, with the aid of rhetoric, help to focus one's view of moral responsibility in a certain way. These filters or lenses are prescribed by nature for all humanity, and no individual developing normally can pass through life without using some of them. Unfortunately, however, in the process of use they become dirty, difficult to see through, and noncorrective. Each argument favoring abortion except to save the life of the mother represents so much dirt on the lens. This dirt must be removed before the moralizing individual can again see clearly.

The great danger faced by all movement educator/persuaders is that as a society locks into a certain level of morality, it begins to stagnate at that point. The longer a society remains at this point, the stronger become the screens or filters which now act as defenses against the onset of a clearer perception of moral reality. In such a corrupted state of mind, those features of the social world which are thought incongruous (but are really healthy stimulants to growth toward the next mode) are increasingly filtered out and so do not serve their natural function of promoting moral growth. In any social movement it is important that the tempo of education be speeded up constantly so that society does not stabilize and develop an intractable filtration system which always frustrates the normal path of moral growth.

MATCHING

In cognitive developmental theory, the physical and moral worlds come fully structured, and the human mind, in processing information about them, exhibits structuralizing tendencies. An important assumption of this theory is that mental development is a constant dialogue between structures of the mind and structures of the environment. Correct thinking occurs when the two become isomorphic, or when a match occurs. Cognitive developmentalists then say that symmetry has been achieved or an equilibrium reached. Matched structures minimize mental discrepancy and make thinking less painful.

From the developmental standpoint, persuasion is an attempt to match structures or to apply content to form. When applied vigorously to a content area the developmentalism of Piaget and Kohlberg becomes a persuasive instrument. And the more effectively content is wedded to form, the more powerful the persuasion. But while the educational theorist will contend that learning readiness depends on match and that a failure in persuasion is usually a failure in match, the practical communicator will simply view this as the need to speak the language of the audience or to track with their prejudices. And this, the communicator will contend, is what successful audience adaptation is all about. Speakers induce structural change when they meet the audience at its preferred level of processing moral information. After determining the proper mode, they modify their instruction accordingly. And when the developmentalist says that the higher the mode the greater the consistency between thought and action, the speaker's task becomes the creation of such a consistency. In practical terms, if the reasoner is at Mode 3, the communicator must speak to him or her in Mode 3 language with an invitation to move to Mode 4. Only then can a developmental moral persuasion fulfill its purpose.[5]

CUING IN

Although the specific techniques of intervention have yet to be worked out, some general recommendations are still possible. One technique involves what might be called "cuing in," or opening the appropriate developmental structures to discussion. Whatever cues in is like a "releaser," to use a term from the new science of ethology. To borrow a term from computer technology, whatever gains attention has the potential to "access" the growth process. On the broad scale of mass persuasion which utilizes both the print and broadcast media, sloganeering often serves this cuing in or accessing purpose well, at least when the slogans are fresh and provocative. With an individual or small group, however, the Socratic method of questioning should prove more helpful. Posing dilemmas has always been a core vehicle of developmental moral education since the time of the Greeks. It is transcultural and certainly ahistorical. By stimulating moral reasoning, the dilemma exposes the developmental structure to some corrective therapy, if necessary. Moral dilemmas, then, are both diagnostic and growth tools.[6] As one commentator states: "Moral education involves simply showing people what they are really doing. And it is aimed, not at those who lack practical wisdom or moral virtue, but at those who, possessing these characteristics, nevertheless fail to do as they ought because 'they do not know what they do.'"[7]

The role of rhetorical theory is to make the entire system of movement rhetoric understandable and to help communicators induce or spur progress through the modes of moral discourse. The teacher/persuader accomplishes the latter by effectively communicating at the audience's level of moral competence. Certain modes are emotionally central to specific audiences, and the communicator must cue in to them. If an individual cannot rise to a more effective level of moral decision-making unless he or she first understands this level, it is the teacher/persuader's task to help the individual see and understand it. And if moral development is the result of an increasing ability to organize social reality, it is the task of the rhetorician to show how that reality can be best organized.

☐

The Socratic method of teaching virtue exposes the reasoner to situations of moral conflict. It is a gentle but effective argumentation that generates dissatisfaction while avoiding head-on confrontations. It is based on the premise that thinking is stimulated by the problematic, and it blends well with Carl Rogers's peer-group counseling.[8] Kohlberg himself calls it "a model of the progression of ideas in discourse and conversation." [KM72b-456] Ideally employed, it makes the moral mode under discussion seem untenable and paves the way for structural reorganization. Its great strength as an educational technique is its subtlety. It is an almost denatured type of argument that teaches moral reasoning indirectly and, perhaps, because of this, more lastingly. Another word for Socratic probing is dialectic.

A healthy moral growth brings with it a deep respect for human life and a willingness to defend it when threatened. In stimulating such growth, educator/communicators become more than moral guides or peer-group counselors as they seek to enter the normal trajectory of moral development. They are not restricted to the passive Socratic-Rogerian tradition. They become active instigators to goodness. They understand the necessity of dealing with the audience as it is and not merely as they would like it to be. Their intervention is carefully orchestrated as they assist actively in the unfolding of morality. Their action is analogous to the work of insects in propagating flowers. An instigator to goodness, working through a social movement, is needed to complete the process.

Because the principle of justice is a natural outgrowth of the human's attempt to understand his or her social world, the system of moral development we have discussed cannot be imposed—it can only be exposed. Higher levels of moral reasoning are either freely chosen or not chosen at all. An audience is moved in the only direction it can go. Rhetoricians assist the choice of moral advancement by helping morality to develop naturally. This is why human freedom is so important. Freedom of thought creates a facilitating atmosphere where truth and falsehood can associate in a purifying dialectic struggle. The rhetorician's task is to help the social environment provide a smoother passage for the natural trajectory of moral growth.

In brief summary, the key to successful teaching is organization and control of the educational environment. Ultimately, from a social-movement perspective, this organization and control are gained through constant peer interaction or involvement with the rest of society in the moralizing enterprise. By breaking down destructive egocentrisms, this interaction provides the essential ingredients for a more perceptive moral awareness. And since audiences will more than likely exhibit a variety of modal thinking at any given time, though one or two modes may predominate, the teacher/rhetorician may often be well advised to employ a buckshot or cafeteria style of moralizing. In so doing he or she may run the risk of talking beyond an audience, but even the expression of a mode which is temporarily out of reach should not create undue apprehension. The mere mention of a higher mode can introduce a new verbalization and thinking process which could be summoned later when actually needed.

ROLE-TAKING

One of the crucial strategies associated with moral development is role-taking.* As we have already concluded, social reasoning is different from the reasoning which pertains to the physical world. A prin-

*Although "role-playing" seems to be a more frequently used term, it has a slightly different meaning and should not be confused with "role-taking." The former implies a conscious awareness and an actual observation of a process, while the latter implies an unconscious participation in the process, i.e., naturally or without intention, practice, or artifice.

cipal difference is that the former involves role-taking or putting oneself in someone else's shoes. This peculiar way in which humans structure their actions toward one another is characterized by the tendency to treat others like oneself or to treat one's own behavior from the vantage point of the other person. Role-taking links cognitive to affective functioning; it is necessary if one is to understand another's moral perspective. It gives value to others, a value proportioned equally to everyone and protected by inherent rights. Moral development means growth in the ability to take the role of the other, which, in turn, is integral to the proper functioning of society.

A fundamental aspect of role-taking is empathy: the art of placing oneself into what one perceives. Empathy requires an ability to reverse logical relationships. Translated into the language of moral development, an empathic response is that which exhibits a concern for the welfare of others. It is an important dynamic which influences moral judgment. [HK77f-57] The receiver of moral growth-inducing messages begins to feel as the communicator wishes him or her to feel—to react to others from the others' points of view. Let us apply this to the abortion controversy: Harm to others (including fetuses or pregnant women) is considered as though it were harm to you. Under the full impact of successful empathy, the only abstractions governing your moral outlook are the inalienable right-to-life and a woman's right-to-choose. That there is no middle ground does not mean that each must be played off against the other. One can indeed be pro-fetus and pro-woman simultaneously.[9]

In more technical language, empathy is the cognitive awareness of others and the affective or emotional response to their happiness or distress. It is generally considered to be the result of time and space, and, some would add, attention. Most who read these pages, for example, are not particularly concerned about the wars and the inevitable dislocation of peoples which may have ravaged Vietnam and the rest of Southeast Asia a thousand years ago. The human violence that ravages that unhappy region today, however, is another matter. America became deeply concerned with its own involvement and continues to show a concern for the many refugees expelled or forced to flee their homelands. With the passage of time, deep emotional attachments seem to disappear. Unless there is some strong ethnic or cultural association, who now mourns the bloody confrontations at

Thermopylae, Masada, or Gettysburg? Time slowly, but inexorably, dulls the empathic impulse.

Evil committed at a distance also seems easier for the average person to accept. Milgram's classic experiment with obedience to authority is a case in point.[10] In one of the more important psychological studies conducted within recent years, it was found that the closer one experimental subject was to another, the greater was his or her reluctance to inflict severe pain (65% consented to inflict pain when in another room and only 30% when actually touching the victim). The more proximate the victim, the more powerful one's conscience became. This revealing disclosure has direct and inherent relevance for an understanding of the idea of empathy and ultimately for the abortion dilemma. Getting close to the woman in a stressful pregnancy or to her soon-to-be aborted unborn child changes the moral perspective for good or ill. With the impersonal there can be no empathic involvement. "Out of sight, out of mind."

Yet, it might be equally true that "absence makes the heart grow fonder." In contrast to the impact of time and space in generating an empathic response, there are those who would contend that a lack of attention is the main factor. One can shed fresh tears over the memory of a parent who died twenty years ago and fail to heed the anguish of a neighbor. One can weep over a 2,000-year-old crucifixion and still ignore the plight of an indigent slum dweller. Empathic response, therefore, seems to be linked to whatever captures the strongest and longest attention span.

□

Some of the best examples of moral growth as a function of role-taking can be found in the classics of world literature. One such classic is Mark Twain's *Adventures of Huckleberry Finn*—a book which Hemingway claims was the progenitor of all modern American literature. In the Twain narrative, the main character is faced with an occasion of great moral crisis and grows in ethical stature because he is finally able to recognize something that really matters—a man's freedom and a man's future—and changes for the better because of it.

Huckleberry Finn centers around two fugitives on a raft floating down the Mississippi in pre-Civil War America. A young white boy,

Huck, and Jim, the black runaway slave, are genuine down-and-outers to whom life has not been good.

In Chapter 15 Huck plays a trick on Jim and, after apologizing when learning how much Jim was hurt, concludes the chapter by saying, "I didn't do him no more mean tricks, and I wouldn't done that one if I'd 'a' knowed it would make him feel that way." In Huck's developing moral thought, Jim now begins to assume the role of a significant other.

In the next chapter, Huck's conscience really begins to bother him. He is torn between the desire to continue aiding and abetting Jim's escape to a free state or, in preserving an allegiance to conventional morality, to turn him in as a runaway slave.

Just as Huck finally decides to turn Jim in, Jim says something that reminds Huck of their friendship and of Jim's deep appreciation of Huck's help. "I was paddling off, all in a sweat to tell on him; but when he says this, it seemed to kind of take the tuck all out of me." Huck is caught in the web of conscience and cannot extricate himself without doing violence to something noble inside him. What Jim says to Huck is very humanizing and eventually prevents Huck from turning him in. It is only when Jim is looked upon as human, vulnerable, and in need of help that Huck begins to free himself from his apparent moral dilemma. Says Huck: "But somehow I couldn't seem to strike no places to harden me against him."

This story is a powerful description of successful role-taking. The classic narrative portrays rights in conflict. Huck grows morally because he is able to think in terms of someone else's needs.

☐

The Harvard philosopher John Rawls has provided another cogent and compelling example of role-taking. Let us suppose there are two parties engaged in dividing a cake between them. In discussing the best possible procedure, both could sensibly agree to have one person cut the cake and the other select the first piece. This procedure would be logically sound and fair because each individual could change place with the other and still be assured of getting half the cake. By taking the potential role of the other, one can realize intuitively that the procedure to which both can agree has the built-in corrective of complete equality and reciprocity.[11]

As the Rawlsian example indicates, such complete or universalized reciprocity is necessary for simple justice to prevail in even so mundane a matter as sharing a cake. Much more is at stake in the abortion controversy, however, though the same role-taking procedure holds true. Complete equality and reciprocity are achieved only when a full human bargaining status is given to the unborn child. Having granted this status and assuming a veil of ignorance in the initial position, i.e., not knowing whether you are to be a fetus or a pregnant woman, the rational social response would be to choose not to abort, since realistically at least 50 percent of the time (assuming sex is only one of the characteristics to be apportioned), one could be the person to be aborted. From the abortion controversy, the role-taking message of complete reciprocity is starkly clear: If you wouldn't want to be aborted, then don't abort or, by extension, condone abortion.

Ideal role-taking rarely occurs in human relationships. The complete equality and reciprocity envisaged by the Rawlsian formula can be seen only at the highest levels of moral thought. With each prior level, the roles fail to reach the most appropriate expression. They become stunted or distorted because the mental perspectives necessary to sustain them are limited by motivational factors which are external to the moral decision-maker. At the lowest level of moral sensitivity, there is only a primitive structuring of emotion. And motivation, being governed solely by outwardly directed pain and pleasure, is overwhelmingly egocentric. At the median level, motivation is determined by what others will think, i.e., by simple peer-group pressure or by the desire not to violate the peer group's law. It is not until the moral agent looks inside him- or herself and is governed by feelings of moral outrage that he or she truly thinks in terms of and assumes the role of the significant other.

The unresolved problem of capital punishment continues to be an issue in which the significant other is often forgotten. Recent U.S. Supreme Court decisions have moved the issue from the periphery to the center of public attention.[12] When these lines were first written, over 500 convicted criminals awaited execution in American prisons. One of them, John Spenkelink, on Death Row of the Florida State Prison, appealed to his governor for a stay of execution. Although his appeal was unsuccessful and other legal maneuvers finally proved futile, a national television news program helped convey to the general public the condemned prisoner's invitation to his executioners to take his role. "How can you kill my son?" his mother was pictured as saying. "You don't even know him." And in a statement made public through his lawyer, Spenkelink himself said of the judge, "If he is to judge me, let him know me." This is a clear invitation to increase one's moral sensitivity through role-taking.

Now consider another illustration of role-taking. I use the case of rape because it is probably the most difficult item to handle in the whole abortion debate.

A CASE OF RAPE

Laura and her girlfriend Jennifer (names fictitious) stopped at a filling station one summer evening on their way to a shopping center. While at the filling station, they were approached by nine men in another car. After forcing their way into the girls' car, the men told the two girls to drive to a desolate area near an inland canal in a neighboring state. There they were taken from the car, knocked to the ground, and forced to engage in all kinds of perverted sexual acts with the men. Several weeks later, Laura discovered she was pregnant and threatened suicide.

This illustration, partly hypothetical, is typical of those found in pro-abortion literature. It was adapted from the private files of a midwestern psychiatrist.[13]

With opposing demands that the woman be allowed to abort and that two wrongs do not make a right, anti-abortion rhetoric has always had trouble dealing with pregnancy from sexual assault. The standard pro-life reply once stressed the extreme rarity of pregnancy in this circumstance and the ready availability of certain medical treatments to obviate it (like dilatation and curretage). This reply was usually accompanied by appeals to the principle of the double effect.*
Now, however, recent scholarship has tended to broaden the definition of rape, and we are faced with the possibility that pregnancy does occur and may, in fact, not be so rare. Yet, we are also advised that the woman pregnant through rape can, with the proper counseling, be helped to carry her child to term.

It is very difficult for audiences to take reciprocal roles in the case of rape. Despite all the medical and statistical data available to anti-abortion speakers, there is always the possibility that a woman can get

---

*The principle of the double effect, as applied here, means that if the D and C procedure should happen to kill a fertilized ovum, the act itself bears no moral onus because the intended purpose was to eliminate uninvited sperm from the woman's uterus.

pregnant. To bypass such an emotionally loaded fact, the most successful counter-role-taking I have witnessed dispenses with the standard response and instead concentrates on the actual principle involved. The idea is advanced of not abandoning any child, born or
unborn, who has no choice of parentage and whose fate is left to basic
human kindness, the idea of responding in a noble way to an unex-
pected and unwanted predicament involving deep human concern.[14]

The Uninvited Guest

Suppose one wintery morning you are leaving your house on the way to the
most important job interview of your entire life. Assume that this interview
really guarantees a job and that if you fail to show up for any reason, all is lost.
On the way to your car you notice a bundle on the doorstep. Upon inspection
it turns out to be a newborn infant in need of immediate medical attention. If
you arrive late, the job will be given to someone else; if you arrive on time the
child will die. This is your terrible choice. What will you do?

The thrust of the previous illustration goes to the heart of role-
taking. It requires placing oneself in another's moral shoes for the
purpose of understanding a particular human relationship—one's relation to another in the context of need and inconvenience. This
role-taking illustration answers the unanswerable by reducing the
emotional component to its cognitive core. Simply put, the hypothetical situation poignantly asks a crucial question: How should one
human treat another? The entire abortion controversy ultimately
hinges on such a question. And the question is entirely moral.

Nowhere is role-taking more needed than in the abortion controversy. While pro-abortion literature seemingly abounds in moral
situations readily identified with the plight of pregnant women, there
appears to be little anti-abortion literature that significantly identifies
with the plight of unborn children. Perhaps this is because those who
oppose abortion have an additional burden prior to assuming the role
of the fetus—the responsibility of making the fetus appear human.
This problem, as we have noted several times throughout the book,
resides primarily in one's perception of the physical world. And
although our treatment has not concentrated on this aspect of mental
functioning, now is an appropriate time to make some general
observations.

☐

From the very beginning of the organized effort to repeal liberal or relaxed abortion laws in America, an instinctive assumption of pro-life rhetoric has been that human characteristics must be attached to the being *in utero* so that audiences may perceive it as human. As of this writing, in fact, these humanizing characteristics are still being collected assiduously by pro-life educators and shared with colleagues. Pro-life literature points out that the unborn child moves (changes position to avoid discomfort), sucks its thumb, reacts to the altered composition of the amniotic fluid (drinks more if sweet and less if bitter), is startled by loud noise, has a heart that begins beating at 18 days and brain waves that can be detected at 8 weeks, etc. The *in utero* offspring grows rapidly (proportionately faster than at any other time in human development). Withdrawal from painful stimuli indicates that pain is felt. All of these developmental facts are humanizing and some can be supported with the latest audio-visual technology. For example, real-time ultrasound, a live motion videotaping technique, can detect heartbeat and show gross bodily movement. All are helpful in the process of role-taking because they help establish the humanity of the unborn and therefore set the stage for normal moral growth.

Obviously, the role-taking we are concerned with here starts with the assumption that the unborn is human. Why even discuss the rape problem if a dilemma involving a life is not posed? The real question is (or should be) under what circumstances may human life be taken? References to the humanity of the unborn are merely a reminder—a cognitive reinforcement of what most people believe anyway. Why even talk about abortion if the unborn are not human? [15]

☐

Role-taking in the abortion controversy involves intense human emotions. Appeals to rights and duties, whether viewed as authentic or counterfeit, are accompanied by even greater appeals to sympathy. "Never to laugh or love, nor taste the summertime" is a pro-life slogan noted earlier, designed to project the loss and sadness of abortion in denying life to smiling, contented babies. Its pro-abortion counterpart is the symbol of the rusty coathanger, placed on many a legislator's desk, emphasizing the tragedy of women enduring illegal abortion. Each appeal is a poignant invitation to the moral bystander to take a role—to exchange places with a significant other. These powerful urgings fuel the vehicle of social change and contribute to the moral sensitivity of those who experience them.

Role-taking, however, has a deeper meaning in the abortion controversy. Not only does each mode of moral thinking increase the opportunity for the unborn victim to become a factor in the decision to abort, but each mode also provides the moral communicator with a new opportunity for role-taking. Each mode of moral development provides a slightly different perspective of the needs of and duties toward the other. Each treats the significant other in a different way. This continual refocusing of perspective is called decentration and leads to moral growth.[16] An understanding of moral growth points to the importance of role-taking and helps the communicator to employ it effectively.

Each mode of moral development, from a strictly interpersonal context, of course, assumes the humanity of the unborn. Throughout the developmental sequence, this assumption has a variable but profound influence upon the moral perspective. In general, at Phase I role-taking is dominated by what is considered good for the woman; at Phase II, for the peer group; and, finally, at Phase III, for the unborn victim. More specifically, putting oneself in place of the other at Mode 2 generates the following hypothetical fetal monologue, "Hey, I smile and do all sorts of cute things. I'm soft to touch and kiss and someday I'll repay you with kindness;" at Mode 3, "Hey, let me live and I'll add to the nation's resources. I think I have a little musical talent and could entertain millions while bringing great honor to parents and country. Why, I might even grow up to be President." From these limited examples, the practical strategy of pro-life rhetoric has been to maximize role-taking opportunities.

In sociopsychological jargon, the abortion debate may be likened to humanity's collective search for the significant other.[17] Without a significant other there can be no real experience of a moral conflict. Moral decision-making calls for the assumption of another's role before a valid and impartial judgment can be made. In the abortion debate, however, the tension between self and other has largely disappeared. The *Roe* v. *Wade* decision has all but destroyed this necessary tension by ignoring the unborn's claim to be a human other and by elevating the woman's claim to be a supreme self in disposing of her offspring. The result is an encouragement of egocentrism whereby the woman beguiles herself into believing that she cannot really separate herself from the other. The assertion "I can do whatever I want with my own body," is a clear example of this egocentrism.[18] Healthy role-taking is stifled when reciprocity in human relationships is denied. As a result the unborn child becomes a quite insignificant other and no golden rule obtains.

The Golden Rule, a universal precept adhered to by most cultures, has profound significance in the abortion debate. The moralizing value of "Do unto others as you would have them do unto you" lies not so much in its expression of an equality and reciprocity of relationship as in its attention to the social symbiosis of self and other. In a smoothly functioning society, such an intimate association becomes tacitly accepted; and the occasions for serious conflict are thereby minimized. At a tumultuous time in American history, Lincoln expressed role-taking in very personal terms—through an aphorism we have already quoted: "As I would not be a slave, so I would not be a master."

In addition to equality and reciprocity, there is also the concept of reversibility to be considered. In Piagetian theory, reversibility is the fundamental condition of equilibrium in the way we view the physical and moral worlds. Kohlberg contends that "we can only define a more moral solution in terms of fairness or reversibility." [K79c-267] By definition, it means the willingness to live with our moral decision once we trade places with the other in the situation being judged. It implies that each stage of moral judgment defines equality and reciprocity in a more reversible way. It implies that the higher the degree of reversibility, the more mature is one's moral thinking. In short, it indicates that complete reversibility is ideal role-taking.

Reversibility means the ability to return to one's original position. In the principle of the right-to-life, role-taking is completely reversible: If I would not be aborted, I should not abort or allow another to be aborted. The pro-abortion slogan, a woman's right-to-choose, on the other hand, is totally irreversible, since it advocates the absolute dominance of a single party and the death of another. Death, of course, is the ultimate irreversibility. And abortion, in its barest moral terms, is the end of reciprocity.

☐

If role-taking is so important to moral growth, then what impedes its progress? The answer to such a question, of course, touches profoundly the mysterious interrelationship between how one views the social and physical worlds, and needs much greater study than this book is designed to give. From my experience, the most logical answer is to be found in the thwarting of essential role-taking opportunities by the print and broadcast media. For one reason or another, these influential carriers of social change have not permitted adequate portrayal of the unborn child as truly human and, thus, deserving of protection. Instead, the movement which would give the unborn child the status of significant other is pictured as reactionary and out of step with current thinking. All that the movement would ask is that the media treat the victims of abortion the same way they treat baby harp seals. The simple truth of the matter is that while the myth of progress may resonate through the media to the demand of our contemporary culture, the stark reality of justice does not.

The answer to the decline or ineffectiveness of role-taking, I think, goes much deeper than this. Apart from the fact that variations in the amount and type of role-taking opportunities are obviously needed, what may be of greater urgency is a clearer understanding of how role-taking opportunities are best structured. This book has been written to help provide such an understanding. The categories of moral thought, which follow a carefully researched growth pattern, offer role-taking insights heretofore not applied to abortion. In short, ignorance blocks role-taking opportunities on the part of those who wish to persuade. The only remedy is more and better messages.

A social movement like the pro-life movement should help society construct (or reconstruct) the rights of all significant others. By championing the rights of others, every social movement extends an invitation to the uncommitted to take a role. In the anti-slavery crusade, the attempt was made by those involved to help the black become a significant other. It is now generally accepted that blacks were denied basic civil rights because they were not considered human; they were given no place in the vital social equation of self and other. Much like unborn children today, blacks were, and in many cases still are, treated as insignificant (or even nonexistent) others. What some have called a "war on the unborn" will end when the unborn child is recognized as a significant other—especially as an aggrieved fellow human being who feels pain.

Morality deals with human relationships and the conflicts they engender. Moral concepts are ultimately social concepts that can be conveyed only through role-taking. In Kohlberg's thinking "The precondition for a moral conflict is man's capacity for role taking." [K71b-192] He places, as I do, a high value upon those activities which, if structured properly, are conducive to moral growth. He maintains that role-taking is one such activity and considers its opportunity of expression as a fundamental social input. [K69a-399] Kohlberg's greatest contribution to the theory of moral growth may well be the centrality he gives to role-taking. This feature of his developmental theory is largely ignored by commentators, but can never be omitted from any comprehensive theory of persuasion for social movements.

Successful role-taking is central to any solution to moral conflict. In fact, it is central to any real understanding of the abortion controversy. Social injustice is really role-taking denied. And the extent to which role-taking can be denied is (or should be) clearly apparent in the euphemistic and misleading reference to abortion as a crime without a victim. It takes little imagination, of course, to conclude that any definition of crime is absurd without victims. But what is more tellingly significant is that without a victim there can be no authentic moral conflict and, hence, no resolution through principles of justice, perceived by role-taking, of a pressing moral problem. While role-taking does not provide a determinate solution to the question of abortion, in that per se it does not necessarily establish whose role to assume, it does point to the incontrovertible fact that one party to the dispute, at present, is being totally ignored—namely, the unborn child. The controversy continues because no one has devised a way of asking an unborn child whether or not he or she wants to be aborted. In accepting without challenge the idea of crimes without victims, society is now faced with the inevitable alternative of victims without crimes.

To sum up in a very practical way, ask a pro-abortionist sometime if he or she would like to engage in some realistic role-taking and give him or her the role of a fetus. Have the pro-abortionist build a case for not being aborted and challenge him or her to be objective and fair. Chances are rather slim that hardened abortionists will not deny that this is thoroughly unrealistic role-taking; in their own minds they are forced to deny the very existence of the being whose life you ask them to uphold. But, by contrast, if this scenario of role-taking is valid, the authentic anti-abortionist should have no difficulty assuming the position of a pregnant woman who is considering abortion. To the extent that the pro-lifer is unable to take the opposite role and suggest alternatives to abortion which show genuine concern for the woman, to that extent role-taking breaks down and moral growth is stunted. A growth in public morality demands that stressful pregnancies receive society's most compassionate and immediate attention.

In conclusion, one final observation is in order. The moral educator does not create role-taking; it is a primary social datum. What he or she does is to help organize it in a consistent manner, preferably through peer-group interaction, so that it contributes to the moral growth of society. Rhetoric helps organize empathy, an ingredient of role-taking, in socially constructive ways.

PROMOTING ALTERNATIVES

In a manner peculiar to the way American society is structured, questions of value have a strong tendency to be polarized into win-lose configurations. Arguments over slavery and prohibition are prime examples of this peculiarity.[19] Both questions were finally transformed into a noncompromising type of political action and were settled only after years of social turmoil, and in the former instance, only by a massive shedding of blood. Perhaps, in the American context, this is all that can be expected of issues which divide a nation so profoundly or which disturb so fundamentally the agreed-upon hierarchy of values. If this is so, the prospect for a quick and amicable settlement of the abortion issue is remote indeed. Victory may come only after one side clearly shows a preponderance of popular support and has the political muscle to prove it. To date, that preponderance is not evident, nor was it evident prior to *Roe* v. *Wade*.

As noted in the introduction, a large part of the difficulty in solving the abortion problem can be traced to the mass media. The print and broadcast media always seem to want to talk about priorities that create some type of confrontation. And thus true conflict resolution gets pushed into the background. In their hands, social priorities are presented as dramatic events that capture the public's attention and create a reader-viewership that ultimately generates more advertising dollars. Social movements live by slogans (and sometimes die by them). Many of these slogans, like the "right-to-life" and the "right-to-choose," are designed to identify ideology but also, as a bad side effect, happen to magnify rigidity. Photo journalists and television camera crews seek out confrontation. They especially delight in protest rallies showing opposing activists locked in some bitter curbside debate (and preferably hitting one another). One favorite newsgathering technique I have observed many times over the years is for a journalist to extract a strong statement from one party to the dispute and then use it to goad an opposition leader into an equally strong counterstatement. This may be good for theater journalism, but it is not good for serious conflict resolution. What really happens is a hardening of positions which makes constructive negotiation more difficult—and some might say, all but impossible.

Using a diagram developed by social scientists, it is possible to visualize the polarities in the abortion controversy.[20] These polarities, with each dominant or winning solution represented by a shaded or darkened circle, are depicted in Figure 15. While each solution can be translated into appropriate social action, what is important to successful conflict resolution is that each side views itself as the winner. Where there is an imbalance or perception of loss and the power differential shifts from self to other and back again, social conflict will continue. (Prior to *Roe* v. *Wade*, of course, the other was emphasized; now it is the self.) An either/or-type solution (Types I and II) must somehow be made to appear transformed into a both/and-type solution (Type III). Put in the standard language of conflict resolution, the I Win—You Lose approach becomes a We All Win approach. Obviously, no quick and painless social legerdemain can accomplish this. The answer requires time and patience. Type I and II solutions are not subject to a fast television fade-out. They are basically power struggles that must somehow be bypassed in favor of building and strengthening relationships. This is the function of the preferred Type III solution.

In contrast to Figure 15, if one were to place the self (woman)—other (baby) circles in a relationship reflecting the real world, they would actually overlap as in Figure 16. The area for teaching and learning is the no-problem area. Here is where negotiations can take place and where they must if the larger value conflict is to be resolved. Any responsible citizen imbued with only a trace of civic awareness would choose to expand this area of overlap. If such an effort is successful, at some future time everyone will become a winner and, more importantly, there will be no losers. There will have

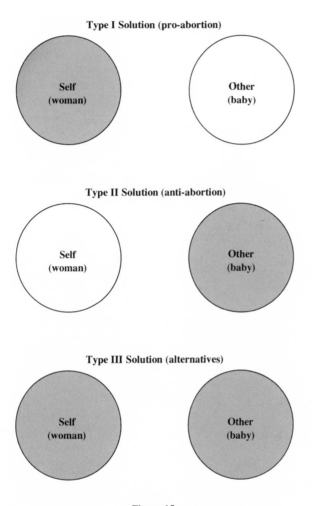

Figure 15.

been a fair exchange of benefits, and the needs of both factions will have been accommodated. In short, there will no longer be a problem.

Linked closely with the We All Win problem-solving method is one of the core ideas of moral development—the idea of justice. As our

Figure 16.

previous analysis has shown at considerable length, internalizing the idea of justice is what moral development is all about. Justice has an appeal of its own. All that is needed are enough people to subscribe to it in order to make it socially effective. Both sides to the abortion controversy would be untrue to themselves and to commonly held values if together they did not search for justice. A partisanship that begins, however feebly, with the idea of justice, ends with the idea of love and a caring society. To teach justice is to teach moral growth and to lay the foundation for the We All Win solution.

Increasing the size of the no-problem area means exploring all the possibilities leading to cooperation and mutual satisfaction. The history of this exploration as related to the abortion problem has shown that solutions can be found for providing pregnancy care for working women, help for unmarried women who wish to keep their babies, programs for rape prevention and the outlawing of forced sterilization, etc.[21] With hardly any imagination, this list could be expanded. That it has not been expanded indicts the nation's general level of moral reasoning. A society locked into a conventional morality discerns a common ground only dimly, if at all. A more mature or advanced level of moral reasoning is really needed to see clearly this common ground and the alternatives to abortion attached thereto. Without enough key people (national opinion shapers, legislators, judges, etc.) seeing and then vigorously supporting alternatives, the problem of abortion will remain largely unsolved. Comprehending an alternative is an essential component of moral reasoning and constitutes the difference between moral blindness and moral vision.

Helping society solve its needs in the matter of abortion is largely the task of alternatives. Satisfying the best interests of pregnant women and their unborn children would establish a middle or common ground on which both sides could agree. Although admittedly some abortions are obtained for no reason at all, the real problem is not abortion per se, but stressful pregnancies. More specifically, unwantedness is the manifest problem, or in a clinical sense, the presenting problem. Of deeper significance is the question, Why is the child unwanted? Only by posing this question can we accurately identify the underlying difficulty; only then are we doing more than merely treating symptoms. In short, we must free ourselves from the stultifying I Win—You Lose approach. Society must be willing to assume the cost of an alternative solution which ultimately boils down to a no-abortion policy. But if we remember that with rewards there are always expenditures, the social equation of self and other will be balanced when there is more empathy toward pregnant women. (And surely the new feminist consciousness can help us here!)

Although it is easy to conceptualize, the actual application of the We All Win problem-solving method will be difficult. The idea is not very appealing because, as we've noted, our national moral level is so conventional. Without at the same time thinking about alternatives, it is far easier to assume an inflexible pro- or anti-abortion position. But without adequate compensation for women and unborn children, either a strictly pro- or anti-abortion position is a nonsolution. Each subtly presents the destructive hidden message: I've got the whole truth; aren't you stupid for believing as you do! As a result, all the general public seems to see is the abortion—no abortion polarity, which is outside the negotiable area of free agreement. Conceptually, neither end of this polarity contains the solution to the problem of stressful pregnancies. Only concrete alternatives from a caring society can ease the tension surrounding abortion. In the practical realm, with neither side willing to give in to a decision deemed acceptable to the other, the common-ground approach is the only answer. Both sides must be willing to pursue the negotiable area at the bargaining table.

☐

To use the word "weapon" to describe metaphorically the practical application of cognitive moral development is to risk the possibility of describing rhetoric as a potentially violent enterprise. Yet, we must take this risk to make a very important point: The paradigm of cognitive moral development can indeed be used as a rhetorical weapon, but only for the good (except by those who would maliciously frustrate it). Like the legendary sword Excalibur, this weapon can be pulled from the stone of human understanding only by those who know the truth and have the courage to defend it. Only certain of those who come from a tradition of religious or secular humanism may extract its power; no intellectually dishonest person may do so. It must advance the cause of humankind, and only those who have humanity's best interest at heart can put it to use in acts of persuasion. As a rhetorical weapon, the paradigm of cognitive moral development represents education in personal involvement at its very best.

The result of successful intervention will ultimately be the building of a national consensus, not only regarding abortion but regarding respect for human life generally. Helping people to understand our commonly held values or simply showing that these values are still widely held and have been so throughout history is in itself a great incentive to moral growth. What this implies is the creation of a consistent moral atmosphere. And with a restored and expanded sense of the other comes a strengthened and enlarged sense of community. A healthier society is the goal of most social movements, and a healthy society cares for its weakest members. The organic sense of community postulates that an attack against one is a threat against all. The abortion controversy verifies the dictum that no one is an island.

As we have mentioned in one form or another throughout this book, the theory of persuasion herein advanced assumes that humans prefer logic to illogic and that the physical and social worlds we inhabit are basically rational. The heart may have reason that reason knows nothing about, but this poetic fancy is true only for the moment. A heart that consistently contradicts reason is destined for heartbreak—a condition that normal humans attempt to avoid. Our educational assumption is that since truth is usually more attractive than falsehood, audiences will gravitate, sooner or later, toward the truth. It follows that the responsibility of the rhetorician, then, is to understand the truth and help make it more attractive.

One of the axioms of a developmental rhetoric is to make truth more attractive by making falsehood less attractive. One persuades by confronting audiences with the prospect of endless inconsistencies. Without wanting to be irreverent I have composed a prayer for the developmental persuader:

A PERSUADER'S PRAYER

Oh, Lord! Create for my audiences a world of nagging doubts and painful inconsistencies. Help me show them how their moral position is logically untenable and unpleasantly inadequate. Provoke in them the desire to grow through the slightly incongruous and to achieve higher levels of moral thinking. Give them a firm rationality and make them earn their righteousness. For morality's sake, Amen.

Engaging in moral education through a social movement is like taming a wild horse. In the mind of C. S. Lewis, those who tame horses become victims themselves while turning the horse into something a future rider can trust. By a similar token, social activists are subject to the same ongoing moral growth processes as the people they wish to influence. An unalterable fact of life is that a social movement is itself a catalytic agent for the social activist's own personal moral growth.

Those who wish to understand the current abortion controversy must search for a broader vision. It is my contention that moral-development theory can provide such a vision. Without reference to a developmental perspective, we are much like an observer standing on an unknown shore with the sun barely visible over the horizon. If such a person were part of a painting, with no reference to time, one could not tell (as in the Franklin episode mentioned earlier) whether the sun were rising or setting. In similar fashion, a developmental view of the abortion controversy is like the missing time of day for the observer on the unknown shore; it gives us our bearings and provides a broader vision.

Some would argue that a woman's choice in the matter of abortion is the inevitable wave of the future. I would argue the contrary. From the developmental perspective we have studied, it is much more reasonable to believe that the current abortion controversy represents a temporary regression which will eventually give way to new moral growth. It is an axiom of developmental theory that there must be a breaking up before a new level can be added to one's moral stature. A broader perspective would show that an increased respect for life is a more likely developmental outcome. Justice, the core of moral development, nurtures such a respect for human life. This respect is ordained by the weight of scientifically based developmental evidence and is arguably a part of nature's grand design.

DECALAGE

We have left to the final and perhaps most important section of the book a developmental concept that is critical to the success of a social movement. The concept, "decalage," taken directly from the French, means an "uncoupling." In Piagetian developmental psychology, it refers to the natural connectedness among certain mental operations, or the generalization of certain mental abilities used to order the physical world. Take, for example, the Piagetian notion of conservation. The ability of the human mind to realize that a given quantity of a liquid like water remains constant as it is poured into containers of different shapes is the ability to conserve. While children under the age of six cannot conserve, such an ability, once mastered, is potentially generalizable to other areas, including weight and volume. The Piagetians have investigated this linking phenomenon through a series of dramatic experiments which support the conclusion that if a conservational ability is mastered in one area, the natural course of mental development is to master it in others. Conservation of continuous and discontinuous quantity initiates the sequence, and conservation of volume usually ends it. This potentially unified ability, as its name implies, becomes "uncoupled" or strung out over a period of several years.

As applied to moral development, the concept of decalage refers to the spreading of certain key ideas used to order the social world. [K71g-32][22] In the light of developmental theory, it suggests that there is an option to a strategy of accelerated moral growth which, as we know from common sense, is a very slow process when extended over the landscape of an entire society. [K70d] The option, specifically in terms of a social movement, is to extend whatever constitutes the core ideology to other content areas. With respect to the question of abortion, the core ideological concern is respect for human life as embodied in the slogan "right-to-life." Through the concept of decalage, this core ideological concern, because it can be found in other

contemporary social problems, can be transferred to their associated
movements. In the anti-war movement, in the ecological movement,
in issues involving the use of nuclear energy, women's rights, capital
punishment, to name but a few, there is a common concern for respecting human life. When applied to the social world, broadening or
deepening this concern is what decalage implies.[23]

Technically, the coupling of existing thought structures to new content areas applies standard methods of social role-taking and elabo-
rates them to other social movements. The abortion controversy
abounds in generalizing opportunities. Two vivid examples can be
drawn from my own experience. The first example arose from a
formal debate format and the second from a picketing episode.

Several years ago I participated in a debate on a college campus
with a well-known secular humanist. The debate took place at the
height of the ecology crisis and thus afforded an opportunity for
some anti-abortion tie-ins. One of my three principal arguments was
that abortion was ecologically unsound. I emphasized the fact that the
womb, as a part of the seamless web of life, was also an environment
in need of protection, and that through repeated abortion the womb,
so to speak, could be polluted. Statistics were marshaled which
attempted to show possible long-range health problems associated
with abortion which could render the womb incapable of bearing
future children. The campus paper, reputed at the time to be one of
the largest in the country with a staff of competent student journalists, chose to play up this part of the debate and featured it in the next
day's article headline. This emphasis also had a word-of-mouth impact which is the point of our example. Later in the day of the debate,
before the news article appeared, I received an anonymous phone call
from what seemed to be a deeply disturbed student ecologist who
believed in unlimited abortion but who was also committed to environmental protection. In a voice etched with anxiety, he asked me
what kind of car I drove and how absolute was my opposition to
abortion. When I indicated that I drove a small foreign car and that I
favored abortion only to save the physical life of the mother, the caller
became almost incoherent. My abortion/ecology linkage had cut too
deeply and created overpowering psychic turmoil.

The second example occurred during a Democratic presidential
primary in the spring of 1972. A group of students from several
nearby states who, along with me, belonged to the National Youth Pro-

Life Coalition (NYPLC) confronted with pro-life chants and placards an extreme right-wing candidate from a southern state who had a states' rights position on abortion. This small anti-abortion group—never numbering more than 50—shared the demonstration site with a much larger contingent of anti-war protesters who opposed the candidate for his views on the Vietnam War. The combined demonstration involved two marching circles moving clock- and counter-clockwise and tangentially for a short distance. Since both lines of march passed each other continuously, each other's presence was clearly felt and there was tension in the air. The pro-life group, chanting such slogans as "Stop the war on the unborn," criticized the candidate's declared preference for letting each state decide the abortion question. This and other ideas showing the candidate's general disdain for human rights created concern among some of the nearby anti-war protesters who, when the opportunity arose, attempted to destroy some anti-abortion placards. These protesters, believing strongly in abortion, could not accept the idea that the candidate they despised could in any way favor it. Their hostility reflected the potency of relating one movement to another through rhetoric.

These two episodes highlight the ability of movement rhetoric to elaborate those core ideas, like respect for human life, which resonate in other movements. The emotional and physical reactions cited arose because the reactors wanted to accept two contradictory ideologies which, when shown to be untenable, precipitated the behavior. The fact that they reacted the way they did displayed the sensitivity to a social problem which is the first step toward regaining cognitive balance and a consistent moral stance. Such a first step so dramatically witnessed by me can easily evoke a cry of pain if the rhetoric of the decalage is poignant enough. These examples clearly show that exploiting this developmental phenomenon can be a powerful rhetorical strategy. Educationally, a deepened knowledge of such a strategy goes far toward penetrating the rhetorical complexity of social movements.

An important rhetorical strategy, then, might be to forgo the general acceleration of moral growth and concentrate instead upon building strong linkages among those social movements sharing a common ideological core. From a practical educational standpoint, this may actually be the best way to approach total moral growth. Movement rhetoric should be directed to expanding the demographic base by communicating with kindred movements. The activist personnel from other movements may have surplus energies which can be redirected. Getting these companion spirits to march with you should be a high priority, although much can be gained by simply opening a straightforward dialogue to acknowledge shared values. Even a neutralization of incipient (though misplaced) hostility is an advantage. The concept of decalage, even when it does not achieve cooperation, can be harnessed to play down hostility.[24]

The responsibility of each movement communicator should be to help listeners extend their moral reasoning to new situations. While such a strategy may be unacceptable to those who are oriented to a single issue, the possibility of decalage is still an unalterable reality of social movements. Unfortunately, single-issue people often fail to see the potential in communicating with activists in other areas of social concern. Their narrowness, instead of strengthening their cause, brands them as rigid fanatics who have no other social interests. Sharpening a movement's ability to converse with other movements traveling in the same direction would appear to be a priority.

To sum up, what is needed for the successful communication of a movement ideology is not the accelerated acceptance by the society as a whole of the final stages of moral growth, although for obvious reasons this would be highly desirable. Rather, what is needed is the stimulation of decalage. An across-the-board speedup of total moral development throughout society is an enormous undertaking, while generalizing a respect for human life (one facet of total moral growth) is a less formidable task. To be maximally effective an educational/ rhetorical strategy should reflect social reality. It is likely to be easier to seek new converts among the already converted in some other movement than to move the mass of humanity to a more advanced moral position. Helping audiences become responsive to higher levels of moral reasoning is a good long-range developmental goal, but, for the short range, it ignores the nature of educational reality.

The modes of moral discourse are nexes of rhetorical strategies which have clusters of symbols attached to them. The task of the educator/communicator is to discover what these symbols are and consciously to employ them for humankind's moral betterment. It has already been intimated, for example, that a respect for life at every mode may be generalized to a number of other problem areas, including proper care for the elderly, the handicapped, etc. How the activists associated with these problems can be united in one common social movement remains an important unanswered question.

Also worth exploring is the question, "What do moral education and persuasion have in common?" It would appear (to extend comments made previously) that any response to this question should include the following: Both help structure the experiences necessary to make and defend moral decisions. Both deal with rational thinking and consider being rational in morality no different from being rational in science. Both help audiences understand why certain principles of action are sound, and both assume that these principles should be followed more consistently. Both can inculcate without indoctrinating. And at the very least, both can help prevent moral stagnation through acknowledging that each person has the capacity to develop a sense of justice. If a social movement provides the raw material of moral experience, both education and persuasion transform it into something useful for everyone. And, finally, if education and persuasion have a common goal, it is to actualize the seed of justice by stimulating and releasing its capacity to grow.

CREATIVE UNCERTAINTY

Social movements deal with moral situations in disequilibrium. Although no one really knows how this disequilibrium takes place, one thing appears certain: the individual normally experiences it through cognitive conflict. Such conflict, or imbalance as it is sometimes called, is produced by certain kinds of environmental stimulation interacting with the individual's mode of thinking. Developmental theorists describe this conflict as the central "motor" or condition for moral reorganization. Thus, cognitive imbalance has a positive effect upon restructuring and transforming thought processes. For the movement activist, it becomes the core of an educational strategy. Given enough time and enough teachers, the communication of cognitive uncertainty can be one of the best antidotes for the misuse of moral reasoning. The listener who is dissatisfied with his or her existing pattern of moral thought is a prime candidate for some mental readjustments. Cognitive errors seem best remedied through creative cognitive uncertainty.

The creative use of uncertainty is necessary for those who educate for social justice. This does not imply that communicators willfully confuse their audiences; it rather means that they take advantage of the natural pressures for dissonance reduction existing in every human. Audiences modify beliefs and behaviors only when they are made to feel uneasy or unsure of them. Creating cognitive dissonance simply adds to what is already there by nature and moves listeners more rapidly to abandon their outmoded patterns of thought. It is the task of each movement leader, in association with peers within the larger society, to stimulate society's moral growth to more advanced levels. Through the creation of an uncertainty that casts doubt upon existing moral structures, movement communicators help their neighbors grow to a deeper understanding of justice and of what it means to be human. The pros and cons of abortion become academic, if not meaningless, without a broader understanding of how the individual, through creative cognitive uncertainty, can be persuaded to accept one side or the other. This view of persuasion is really at the heart of moral growth.

Education in the truest and classic sense (from the Latin *educare*) is a "leading out." A social-movement activist in some way enters every human being's moral biography to stimulate a growth pattern that has been neglected, distorted, or both. The developmental moral sequence and associated categories of thought, which we know occur naturally, can be influenced with the right educational program. Such a program recognizes that educational outputs are determined largely by educational inputs which, in turn, must be adapted to the characteristics of the learner. The successful teaching of virtue within a developmental framework creates the impression in the learner of something vaguely familiar. Each successive mode of moral thought becomes a more adequate expression of what is waiting to be expressed.

The creative rhetorician will capitalize on the truths of developmental psychology and anchor the elements of moral persuasion to a rigorous rationality. But to exploit uncertainty within the context of a social movement already generating ambiguity is to be aware of uncertainty in oneself. Persuasion grows out of uncertainty and can best originate from those who have themselves experienced it. As has been said many times before, if there were perfect justice, the world would need no courage. By the same token, if a complex moral issue like abortion could be solved by a simple demonstration of fact there would be no need for persuasion. And the interactional world of subjects would be graced with certainty in its development.

It is a truth worth repeating that uncertainty about specific aspects of moral behavior resides in all people. Complete moral maturity is the mark of a saint or a God and not of ordinary mortals. Less self-righteousness in the communicator not only fosters a healthier mental attitude but makes persuasion possible. Such an attitude creates the best atmosphere for rhetoric to do its work. An awareness of our own uncertainty is the product of moral insight and a determinant for increased maturity. Recognizing our own feelings of uncertainty can be sanctifying and can be the prologue to stimulating an understanding of it in others. This is the essence of moral growth and a lodestar for those who hope to persuade.

Finally, we must emphasize that a self-righteous attitude is the enemy of true persuasion. The genuine persuader knows that listeners tend to be selectively insensitive and that all humans exhibit immaturity in some areas of moral decision-making. One person's certainty in one moral matter may well be someone else's uncertainty. A knowledge of developmental morality should impress upon the persuader the need to approach any rhetorical task with an enormous degree of humility, for it is only in humility that a genuine persuasion can be ultimately fashioned. Whoever hungers for social justice and is determined to persevere must be willing to accept the challenge of the religious paradox that in humility there is strength.

□

Those who oppose abortion are often caricatured as nervous, sexually frustrated, beady-eyed zealots ready to emblazon the world with scarlet letters. They are described in the popular media as right-wing fanatics with little care for anything but their own moral certitudes. They have the look of the smugly self-righteous and are a definite throwback to the archetypal extremists who lured the nation into Prohibition. They are easily the American version of history's moral tyrants. Of course, this image, like many of the portrayals relating to the pro-life movement, is overdrawn. Yet, with the proper rhetoric even this distorted image can be changed. There will always be room in a social movement for the sincerely righteous who are sensitive to the feelings of others.

CONCLUSION

Those that I fight I do not hate.
YEATS

THE PATH TO PERSUASION

Without shared human values and a common core of accepted moral practices, society becomes destructive of individual rights and suffers from a pernicious malaise. The slavery issue (in which liberty was compromised) and the abortion issue (in which life is compromised) represent two moral watersheds in the American experience. In both cases, social movements arose to rectify the compromise and heal the painful discrepancy between reality and the ideal.

It is the generation of new life itself which concerns us here. Pregnancy, fraught as it is with uncertainty, has come to be seen as a predicament rather than as a natural event. Abortion has become an accepted alternative. Yet when all the arguments for abortion have been made, considered, and finally discarded, our persistent need to understand our relationship to nature will remain. Induced abortion, like the epicenter of some hidden fault plane, introduces a primordial tension between nature and culture. It is an unseen crisis of the human spirit. And to lessen the pain and misery, ethics, with the help of rhetoric, must emerge to heal the rift that arises whenever the interface between nature and culture is disturbed. Abortion is indeed a "civilized" revolt against nature that comes with a high price tag.

This book is a response to the decline in morals signified by the issue of abortion. It was written on the assumption that moral development is a path as well as a destination, a process as well as a goal, and that the social environment should provide an easier path toward its achievement. Strictly speaking, abortion represents a detour along the way.

Yet, few natural phenomena occur all at once. Even earthquakes have a gestation period before the final cataclysm. So it is with moral reasoning. Societies that decide to pursue a policy of abortion are oftentimes as much the victims of environmental pressures as of ideology. And most individuals likewise experience a period of doubt regarding the decision to abort. With few exceptions, that decision is not taken lightly, and sufficient reason must be advanced to satisfy even the most life-hardened conscience. What takes time to do must take time to undo. Thinking and rethinking about abortion can be evolutionary or devolutionary, but the process of moralizing itself is gradual.

It has been said that individuals and societies tend to develop toward the ideal type—that given enough time, the outcome would be a perfect sense of social justice. Yet, as we have seen, a growth in justice can be stimulated. Humans can be helped to realize their natural inclinations to live in harmony with their fellows; they can be educated in justice.

What I have just said, however, demands an important limitation: no society can be based on justice alone. If all human creatures are social animals who strive toward union with their kind, then this tendency is surely mediated more by love than by justice. If communion is humanity's fundamental social tendency, then love is really the supreme social virtue and should be so acknowledged by those who wish to persuade.[1]

Both justice and love are indeed moral virtues, but justice becomes meaningful only in contemplation of "the other." It starts with the given datum of the other and loses its essential meaning when the other becomes one.[2] Justice mediates vindictiveness and belligerent self-defensive posturing. It prefers merely to discuss the violation of one's rights instead of concentrating on respect for the rights of others. In truth, justice, while trying to create the minimum conditions for love to grow, becomes anemic, if not moribund, without love. Tillich said it wisely: "Justice is fulfilled in love."[3] Though justice makes love possible and is love's social foundation, it must yet be tempered by love.

A failure to respect human life is largely a failure in moral education. When home, school, and church are functioning properly and

peer-group interaction exerts its moralizing influence, society benefits. There is an increase in cohesiveness brought about by an
actualized concern for others and a greater sensitivity of the strong
for the weak.

□

Now, I would like to return to a theme first mentioned in the introduction—the theme of the rhetorical imagination. The intervening
pages have been an attempt to explore a portion of social reality
through an understanding of rhetoric. And we have used a knowledge of cognitive moral development to aid us in this exploration.
Allied with the inspired work of William Lynch, our prime assumption has been that it is only when we remain in "complete and undis-
torted touch with things as they really are" (in this case our bioethical
responsibilities) that we can begin to gain the kind of insight needed
to solve our moral problems. Our first premise is that reality itself is
curative and that knowledge of moral growth, as a reflection of reality, can and does indeed possess a healing power. An important corollary to this premise is that to communicate effectively, i.e., with imagination, one must communicate in relation to a clearly perceived
reality. We assert unabashedly that true rhetoric clarifies reality and
liberates the imagination so that people can act. Simply stated, rhetoric is a creative tool for the exploration of social reality; it provides the
individual with interpretative resources that help him or her to make
sound moral choices.

I would agree with all those who claim that humanity cannot live
without a healing vision.[4] The principal task of the rhetorical imagination is to create this vision by helping us realize what it means to
be good. By forging a path through the atrocities of public and private injustices, the rhetorical imagination also helps us realize the
consequences of evil. As the symbolic expression of social movements
that are possessed of a healing vision, the rhetorical imagination
assembles those features of reality that correspond with our inherent
need to extend the boundary of human understanding. The rhetorical imagination is best characterized by its openness to the future. At
home, school, or church, in community or nation, or wherever the
individual may grapple with critical moral problems, the rhetorical
imagination always kindles hope.

Rhetoric as we have conceived it is the enemy of hopelessness; it postulates a way out of difficulties. By helping society imagine what it cannot imagine, rhetoric rekindles hope when hope is lost. And by providing a new context for viewing moral problems, rhetoric directs the movement of human beings to reality. In fact, one could even say that the principal task of the rhetorical imagination is the actual creation of reality. Within the parameters of a developmental theory, it strives to communicate autonomy to moral decision-making and urge humanity to face its problems.

The abortion decision confronts all of us with two versions of human existence. Here in the confrontation between the right-to-life and its opposite is the age-old conflict between thesis and antithesis. To integrate these opposites in their full import is a major challenge to society and a challenge to the rhetorical imagination.

Since humanity's future is intimately involved with the begetting of offspring, and since the urge of all nature is toward birth, abortion therefore is biologically maladaptive. More importantly, it is a tactic of the hopeless—of those who have given up looking for answers. This lack of confrontation with reality results not in the breakdown of egocentrism, but in the breakout of bizarre behavior: the deliberate destruction of one's preborn children. Yet, in any workable solution to this problem, the rhetorical imagination must confront the sobering fact of stressful pregnancies and show that abortion is neither the only nor the best way to handle them, that abortion, in fact, is really a nonsolution. Abortion is a double tragedy; it represents not only the death of human offspring but the death of a people's imagination.

The great human enterprise has always been the relentless struggle out of darkness into truth. Loren Eiseley described this struggle poignantly. He pictures us as prison breakers who, because of ignorance, find ourselves moving from one terrible incarceration to another. We all get locked into rigid moral thought patterns which because of their limited view of reality become so many prisons of the human spirit. These prisons are the modes of moral discourse that when correctly understood, with the help of rhetorical analysis, can purify our collective vision. When misunderstood and uncontrolled, the innate egocentrisms of these modes become our painful undoing. As we have seen with the question of abortion, starting with small errors, we inevitably end with large ones. Initially, a woman gets an abortion because a normal pregnancy is thought to be more harmful and then, finally, she gets one purely as a matter of choice. If authentic social movements do anything at all, they must help us to become emancipated from our small errors that inevitably lead to monumental breaches of moral action.

This book will have succeeded if in some small way it has shown how rhetoric can be liberating and creative. By helping us escape from debilitating egocentrisms, the rhetorical imagination leads society out of its entrapment on key moral issues. It helps us to explore new possibilities, to invent our future and move into it with courage and confidence. The rhetorical imagination is a gift to envision what cannot be seen.

☐

The reader has already been forewarned that it is not my purpose to write a book on specific pedagogy. Those details are best handled in some other format. Rather I have attempted to introduce the reader to the general outlines of a pedagogical method or process—not necessarily to show how to be a good practitioner. At this point in the construction of theory, my goal is achieved if I can show the soundness of the approach. Self-discovery, the cornerstone of developmentalism, is the favored technique to use in encouraging the application of sound ethical reasoning to specific cases. The likely carryover will be the enhancement of moral sensitivity and judgment generally. This book, then, is primarily a treatise of justification.

My purpose is to help people become more ethically aware—to foster clearer thinking about morals. Before the details of an effective pedagogy can be worked out, there must first be a careful analysis of the logic and psychology of ethical thinking itself. I will be satisfied if this book enables those who may apply the developmental insights presented herein to get their listeners to attend more enthusiastically to the moral dimensions of the abortion problem. To borrow a phrase from liberation theology, my aim is to raise the reader's consciousness to the presence of the moral. After all, to stimulate growth through reflective moral tensions, one must first be able to reflect.

In candor, I would emphasize that a developmental pedagogy is probably more difficult than other methods because it requires a greater alertness and sensitivity. Most people are not used to reflecting morally. Since with the abortion question one is dealing largely with moral blindness, great care and consideration must be taken. The communicator's main task is to help the listener develop a heightened moral insight.

☐

From these general pedagogical considerations, let us now briefly extrapolate the developmental perspective to the persuasive goals of a social movement. We will use the American pro-life movement as a real-life paradigm.

As these last sentences are written, two proposals have emerged which seem to embrace some of the important empirical findings of cognitive moral development. One has been labeled the "Human Life Federalism Amendment," a proposal embodied in Senate Joint Resolution 110,[5] and the other the "Power to Protect Life Amendment" (sometimes called the "two-step" approach).[6] Although neither proposal has yet been perfected by the legislative process, even in preliminary form, each seems to contain the basic ingredients of a sound rhetorical strategy. Without considering them in any great detail, we can see that they reflect strategic good sense: they are couched in terms that can be readily understood by a majority of Americans as well as by their elected representatives.

The current wording of the two proposals is closer to the way we as a society are likely to make moral decisions. By asserting that abortion is not a right secured by the Constitution and by authorizing the Congress to protect unborn human life while allowing concurrent state legislation, the proposals construe the terms of the social contract to favor legislative rather than exclusive judicial action. With American society so deeply divided on the issue of abortion and with most of the nation's moral reasoning confined to the conventional phase, it would appear that lofty appeals to personhood and to an inherent right-to-life will likely go unheeded. Something less than an unqualified adherence to principle combined with pedagogically sensitive language stands a better chance of being adapted to prevailing moral thought structures and of ultimately reflecting the legislative will of the people.

Since the language of a constitutional amendment helps define the parameters of the national moral debate, the wording should be chosen to reflect the highest stage of moral reasoning of which the audience is capable. It is clear, and the evidence is substantial, that the majority of Americans cannot assimilate the highest identifiable stage of moral thinking—namely, Mode 6. The U.S. Constitution with all its wisdom is only a Mode 5 document. In its present form it does not define or classify people as persons; in fact, it does not go beyond providing equal protection and due process, the basic ingredients of our constitutionally based social contract. Only with considerable difficulty can we as a nation escape the blandishments of law-and-order moral thinking (Mode 4). Inserting the highest expression of justice into the wording of a constitutional amendment without at the same time raising the moral expectations of the people to that level would appear to be self-defeating. It is politically and rhetorically unsound to attach a Mode 6 amendment to a Mode 5 constitution. The parts should be compatible with the whole.

It is not enough merely to observe, as did Chief Justice Earl Warren, that the American Constitution floats in a sea of ethics. The Constitution itself is a living part of the sociomoral thinking of a people—a mirror of how a nation wishes to think of itself socially and morally. As such, an alteration of it through amendment may be likened to the transplant of an organ. If the transplanted organ is to be accepted by the host body, that body's immune system must be properly conditioned. Any incompatibility will mean a rejection. In like manner, for an amendment to be attached successfully to the Constitution, the nation's sociomoral vision (its immune system) must be properly conditioned through education.

What I have tried to impress upon the reader is that messages should always be adapted to audiences. If a psychology of moral development outlines the way audiences can listen, it is the better part of wisdom to frame amendments in terms that are agreeable to those audiences while still permitting a social movement to attain its major objectives. Wise communicators are sensitive to what the rhetorical traffic will bear and realize, sometimes painfully, that there are inherent limits to rhetoric, built-in constraints to persuasion arising from the moral reasoning process itself. The evidence from moral-development research points to the fact that the moral-reasoning capacity of individuals is restricted to what they can understand. This is a simple pedagogical truth.

We have seen how an individual's moral behavior can be modified by the right pedagogical method, one that is appropriate to the capacity of those who receive moral messages. There is a danger in any persuasive campaign that communicators imbued with a keen sense of social justice will try to raise the level of moral discourse beyond the capacity of audiences to comprehend. Such communicators fail to realize that using a less mature mode of moral thinking is not a compromise but only a concession to social reality, and that an inability to understand a moral message should not be confused with actual hostility to it. Saints and the nations in which they reside are not made morally mature overnight. Political and rhetorical strategy should work together on what is possible.

The developmental moral perspective deals with finely tuned audience adaptation. As a framework for a comprehensive rhetorical strategy in a social movement, therefore, it should have something to say about how the basic issues are framed for public discussion—not only how they are brought to general public awareness but how they are officially defined for legislative debate. Since most authentic social movements strive to create an appropriate climate for principled moral thinking, the empirically valid idea of progressing to more mature levels of thought should help govern educational practice, including over-all campaign strategy. A movement's educational approach demands the contributions of modern rhetorical analysis.

☐

And now for some final thoughts about persuasion. Social movements engage in moral discourse from which a rhetoric can be fashioned that can provide a clearer understanding of what it means to be human. I hope this book, dealing as it does with one of life's central problems, will aid our search for our true selves.

Throughout our analysis we have assumed that human beings are free to choose how and why they will act—their means and their ends. In this freedom, the principle of justice becomes a critically important coping mechanism making it possible for the individual to deal with social reality. We have also maintained that social movements are open systems and that rhetoric helps preserve the character of these systems by enhancing the power and appeal of justice. If times of moral upheaval can be viewed as times of eloquence, then rhetoric has a vital part to play in achieving social equilibrium.

Rhetoric is both a cause and an effect of dynamic developmental processes which embrace the human life-span. A social movement is a conscious moral striving, a great morality play expressing our innermost feelings about such themes as the proper role of parents in begetting and rearing offspring and, on a grander scale, the proper relationship between nature and culture. These questions inevitably lead to others, one of the most important being: why be moral in the first place? All are universal themes which must be answered by each individual in every age, and, collectively, at certain periods in history through the instrumentality of social movements.

Arguments by themselves rarely win debates. On the other hand, over the long run the right attitudes, in conjunction with the right arguments, do. Arguments at best only justify attitudes. It is the way we perceive our moral obligations that more often than not determines the stands we take and the arguments we make on critical social issues. Abortion is a prime example of this. The quality-of-life ethic that pervades pro-abortion thinking represents an elitist attitude toward one's fellows. Discarding the less than perfect under any circumstance is the ultimate end point of moral reasoning patterns that are both distorted and tragic. And, if taken to its logical conclusion, the quality-of-life ethic will mean that only "perfect" specimens will ever be allowed to grow to full maturity. This elitist attitude runs counter to every normal feeling about the biological meaning of human equality.

The best remedy for an elitist attitude is a countervailing attitude of love. And also a genuine humility. We should realize that true morality does not impose itself, it lives itself;[7] and that social movements first grow and die from within. Those who oppose abortion, for whatever reason, must first live the order they envision for the rest of society. To bring order out of chaos, social activists must become more enamored of humility than of power; they must love even those who hold elitist, anti-democratic views.

We seem to have lost sight of the old idea that only in humility is there strength. As the Apostle Paul said two millennia ago, and the philosopher Kierkegaard repeated more recently, the truly humble person will realize that all humans act in ambiguity and work out their salvation in fear and trembling. Perhaps the growth-inducing uncertainty we spoke of earlier is also the expected cause of our own moral growth. If both sides to the abortion controversy reasoned with humility and spoke the truth with love there would be no reason to debate.[8] Abortion is as serious a threat to the meaning of a universal morality as the human community has ever faced. Its anti-life elitism demands a response that is truly heroic and that represents the best that is in us.

Those who actively oppose abortion are the drum majors of justice. What they must become in order to moralize effectively, however, are the artisans of love. And although our treatment emphasizes growth in justice, a corresponding growth in love is mandatory for those who desire to instigate others to goodness. As the encyclical *Quadragesimo Anno* pointedly makes clear: ". . . [J]ustice alone, even though most faithfully observed, can remove indeed the cause of social strife, but can never bring about a union of hearts and minds."[9] Those who teach a genuine respect for human life through justice must learn to cultivate a biblical righteousness which goes beyond justice and, in Rabbi Heschel's words, "implies benevolence, kindness, generosity" and "a burning compassion for the oppressed."[10]

A national union of minds and hearts is needed to solve the abortion problem. Moreover, the world needs exemplars as well as guides and helpers in moral reasoning. We must reason lovingly if the cause of justice is to be well served. A true and lasting justice will reside throughout the land when the ancient maxim is finally realized: that the greatest of teachers are also the greatest of lovers.

POSTSCRIPT

This study is really open-ended, but it must end someplace so it ends here. The motivational theory I have used is a dynamic one that is quite impossible to explore fully within the covers of a single volume. Keeping pace with such a rapidly growing area of knowledge and applying it to a living social issue has been a major preoccupation of mine for nearly a decade.

In my darker moments I have often wondered whether the study of rhetoric had any inherent meaning, or whether rhetoric in its traditional form did in fact bear any significant relationship to the cultural transmission of important human values. When the gloom lifted, however, I was able to conclude that rhetoric is certainly not meaningless, but that, in fact, it has a crucial part to play in the moral development of society. Meaning, of course, is also in the mind of the beholder, and if what I have written brings insight to those who sincerely wish to understand the meaning of persuasion within the context of social movements, my time has been well spent.

From the outset, my principal concern has been the proper blending of partisanship and objectivity. Obviously, I may have succeeded only partially in this concern, perhaps not at all. The decisive question for me has been: How does one write knowingly about a subject without first feeling it deeply and becoming totally immersed in it? That question has no easy answer; it may, in fact, be impossible to answer. What is the meaning of objectivity? When does partisanship become an obstacle or a burden? These are exceedingly difficult questions to answer.

At the height of my perplexity, and to soothe a troubled conscience, I went back to the Greeks, to the beginning of rhetorical speculation within the Western tradition. I reread Plato's *Phaedrus*, which had first nurtured my most intense curiosity about rhetoric. There I found strong confirmation that I had been moving in the right direction. My rereading was, as it were, a revisitation to the philosophical underpinnings of my rhetoric. What I found bears repeating, and the reader will recognize it as a theme I have pursued throughout these pages.

Plato's powerful dialogue contains the crucial insight that there can be no such thing as a neutral rhetoric. Rhetoric by its very nature is partisan, a fact exemplified in the idea that love itself can never be neutral. I would agree with those who believe that the very language we speak is not neutral, but exhibits tendencies of one sort or another. Those who read Plato's *Phaedrus* with discernment soon realize that Lysias, while praising the nonlover, really had his eye on Phaedrus, which by way of allegory says that those who protest a dispassionate neutrality may secretly have attachments to hide or even axes to grind.

I would agree with Iris Murdoch that "Moral philosophy cannot avoid taking sides, and would-be neutral philosophers merely take sides surreptitiously." The same is true of rhetoric and of those who analyze the form and content of persuasion-laden moral discourse. I for one have yet to read a totally nonpartisan, unbiased, critical view of bioethics, or, for that matter, of induced human abortion. Can it be that as with patriotism, a self-proclaimed neutrality is the last refuge of a scoundrel?

My greatest apprehension is the possibility that I may be making Kohlberg's theory into something it is not—an ideology. However, I have become increasingly convinced that the Kohlbergian system, as currently propounded, is itself an ideology. It exposes and promotes the ideology of liberal moral philosophy. As a number of his leading critics have so ably shown (including Hogan, Sullivan, and Vitz), Kohlberg is really not impartial. While claiming moral neutrality, he places a very high value on the principle of justice and on human life. Moreover, individualistic values like private property and civil rights creep into his theory repeatedly. Thus I find no basic imcompatibility between this ideology and a pro-life ideology. My deepest feelings have always been from the first moment of my anti-abortion activism that the truest and most laudable liberalism — indeed, the highest idealism—is to protect innocent human life and encourage its development.

Rhetoric is a mixture of both good and evil but is most effective when it deals with the truth. It is good if it gives us a clearer picture of what we can become, or if it reminds us of our nobility as moral agents. On the other hand, rhetoric is evil when it frustrates the realization of our moral potential or when it skews or twists the normal trajectory of moral growth. Because rhetoric inherently takes sides, therefore, ineffective persuasion can in large part be attributed either to falsifying nature or to mimicking its features poorly, either by accident or by design. A resourceful rhetoric works with nature.

Behind every rhetorical theory are certain key assumptions about the general persuasive characteristics of human beings. We have explored the cognitive-developmental assumption as it pertains to the moral dimension of a contemporary social movement. This motivational theory, of course, is incomplete. It would be naïve and possibly unfair to hope or wait for a perfected one. Rhetoricians must use what is currently available. Rhetoric is an exceedingly practical subject, and rhetoricians tend to be practical people. Rarely do they have the luxury of choice; they must do the best with what they have.

Kohlberg, in the classic Greek tradition, has attempted to tell the truth about the nature of things. His stages of moral growth describe the shape or contour of the human soul envisioned by Plato's *Phaedrus*; they help to delineate its nature. So also a developmental perspective can help communicators adapt to the variety of human souls, or, in more modern terminology, exhibit a greater sensitivity to audiences. Of course, there is no guarantee that a cognitive-developmental approach will work. Yet, I am inclined to agree with Wolterstorff, whose work on Kohlberg is an unalloyed example of cautious scholarship, that even in view of all its shortcomings, a moral-developmental outlook should increase the likelihood that certain favorable results will follow.

The cognitive-developmental approach to moral decision-making has a number of critics. Yet, in my opinion, many of those who criticize it seem to lack a detailed knowledge of what scholars like Kohlberg have really said. It is incumbent upon those who criticize a theoretician first to read him or her thoroughly. There is evidence that the two Kohlberg reviewers cited in the bibliography have not done so. A detailed reading of his work would have produced a better understanding of the cognitive-developmental paradigm. It will be unfortunate now that his theory is fairly well fleshed out that he will be forced to spend an increasing amount of time responding to those who have quoted him out of context.

Kohlberg's theory is at least as heuristic as Dewey's pattern of reflective thinking, of which it is a far more complete expression. It is certainly of greater potential application than Monroe's motivated sequence. But if the empirical support for it should somehow evaporate or become seriously weakened, it would still have inherent value in organizing messages. A psychological disposition of persuasive materials is important in itself. In this respect, then, it is not absolutely necessary that Kohlberg survive his critics. It is enough that he has provided a new way of organizing the parameters of complex moral issues.

Though I have tried in this postscript to be honest with the reader in expressing certain misgivings, it is not intended as an apologia for what I have done. My analysis is incomplete because it says nothing about the philosophical and rhetorical dynamics of viewing the physical world, i.e., the humanity of unborn human life, nor does it deal with the manifold cultural barriers to communicating moral and scientific truth. Each of these scholarly tasks would necessitate separate volumes, and I hope someday to produce them. In the pages of this volume I have attempted to justify moral developmentalism as a guide to rhetorical analysis. How well I have succeeded now depends on the reader. How well the reader succeeds depends upon his or her openness to new ideas and upon a sincere desire to get to the bottom of things.

APPENDIX

This appendix is divided into two sections. Section A includes sources from which a theory of persuasion for social movements might be fashioned. Section B is a summary of the pertinent criticism leveled against the Kohlbergian theory, along with a list of selected essays.

SECTION A

Other models from which rhetorical theories might be imaginatively and profitably drawn include the interactional, maturational, psychosocial, and typological. Used singly or in combination, these as well as life-span models emphasizing the adult years provide a wealth of potentially useful material for enterprising rhetoricians. The following list of representative books includes other cognitive-developmental formulations which should help to place the Kohlbergian model into proper perspective. Also included are a few titles reflecting values clarification, normative ethics, and general value theory. These latter approaches, as well as the behavioral, social-learning, and psychoanalytic models not cited here, are without sufficient immediate relevance to an understanding of the rhetoric of social movements to justify more than passing comment. While these sources do contain some excellent insight, they are not central to our purpose. And this is particularly true of those studies based on conditioning, training, or the dynamics of the unconscious.

Barker, Roger G. *Ecological Psychology*. Stanford, California: Stanford University Press, 1968.

Chickering, Arthur W. *Education and Identity*. San Francisco: Jossey-Bass, Inc., 1969.

Cross, K. Patricia. *Accent on Learning*. San Francisco: Jossey-Bass, Inc., 1976.

Haan, Norma. *Coping and Defending: Processes of Self-Environment Organization*. New York: Academic Press, 1977.

Hall, Brian P. *The Development of Consciousness*. New York: Paulist Press, 1976.

Harvey, O. J., Hunt, David E., and Schroder, Harold M. *Conceptual Systems and Personality Organization*. New York: John Wiley and Sons, Inc., 1961.

Heath, Douglas H. *Maturity and Competence*. New York: Gardner Press, Inc., 1977.

Heath, Roy. *The Reasonable Adventurer*. Pittsburgh: University of Pittsburgh Press, 1964.

Huebner, Lois A., ed. *Redesigning Campus Environments.* San Francisco: Jossey-Bass, Inc., 1979.

Keniston, Kenneth. *Youth and Dissent.* New York: Harcourt Brace Jovanovich, Inc., 1960.

Levinson, Daniel J., et al. *The Seasons of a Man's Life.* New York: Alfred A. Knopf, 1978.

Litwin, George H., and Stringer, Robert A., Jr. *Motivation and Organizational Climate.* Boston: Harvard University Graduate School of Business Administration, 1968.

Loevinger, Jane. *Ego Development: Conceptions and Theories.* San Francisco: Jossey-Bass, Inc., 1976.

Maslow, Abraham H. *Motivation and Personality.* 2nd ed. New York: Harper and Row, 1970.

Moos, Rudolf H. *The Human Context.* New York: John Wiley and Sons, Inc., 1976.

Murrell, Stanley A. *Community Psychology and Social Systems.* New York: Behavioral Publications, 1973.

Neugarten, Bernice L., et al. *Personality in Middle and Late Life.* New York: Arno Press, 1980.

Perry, William G., Jr. *Forms of Intellectual and Ethical Development in the College Years.* New York: Holt, Rinehart and Winston, Inc., 1968.

Raths, Louis E., Harmin, Merrill, and Simon, Sidney B. *Values and Teaching.* 2nd ed. Columbus: Charles E. Merrill Publishing Company, 1978.

Rogers, Carl R. *Client-Centered Therapy.* Boston: Houghton Mifflin Company, 1951.

Rokeach, Milton. *The Nature of Human Values.* New York: The Free Press, 1973.

Sanford, Nevitt. *Self and Society.* New York: Atherton Press, 1966.

Simon, Sidney B., Howe, Leland W., and Kirschenbaum, Howard. *Values Clarification.* Rev. ed. New York: Hart Publishing Company, Inc., 1978.

Stern, George G. *People in Context.* New York: John Wiley and Sons, Inc., 1970.

Tyler, Leona E. *Individuality.* San Francisco: Jossey-Bass, Inc., 1978.

Vaillant, George E. *Adaptation to Life.* Boston: Little, Brown and Company, 1977.

For a more detailed account of some of these and other sources, particularly scholarly journal articles, see Lee Knefelkamp, Carole Widick, and Clyde A. Parker, eds., *Applying New Developmental Findings* (San Francisco: Jossey-Bass, Inc., 1978), and Richard L. Morrill, *Teaching Values in College* (San Francisco: Jossey-Bass, Inc., 1980).

Of immediate educational value would be the following:

Fraenkel, Jack R. *How to Teach about Values: An Analytic Approach.* Englewood Cliffs, New Jersey: Prentice-Hall, Inc., 1977.

McPhail, Peter, Ungoed-Thomas, J. R., and Chapman, Hilary. *Lifeline.* Niles, Illinois: Argus Communications, 1975.

Metcalf, Lawrence E., ed. *Values Education*. Washington, D.C.: National Council for the Social Studies, 1971.

Newmann, Fred M. *Education for Citizen Action*. Berkeley, California: McCutchan Publishing Corporation, 1975.

Newmann, Fred M., Bertocci, Thomas A., and Landsness, Ruthanne M. *Skills in Citizen Action*. Skokie, Illinois: National Textbook Co., 1977.

Shaver, James P., and Strong, William. *Facing Value Decisions: Rationale-building for Teachers*. Belmont, California: Wadsworth Publishing Co., 1976.

For a comprehensive description and analysis of these works, see Richard H. Hersh, John P. Miller, and Glen D. Fielding, *Models of Moral Education* (New York: Longman, Inc., 1980). A less comprehensive appraisal of additional models can be found in Douglas Superka, "Approaches to Values Education," *Social Science Education Consortium Newsletter*, No. 20 (November, 1974). This latter publication, which is sponsored by the National Science Foundation, may be obtained from the SSEC office at 855 Broadway, Boulder, Colorado 80302.

To my knowledge, there is not yet available in book form a detailed application of any of the preceding theories to a specific ethical subject like abortion. The only possible exception would be a psychoanalytic approach. See George Devereux, *A Study of Abortion in Primitive Societies*, rev. ed. (New York: International Universities Press, Inc., 1976). This should not necessarily imply, however, that apart from the Kohlbergian orientation there are no recent influential studies which are capable of creating a coherent picture of how persuasion takes place in social movements.

SECTION B

Kohlberg's theory of moral development has been the object of considerable criticism. While some of this criticism has been constructive in either confirming or extending the theory and some of it has been quite hostile, by and large it has all been helpful to a fuller understanding of the model. Where appropriate, I have mentioned some of this criticism in the main text. Now, in a few paragraphs I will attempt to summarize the leading criticism drawn mainly from the appended list of essays. The list is a modest sampling of what is typically available in the scientific literature and what is sure to proliferate as time goes by.

The interested reader will likely notice that a number of the essays deal entirely or in part with the pioneering scholarship of Jean Piaget. I have included these essays here because comments on Piaget are in some cases applicable to Kohlberg's work as well. A criticism of one is an indirect criticism of the other. The most frequent criticisms can be grouped into two categories: (1) that the theory is weak conceptually, and (2) that it is weak methodologically. (In some places, of course, these two objections obviously overlap.)

(1) The theory is conceptually weak because it is narrow and elitist. Kohlberg's view of morality is criticized for being narrow because it deals with only one aspect of morality, namely, justice, and for ignoring the whole of a person's life in the effort to determine his or her moral status. That justice is the ultimate virtue is merely assumed by Kohlberg and never really proved. Critics ask about the other cardinal virtues, prudence, fortitude, and temperance (in classical ethical analysis, for example, prudence has been traditionally given first place), and about the value or importance of training in good habits. Also, the separation of moral growth from other aspects of development is considered by some to be wholly arbitrary. Can morality be based on reason alone? What about noncognitive development? In some cases, one must act before all the rules are known or before one can make adequate sense of them. Love, which is a synthesis of justice and mercy, is likewise absent from Kohlberg's theory. The idea of the Good Samaritan or of doing more than what justice requires is deeply embedded in Western culture. Compassion may really be more critical to moral behavior than mere justice. Finally, Kohlberg overlooks the climate of trust so necessary to any educational endeavor.

In addition to narrowness, the charge of elitism has been attached to the Kohlbergian construct. With its Platonic emphasis upon an ideal form of justice, it is said to be created for philosopher kings by philosopher kings. (One canard claims *sotto voce* that only three people are definitely known to have reached Kohlberg's highest stage of moral growth, Kohlberg himself and two grad students.) Kohlberg's theory is also labeled ethnocentric and culturally biased. It is criticized for its middle-class orientations and for not being applicable to the ghetto child. Perhaps the most serious charge of elitism is that the theory has a sexual bias. Kohlberg's initial interviewees were all male, as were the main characters in his hypothetical dilemmas. Thus, for promulgating a masculine view of morals, he is open to the charge of androcentrism.

(2) Kohlberg's theory is methodologically weak because it is unrealistic and lacks universality. Critics feel that oversimplified hypothetical conflict situations can hardly elicit meaningful responses from those being tested. Kohlberg's dilemmas are said to deal, not with concrete, but rather with abstract situations unlikely to occur as typical everyday moral experiences. The settings are also considered extreme and the characters one-dimensional (note especially the often-used Heinz dilemma). Real-life dilemmas are much more subtle and complex. It has even been suggested that the dilemmas could

be improved by making them more stage-specific and graduated in complexity.

Of a more technical nature are criticisms relating to Kohlberg's data. There is a basic disagreement about the interpretation of the evidence identifying each stage and about the generalizability of test results. Kohlberg has been criticized for chronically reporting his data incompletely and for mentioning "in press" studies that never seem to materialize. He has been cited for not publishing the psychometric characteristics of his chief measuring instrument. Critics want to know how it was derived, administered, and scored, and what is the evidence for its validity and reliability. Also, there is a scarcity of information about fully one-third of Kohlberg's model (Postconventional Level III—Stages 5 and 6). Not enough subjects were studied to justify really hard conclusions (some say the level is simply too rare to be useful). Other methodological questions left unanswered include the actual number of moral aspects (they vary in Kohlberg's writings) and the efficacy of the stage-transition mechanism (Kohlberg's treatment is considered vague). And, finally, critics question whether the interview technique is in fact the best way to elicit a moral response.

In addition to these two major categories of criticism, my experience as a social-movement communicator (and practical moral educator) brings me to find other problems with Kohlberg's theory. A major problem is that it ignores the facts of the case. Moral reasoning is based upon the truth (or falsity) of certain factual claims made by parties to the dispute. For example, is legal abortion more harmful to women than carrying a child to term? Also, unfortunately, there is no emphasis in Kohlberg's work upon content or the goodness or badness of the moral act being judged. Kohlberg's theory holds that only the reasoning method used to arrive at a moral decision is important. Some critics contend, and I will add my voice to theirs, that the form of reasoning itself is necessary but not sufficient for a full and clear understanding of moral development. Form can hardly be acquired without content. An inevitable result of placing form over content is the absurdity that two people can reason at the same stage and yet come to two different conclusions or diametrically opposed courses of action; or, even more alarming, that a person could reason and subsequently act in one way at one stage and in the opposite way at another. Practically speaking, how could principled moral thinking be both for and against abortion-on-demand, and at the same time? The very idea seems preposterous. History records that many a crime has been committed in the name or guise of principle. (And it is well known that some Nazi jailers took great delight in their children and listened to classical music for relaxation at night in preparation for the next full day of operating the gas chambers.) What this boils down to is that in Kohlberg's theory thinking becomes divorced from action and intent is thereby favored over consequences. At some point morality should come to mean the morally right act for the morally right reason.

Obviously, Kohlberg is more concerned with change than with constancy. In his view of morals, it is never really right or wrong to do anything. There is no correct or incorrect moral action. Kohlberg is interested in patterns, not in answers, in form or process, not in content or outcome. For the committed moral educator, this would be intolerable. Driven to its logical conclusion, it represents a subtle case of antinomianism that ultimately strikes at the heart of the Kohlbergian thesis. By de-emphasizing content, Kohlberg in effect is forced to accept what he most strongly wishes to avoid—moral relativism. While emphatically rejecting moral relativism, he unwittingly accepts it by suggesting that there is no absolute standard. His model permits justice to be interpreted as its opposite at each stage of moral growth—a most serious indictment.

Finally, from both a practical and theoretical standpoint, Kohlberg's theory overlooks a very important audience, the mature older person. More data are needed about adult subjects. Those well beyond late adolescence and early adulthood make some very important decisions in society. It was in 1973, to use a worn and now sexually inaccurate phrase, that "nine old men" on the U.S. Supreme Court decided to relax the nation's abortion laws. Can there be a difference in mature adult moral reasoning? The question remains unanswered.

Before I conclude, there are two final observations that should be made. To begin with, there is no place in Kohlberg's system for evil or moral failure and for the concept of the human will. Critics rightly point out that in Kohlberg's scheme there is no dark side to the human moral enterprise; and in the human spirit there is neither pride, nor impulse, nor personal aggrandizement. But perhaps the most telling criticism of the Kohlbergian construct is the efficacy of revolutionary moral transformations. What about those great dramatic conversion experiences whereby someone suddenly changes a moral position? The Pauline experience on the road to Damascus would be alien to Kohlbergian developmental thinking. Where is the proper place in Kohlberg's scheme for the whole idea of sin and reconciliation, for seeing the light and mending one's ways? How can moral developmentalism explain the behavior of Bernard Nathanson, the notorious abortionist who had a most dramatic change of heart? How, indeed?

Yet, with all this in mind, i.e., the problems yet to be faced by Kohlberg and his school, the reader should not be frustrated or discouraged. If the developmental model seems inconclusive, one fact remains unaffected: many educators will agree (including some of his most vocal critics) that moral judgment does appear to possess a discernible growth pattern and that Kohlberg's attempt to describe it offers exciting new possibilities. Furthermore, a good typology to aid rhetorical analysis is always a helpful addition to any persuader's armamentarium. And now that the reader has been alerted to what objections to anticipate, he or she is left to explore the following, bearing in mind that all the essays may not reflect equal degrees of scholarship or insight and that a thorough critical study of Kohlberg's work by a team of scholars has yet to be made. For variety, I have also included a few well-written "think pieces" which either enlarge the cognitive-developmental model or provide a viable alternative.

Altilia, Leonard. "Education in Christian Morality: A Developmental Framework," *Religious Education*, LXXI, No. 5 (September–October, 1976), 488–99.

Arbuthnot, Jack. "Modification of Moral Judgment through Role Playing," *Developmental Psychology*, XI, No. 3 (May, 1975), 319–24.

Archibald, Helen A., "The Naturalistic Fallacy," *Religious Education*, LXXV, No. 2 (March–April, 1980), 152–64.

Aron, Israela Ettenberg. "Moral Philosophy and Moral Education: A Critique of Kohlberg's Theory," *School Review*, LXXXV, No. 2 (February, 1977), 197–217.

Bachmeyer, T. J. "Ethics and the Psychology of Moral Judgment," *Zygon*, VIII, No. 2 (June, 1973), 82–95.

Bachmeyer, T. J. "The Golden Rule and Developing Moral Judgment," *Religious Education*, LXVIII, No. 3 (May–June, 1973), 348–65.

Bachmeyer, T. J. "The Use of Kohlberg's Theory of Moral Development in Religious Education," *The Living Light*, X, No. 3 (Fall, 1973), 340–50.

Baier, Kurt. "Individual Moral Development and Social Moral Advance," *The Journal of Philosophy*, LXX, No. 18 (October 25, 1973), 646–48.

Bandura, Albert. "Social Learning of Moral Judgments," *Journal of Personality and Social Psychology*, XI, No. 3 (March, 1969), 275–79.

Bandura, Albert, and McDonald, Frederick J. "Influence of Social Reinforcement and the Behavior of Models in Shaping Children's Moral Judgments," *Journal of Abnormal and Social Psychology*, LXVII, No. 3 (September, 1963), 274–81.

Belenky, Mary Field. "Conflict and Development: A Longitudinal Study of the Impact of Abortion Decisions on Moral Judgments of Adolescent and Adult Women" (unpublished Ed.D. dissertation, Harvard University, 1978).

Bergman, Marvin. "Moral Decision Making in the Light of Kohlberg and Bonhoeffer: A Comparison," *Religious Education*, LXIX, No. 2 (March–April, 1974), 227–43.

Brown, Roger, and Herrnstein, Richard J. *Psychology.* Boston: Little, Brown and Co., 1975.

Conn, Walter E. "Postconventional Morality: An Exposition and Critique of Lawrence Kohlberg's Analysis of Moral Development in the Adolescent and Adult," *Lumen Vitae*, XXX, No. 2 (June, 1975), 213–30.

Cowan, Philip A., Langer, Jonas, Heavenrich, Judith, and Nathanson, Marjorie. "Social Learning and Piaget's Cognitive Theory of Moral Develop-ment," *Journal of Personality and Social Psychology*, XI, No. 3 (March, 1969), 261–74.

Crittenden, Brian. "A Comment on Cognitive Moral Education," *Phi Delta Kappan*, LVI, No. 10 (June, 1975), 695–96.

Dooley, Catherine. "Moral Education in a Christian Context," *The Living Light*, XII, No. 4 (Winter, 1975), 510–25.

Dykstra, Craig, R. "Christian Education and the Moral Life: An Evaluation of and Alternative to Kohlberg" (unpublished Ph.D. dissertation, Princeton Theological Seminary, 1978).

Dykstra, Craig. "Moral Virtue or Social Reasoning," *Religious Education*, LXXV, No. 2 (March–April, 1980), 115–28.

Dykstra, Craig. "Sin, Repentance, and Moral Transformation: Some Critical Reflections on Kohlberg," *The Living Light*, XVI, No. 4 (Winter, 1979), 451–61.

Elias, John L. "A Cultural Approach to Religious Moral Education," *The Living Light*, XVII, No. 3 (Fall, 1980), 234–41.

Ellrod, Rick. "Morality and Interests: A Critique of Kohlberg's Ethical Theory," *Communio*, VII, No. 3 (Fall, 1980), 259–68.

Feffer, Melvin. "Developmental Analysis of Interpersonal Behavior," *Psychological Review*, LXXVII, No. 3 (May, 1970), 197–214.

Fodor, Eugene M. "Resistance to Temptation, Moral Development, and Perceptions of Parental Behavior among Adolescent Boys," *Journal of Social Psychology*, LXXXVIII, First Half (October, 1972), 155–56.

Fraenkel, Jack R. "The Kohlberg Bandwagon: Some Reservations," *Social Education*, XL, No. 4 (April, 1976), 216–22.

Gibbs, John C. "Kohlberg's Stages of Moral Judgment: A Constructive Critique," *Harvard Educational Review*, XLVII, No. 1 (February, 1977), 43–61.

Haan, Norma. "Hypothetical and Actual Moral Reasoning in a Situation of Civil Disobedience," *Journal of Personality and Social Psychology*, XXXII, No. 2 (August, 1975), 255–70.

Haan, Norma. "Two Moralities in Action Contexts: Relationships to Thought, Ego Regulation, and Development," *Journal of Personality and Social Psychology*, XXXVI, No. 3 (March, 1978), 286–305.

Haggett, Margaret. "Do Catholics Need Moral Education?" *The Clergy Review*, LIX, No. 10 (October, 1974), 681–87.

Hamm, Cornel M. "The Content of Moral Education, or in Defense of the 'Bag of Virtues,'" *School Review*, LXXXV, No. 2 (February, 1977), 218–28.

Hargadon, Joseph M., and Proctor, John. "Kohlberg for Parents," *The Living Light*, XII, No. 2 (Summer, 1975), 239–45.

Harris, Stephen, Mussen, Paul, and Rutherford, Eldred. "Some Cognitive, Behavioral, and Personality Correlates of Maturity of Moral Judgment," *Journal of Genetic Psychology*, CXXVIII, First Half (March, 1976), 123–35.

Harrower, M. R. "Social Status and the Moral Development of the Child,"

British Journal of Educational Psychology, IV, Part I (February, 1934), 75–95.

Henson, Richard G. "Correlativity and Reversibility," *The Journal of Philosophy*, LXX, No. 18 (October 25, 1973), 648–49.

Hogan, Robert. "A Dimension of Moral Judgment," *Journal of Consulting and Clinical Psychology*, XXXV, No. 2 (October, 1970), 205–12.

Hogan, Robert. "Moral Conduct and Moral Character: A Psychological Perspective," *Psychological Bulletin*, LXXIX, No. 4 (April, 1973), 217–32.

Hogan, Robert, and Dickstein, Ellen. "A Measure of Moral Values," *Journal of Consulting and Clinical Psychology*, XXXIX, No. 2 (October, 1972), 210–14.

Hogan, Robert T., and Emler, Nicholas P. "The Biases in Contemporary Social Psychology," *Social Research*, XLV, No. 3 (Autumn, 1978), 478–534.

Holstein, Constance Boucher. "Irreversible, Stepwise Sequence in the Development of Moral Judgment: A Longitudinal Study of Males and Females," *Child Development*, XLVII, No. 1 (March, 1976), 51–61.

Johnson, Ronald C. "A Study of Children's Moral Judgments," *Child Development*, XXXIII (March–December, 1962), 327–54.

Joy, Donald M. "Moral Development: Evangelical Perspectives," *Religious Education*, LXXV, No. 2 (March–April, 1980), 142–51.

Joy, Maureen. "Kohlberg and Moral Education," *New Catholic World*, CCXV, No. 1282 (January–February, 1972), 14–16.

Keniston, Kenneth. "Moral Development, Youthful Activism, and Modern Society," *The Critic*, XXVIII, No. 1 (September–October, 1969), 17–24.

Kibble, David G. "Moral Education in an Inner-City Comprehensive: Rationality Is Not Enough," *Learning for Living*, XVI, No. 2 (Winter, 1976), 63–67+.

Krahn, John H. "A Comparison of Kohlberg's and Piaget's Type I Morality," *Religious Education*, LXVI, No. 5 (September–October, 1971), 373–75.

Kurtines, William, and Greif, Esther Blank. "The Development of Moral Thought: Review and Evaluation of Kohlberg's Approach," *Psychological Bulletin*, LXXXI, No. 8 (August, 1974), 453–70.

Laney, James T. "Characterization and Moral Judgments," *Journal of Religion*, LV, No. 4 (October, 1975), 405–14.

Lazarowitz, Rachel, Stephan, Walter G., and Friedman, S. Thomas. "Effects of Moral Justifications and Moral Reasoning on Altruism," *Developmental Psychology*, XII, No. 4 (July, 1976), 353–54.

Le Furgy, William G., and Woloshin, Gerald W. "Immediate and Long-Term Effects of Experimentally Induced Social Influence in the Modification of Adolescents' Moral Judgments," *Journal of Personality and Social Psychology*, XII, No. 2 (June, 1969), 104–10.

Leming, James S. "Cheating Behavior, Situational Influence, and Moral Development," *Journal of Educational Research*, LXXI, No. 4 (March–April, 1978) 214–17.

Lickona, Thomas. "Piaget Misunderstood: A Critique of the Criticisms of His Theory of Moral Development," *Merrill-Palmer Quarterly*, XV, No. 4 (October, 1969), 337–50.

Loughran, Robert. "A Pattern of Development in Moral Judgments Made by Adolescents Derived from Piaget's Schema of Its Development in Childhood," *Educational Review*, XIX, No. 2 (February, 1967), 79–98.

McBride, Alfred. "Moral Education and the Kohlberg Thesis," *Momentum*, IV, No. 4 (December, 1973), 23–27.

McKechnie, R. J. "Between Piaget's Stages: A Study in Moral Development," *The British Journal of Educational Psychology*, XLI, Part 2 (June, 1971), 213–17.

MacRae, Duncan, Jr. "A Test of Piaget's Theories of Moral Development," *Journal of Abnormal and Social Psychology*, XLIX, No. 1 (January, 1954), 14–18.

May, William E. "The Natural Law, Conscience, and Developmental Psychology," *Communio*, II, No. 1 (Spring, 1975), 3–31.

Moran, Gabriel. "Beyond the Two Stages of Moral Reasoning," *The Living Light*, XVI, No. 3 (Fall, 1979), 277–89.

Muson, Howard. "Moral Thinking—Can It Be Taught?" *Psychology Today*, XII, No. 9 (February, 1979), 48–49+.

Newton, Robert R. "Kohlberg: Implications for High School Programs," *The Living Light*, XV, No. 2 (Summer, 1978), 231–39.

Orr, John B. "Cognitive-Developmental Approaches to Moral Education: A Social Ethical Analysis," *Education ·Theory*, XXIV, No. 4 (Fall, 1974), 365–73.

O'Toole, John S. "The Philosophy of Christian Moral Education," *The Clergy Review*, LXI, No. 10 (October, 1976), 388–97.

Peatling, John H. "Research on Adult Moral Development: Where Is It?" *Religious Education*, LXXII, No. 2 (March–April, 1977), 212–24.

Peatling, John H. "A Sense of Justice: Moral Judgment in Children, Adolescents and Adults," *Character Potential: A Record of Research*, VIII, No. 1 (November, 1976), 25–34.

Peters, Richard S. "A Reply to Kohlberg," *Phi Delta Kappan*, LVI, No. 10 (June, 1975), 678.

Philibert, Paul J. "Lawrence Kohlberg's Use of Virtue in His Theory of Moral Development," *International Philosophical Quarterly*, XV, No. 4 (December, 1975), 455–79.

Philibert, Paul J. "Some Cautions on Kohlberg," *The Living Light*, XXII, No. 4 (Winter, 1975), 527–34.

Phillips, D. C., and Kelly, Mavis E. "Hierarchical Theories of Development in Education and Psychology," *Harvard Educational Review*, XLV, No. 3 (August, 1975), 351–75.

Potter, Ralph B. "Justice and Beyond in Moral Education" (paper presented at the Regional Conference on the Moral Development of Youth, Spring Hill Center, Wayzata, Minnesota, June 1, 1977).

Prentice, Norman M. "The Influence of Live and Symbolic Modeling on Promoting Moral Judgment of Adolescent Delinquents," *Journal of Abnormal Psychology*, LXXX, No. 2 (September, 1972), 157–61.

Ryan, Kevin. "Moral Formation: The American Scene," in *Moral Formation and Christianity*, ed. by Franz Böckle and Jacques-Marie Pohier (New York: The Seabury Press, 1978), 95–107.

Sams, Janice. "The Ghetto Child and Moral Development," *Religious Education*, LXXX, No. 6 (November–December, 1975), 636–48.

Satterly, David. "Stages of Development: Help or Hindrance in Educating Young Children?" *Universities Quarterly*, XXIX, No. 4 (August, 1975), 379–88.

Schwartz, Shalom H., Feldman, Kenneth A., Brown, Michael E., and Heingartner, Alex. "Some Personality Correlates of Conduct in Two Situations of Moral Conflict." *Journal of Personality*, XXXVII, No. 1 (March, 1969), 41–57.

Scriven, Michael. "Cognitive Moral Education," *Phi Delta Kappan*, LVI, No. 10 (June, 1975), 689–94.

Shields, David. "Education for Moral Action," *Religious Education*, LXXV, No. 2 (March–April, 1980), 129–41.

Sholl, Doug. "The Contributions of Lawrence Kohlberg to Religious and Moral Education," *Religious Education*, LXVI, No. 5 (September–October, 1971), 364–72.

Sichel, Betty A. "Can Kohlberg Respond to Critics?" *Educational Theory*, XXVI, No. 4 (Fall, 1976), 337–47, 394.

Sichel, Betty A. "The Relation Between Moral Judgement and Moral Behaviour in Kohlberg's Theory of the Development of Moral Judgements," *Educational Philosophy and Theory*, VIII, No. 1 (April, 1976), 55–67.

Simpson, Elizabeth Léonie. "Moral Development Research: A Case Study of Scientific Cultural Bias," *Human Development*, XVII, No. 2 (1974), 81–106.

Stanton, Michael. "The Assessment of Moral Judgments: Cultural and Cognitive Considerations," *Religious Education*, LXXI, No. 6 (November–December, 1976), 610–21.

Straughan, Roger R. "Hypothetical Moral Situations," *Journal of Moral Education*, IV, No. 3 (June, 1975), 183–89.

Sullivan, Edmund V. "A Study of Kohlberg's Structural Theory of Moral Development: A Critique of Liberal Social Science Ideology," *Human Development*, XX, No. 6 (1977), 352–76.

Sullivan, Edmund V., McCullough, George, and Stager, Mary. "A Developmental Study of the Relationship between Conceptual, Ego, and Moral Development," *Child Development*, XLI, No. 2 (June, 1970), 399–411.

Vitz, Paul C. "Christian Moral Values and Dominant Psychological Theories: The Case of Kohlberg," in *Christian Faith in a Neo-Pagan Society*, ed. by Paul L. Williams (Scranton: Northeast Books, 1981), 35–56.

Weinreich, Helen. "Kohlberg and Piaget: Aspects of their Relationship in the Field of Moral Development," *Journal of Moral Education*, IV, No. 3 (June, 1975), 201–13.

Weinreich, Helen. "The Structure of Moral Reason," *Journal of Youth and Adolescence*, III, No. 2 (June, 1974), 135–43.

Wilson, Richard W. "Some Comments on Stage Theories of Moral Develop-ment," *Journal of Moral Education*, V, No. 3 (June, 1976), 241–48.

Wolterstorff, Nicholas P. *Educating for Responsible Action.* Grand Rapids, Michigan: Wm. B. Eerdmans Publishing Co., 1980.

Yolton, L. William. "Moral and Faith Development," *Church and Society*, LXVIII, No. 2 (November–December, 1977), 58–60.

Youniss, James. "Kohlberg's Theory: A Commentary," *The Living Light*, X, No. 3 (Fall, 1973), 352–58.

NOTES

INTRODUCTION

1. This information was obtained from a paper presented at the National Right to Life Convention held in St. Louis, Missouri, June 29–July 2, 1978. The speaker was Maris Vinovskis, then associated with the Center for Political Studies of the Institute for Social Research at the University of Michigan. The following month a journal article appeared which contains a useful bibliography of current scientific literature. See Krishna Singh and Peter J. Leahy, "Contextual and Ideological Dimensions of Attitudes toward Discretionary Abortion, *Demography*, XV, No. 3 (August, 1978), pp. 381–88.

2. The exposé occurred during November and December of 1978. The principal authors were Pamela Zekman and Pamela Warrick. So popular was the exposé that the newspaper issued a special reprint also containing reaction stories, editorials, and cartoons. See *Chicago Sun-Times* Special Reprint, *The Abortion Profiteers* (Chicago: Field Enterprises, Inc., 1978).

3. John T. Noonan, *A Private Choice* (New York: The Free Press, 1979), pp. 69–70.

4. Jean Piaget, *The Moral Judgment of the Child*, trans. by Marjorie Gabain (New York: The Free Press, 1965), p. 376.

5. Jean Piaget, *Biology and Knowledge*, trans. by Beatrix Walsh (Chicago: The University of Chicago Press, 1971), p. 29.

6. The following books help to explain Piaget's theory: Ruth M. Beard, *An Outline of Piaget's Developmental Psychology* (New York: The New American Library, Inc., 1969); Molly Brearley and Elizabeth Hitchfield, *A Guide to Reading Piaget* (New York: Schocken Books, 1966); John H. Flavell, *The Developmental Psychology of Jean Piaget* (New York: D. Van Nostrand Company, 1963); Nathan Isaacs, *A Brief Introduction to Piaget* (New York: Schocken Books, 1960); John L. Phillips, Jr., *The Origins of Intellect: Piaget's Theory* (San Francisco: W. H. Freeman and Company, 1969); Mary Ann Spencer Pulaski, *Understanding Piaget* (New York: Harper and Row, 1971); P. G. Richmond, *An Introduction to Piaget* (New York: Basic Books, Inc., 1970); and Barry J. Wadsworth, *Piaget's Theory of Cognitive Development* (New York: David McKay Company, Inc., 1971).

7. For an excellent treatment of the relationship between form and content in the study of ethics, I highly recommend William D. Boyce and Larry Cyril Jensen, *Moral Reasoning* (Lincoln: University of Nebraska Press, 1978). This book provides an important psychological-philosophical integration of the problem of form and content. It is well reasoned, eminently reasonable, and finds some usefulness in nearly all accounts of moral behavior.

8. Adam Clymer, "Nation Votes Today in Skeptical Mood," *The New York Times*, November 7, 1978, p. 1.

PART I. THE DEVELOPMENT OF CONSCIENCE

1. This is the Lane Cooper translation in *The Collected Dialogues of Plato*, ed. by Edith Hamilton and Huntington Cairns, Bollingen Series LXXI (New York: Pantheon Books, 1961), p. 178.

2. Patrick J. Reardon, "McGovern's Antiwar Stand Applauded," *The Milwaukee Journal*, March 24, 1972, p. 14.

3. Rowland Evans and Robert Novak, "Big John on Tightrope," *Chicago Sun-Times*, August 14, 1979, p. 42.

4. William K. Frankena, "Is Morality Logically Dependent on Religion?" in *Religion and Morality*, ed. by Gene Outka and John P. Reeder, Jr. (Garden City, New York: Anchor Books, 1973), p. 295.

5. For a view of conscience as a conditioned reflex, see H. J. Eysenck, "The Biology of Morality," in *Moral Development and Behavior*, ed. by Thomas Lickona (New York: Holt, Rinehart and Winston, 1976), p. 109.

6. Although how one answers the first question is important to the debate (some would also say critical), I have chosen to deal exclusively with the second question initially because it is handled so poorly by most who argue about abortion in the public forum. Another volume would be needed to answer the second question and thus perfect the rhetorical analysis.

7. American Institute of Public Opinion, "Public Is Closely Divided on Court's Ruling on Abortion," *Chicago Sun-Times*, May 31, 1981, p. 20. Several years ago a similar poll was taken in Minnesota with similar results. Respondents were asked about when they thought human life began and about their willingness to support a Human Life Amendment prohibiting abortion. The divergence of opinion, again closely correlated, showed that for those who believed that life begins at conception, 72 percent were for the amendment, 20 percent were against it, and 8 percent had no opinion, while for those who believed that life begins at 3 or 6 months gestation or at birth, 34 percent were for the amendment, 64 percent were against it, and 2 percent had no opinion. See "Most Think Life Begins at Conception," *Minneapolis Tribune*, October 24, 1976, p. 8A.

8. A slight clarification is needed here. In the report of a Gallup Poll conducted two months later than the one previously quoted, views on abortion were again found to be highly correlated with views on when life begins. The surveyed opinion about the Supreme Court's ruling permitting abortion revealed that for those who thought that life begins (1) at conception: 32 percent favored the ruling and 77 percent opposed it; (2) during the first 2 or 3 months: 9 percent favored and 2 percent opposed; (3) later in pregnancy: 25 percent favored, 8 percent opposed; and (4) at birth: 28 percent were in

favor and 7 percent opposed. From these percentages, the AIPO concluded that, because a substantial number of those who favored the Supreme Court's ruling allowing abortion in the first three months of pregnancy also believe that life begins in that period, the abortion issue is not only an issue about when life begins, it is also an issue about how one feels toward that unborn life. This poll does not significantly alter the findings of the previous one. The more recent survey simply has more nuanced categories which seem to have elicited a greater certainty from those who oppose the Supreme Court's ruling, whereas those who favor it seem to be in a quandary. See American Institute of Public Opinion, "American Abortion Views Mostly at Middle Ground," *Chicago Sun-Times*, August 6, 1981, p. 40.

9. Thomas Aquinas, *Summa Theologica* (I–II, Q. 71, A.6) trans. by the Fathers of the English Dominican Province (London: Burns Oates and Washbourne, 1915), p. 274.

10. The preamble to the declaration states: "*Whereas* the child, by reason of his physical and mental immaturity, needs special safeguards and care, including appropriate legal protection, before as well as after birth, ..." See 1386 (XIV). Declaration of the Rights of the Child in Peter I. Hajnal, *Guide to United Nations Organization, Documentation and Publishing* (Dobbs Ferry, New York: Oceana Publications, Inc., 1978), p. 383. A reference to the declaration can also be found in *Everyman's United Nations*, 8th ed. (New York: United Nations Department of Public Information, 1968), p. 360.

11. For readers desiring to pursue further the idea of Natural Law, the following books are strongly recommended. John Cogley, ed., *Natural Law and Modern Society* (Freeport, New York: Books for Libraries Press, 1971). This is a reprint of the book originally published by The Fund for the Republic, Inc., in 1962. Jacques Maritain, *The Rights of Man and Natural Law*, trans. by Doris C. Anson (New York: Gordian Press, 1971). This is a reprint of the book originally published by Charles Scribner's Sons in 1943. Frederick A. Olafson, ed., *Society, Law, and Morality* (Englewood Cliffs, New Jersey: Prentice-Hall, Inc., 1961). Yves R. Simon, *The Tradition of Natural Law* (New York: Fordham University Press, 1965). This book is an edited compilation of Simon's lectures for a course he taught at the University of Chicago. My highest recommendation is reserved for John Finnis, *Natural Law and Natural Rights* (London: Oxford University Press, 1980).

12. John Macquarrie, *Three Issues in Ethics* (New York: Harper and Row, 1970), p. 51.

13. *Ibid.*, p. 91.

14. *Ibid.*, p. 110.

15. Hugh Rosen, *The Development of Sociomoral Knowledge* (New York: Columbia University Press, 1980), p. 97.

16. I am not presupposing an "annexationist" attitude here. Macquarrie's excellent analysis, previously cited, governs my interpretation, however poorly expressed, of the relationship between religion and morality.

17. In his chapter "Reason and Faith" Toulmin says as much: "Ethics provides the *reasons* for choosing the 'right' course: religion helps us to put

our *hearts* into it" (italics in the original). See Stephen Edelston Toulmin, *The Place of Reason in Ethics* (London: Cambridge University Press, 1950), p. 219. See also Peters's chapter "The Religious Dimension of a Rational Morality," in which he says that religion has "the function of endorsing and of emphasizing one or other of the fundamental principles of morality by placing its operation in a setting which awakens awe." Richard S. Peters, *Reason and Compassion* (London: Routledge and Kegan Paul, 1973), p. 118.

18. This is quite similar to Rudolf Otto's notion of the "numinous." See Rudolf Otto, *The Idea of the Holy*, trans. by John W. Harvey (London: Oxford University Press, 1958).

19. See Andrew M. Greeley, *Letters to Nancy* (New York: Sheed and Ward, 1964) and the account of alienation and religious faith in John Powell, *A Reason to Live! A Reason to Die!* (Niles, Illinois: Argus Communications, 1972), p. 74.

20. Shortly before this book was completed I saw the following slogan on a T-shirt hanging in the display window of a Chicago metropolitan area variety store: "I know I'm somebody 'cause God don't make no junk!" Several years earlier I observed a similar slogan on a large banner hanging in the rear of a soup kitchen run by the Franciscans for the indigent of Milwaukee's inner city. The slogan would be clearly ego-enhancing for those who lack basic self-esteem.

21. For a scholarly treatment of what morality can mean, see G. Wallace and A. D. M. Walker, eds., *The Definition of Morality* (London: Methuen and Company, Ltd., 1970).

22. Jean Piaget, *The Moral Judgment of the Child*, trans. by Marjorie Gabian (New York: The Free Press, 1965), p. 198.

23. *Roe* v. *Wade*, 410 U.S. 113 (1973).

24. Reinhold Niebuhr, *The Children of Light and the Children of Darkness* (New York: Charles Scribner's Sons, 1960), p. 125.

25. Rosen, *op. cit.*, p. 4.

26. The perceptive reader should easily recognize the numerous religious and/or quasi-religious journals and publishing houses referred to in these notes as well as in the appendix and bibliography. Paulist Press, in particular, seems to be heavily into Kohlberg.

27. An extension of the developmental paradigm to the realm of religious faith can be found in the work of James Fowler. See James W. Fowler, *Stages of Faith: The Psychology of Human Development and the Quest for Meaning* (New York: Harper and Row, 1981). For a summary and defense of his position see Jerome Berryman, ed., *Life Maps: Conversations on the Journey of Faith* (Minneapolis: Winston Press, 1978). And for a well-written earlier and more general treatment of religio-moral thinking see Ronald Goldman, *Religious Thinking from Childhood to Adolescence* (New York: The Seabury Press, 1964).

28. See particularly Ronald E. Galbraith and Thomas M. Jones, *Moral Reasoning* (Minneapolis: Greenhaven Press, Inc., 1976).

29. See section labeled "Theory of Intellectual Development" in David

E. Hunt and Edmund V. Sullivan, *Between Psychology and Education* (Hinsdale, Illinois: Dryden Press, 1974), pp. 131–38.

30. Ronald Duska and Mariellen Whelan, *Moral Development: A Guide to Piaget and Kohlberg* (New York: Paulist Press, 1975), p. 49.

31. Robert T. Hall and John U. Davis, *Moral Education in Theory and Practice* (Buffalo: Prometheus Books, 1975), p. 91.

32. Erik H. Erikson, *Childhood and Society*, 2nd ed. (New York: W. W. Norton, 1963). For an earlier exposition of his developmental theory, see Erik H. Erikson, "Identity and the Life Cycle," *Psychological Issues*, I, No. 1 (New York: International Universities Press, Inc., 1959).

33. See Chapter 6, "Theories of Development: An Overview," in Richard M. Lerner, *Concepts and Theories of Human Development* (Reading, Massachusetts: Addison-Wesley Publishing Co., 1976).

34. Carol Gilligan and Mary Field Belenky, "A Naturalistic Study of Abortion Decisions," in *Clinical-Developmental Psychology*, ed. by Robert L. Selman and Regina Yando. New Directions for Child Development, No. 7 (San Francisco: Jossey-Bass, Inc., 1980), p. 81.

35. Carol Gilligan, "In a Different Voice: Women's Conceptions of Self and of Morality," *Harvard Educational Review*, XLVII, No. 4 (November, 1977), p. 515.

36. *Ibid.*, p. 487.

37. Rosen, *op. cit.*, p. 39.

38. See Aristotle's *Rhetoric*, Book I, 1354[a], 24. "It is not right to pervert the judge by moving him to anger or envy or pity—one might as well warp a carpenter's rule before using it." From *The Rhetoric and the Poetics of Aristotle*, trans. by W. Rhys Roberts and Ingram Bywater (New York: Random House, Inc., 1954), p. 20.

39. Representative of this agenetic view would be the theory of Chomsky. See Noam Chomsky, *Aspects of the Theory of Syntax* (Cambridge: The Massachusetts Institute of Technology Press, 1965).

40. See Alan L. Lockwood, "Moral Reasoning and Public Policy Debate," in Lickona, *op. cit.*, p. 324.

41. Galbraith and Jones, *op. cit.*, p. 28.

42. *Ibid.*, p. 185. See also James R. Rest, "New Approaches in the Assessment of Moral Judgment," in Lickona, *op. cit.*, p. 203.

43. While writing this, I could not help but note a certain parallel with the concept of parent, adult, and child as formulated by transactional analysis. See Thomas A. Harris, *I'm OK—You're OK* (New York: Harper and Row, 1967).

44. *The Book of Common Prayer* (New York: The Church Pension Fund, 1945), p. 278.

PART II. THE MODES OF MORAL DISCOURSE

1. *Harris* v. *McRae*, 100 S.Ct. 2671, 2680 (1980).

2. For an excellent analysis of this argument, see Stanley Hauerwas, "Abortion: Once Again," in *New Perspectives on Human Abortion*, ed. by Thomas W. Hilgers, Dennis J. Horan, and David Mall (Frederick, Maryland: University Publications of America, 1981), pp. 420–39.

3. There is a peculiar (and some might say unfortunate) use of this mode in a procedure of the American legal system, that of gaining standing in court. In the statement of the case in *Zbaraz*, a case which involved, in part, the question of whether the state of Illinois was permitted under Medicaid (Title XIX of the Social Security Act) to fund only abortions that were necessary to preserve the life of the mother, Mode 2 reasoning became a legal necessity.

Two Chicago physicians, one an obstetrician/gynecologist and the other a pediatrician, who were strongly opposed to abortion, attempted to intervene in the case. To gain standing in court, however, they were forced to indicate some personal injury or harm, such as interruption of livelihood. As a result they claimed in court that the use of their tax money to fund Medicaid abortions might "result in a loss of patients, both mothers and the children they carry."

What disturbs me about this legal requirement is that even though the doctors also appealed to the dictates of the Hippocratic Oath as sufficient motivation for their action, the law compelled them to claim a much less mature motivation, that of financial loss. In short, our legal system colored their motivation with self-centered hedonism, when in fact their motivation was conceived on a much higher plane. See *Williams* v. *Zbaraz*, 448 U.S. 358 (1980).

4. Lynne Olson, "When Government Wants Babies, but Women Don't," *Chicago Sun-Times*, September 1, 1975, p. 30.

5. For documentation, see Fred E. Mecklenburg, "The Indications for Induced Abortion: A Physician's Perspective," in *Abortion and Social Justice*, ed. by Thomas W. Hilgers and Dennis J. Horan (New York: Sheed and Ward, 1972), p. 50.

6. Mary M. Wilcox, *Developmental Journey* (Nashville: Abingdon, 1979), p. 109.

7. In private conversation with me, Victor Rosenblum, Professor of Law at Northwestern University, who argued the pro-life position before the U.S. Supreme Court in *Harris* v. *McRae*, revealed his deep concern over examples of vicious anti-Catholicism he observed during his lecture travels around the United States.

8. Much the same reasoning is used to attack the idea of a convention to amend the Constitution in the area of abortion. As of mid-1981, however, nearly two dozen state legislatures have so petitioned Congress.

9. James E. Adams, "Dilemma of the Pro-Life Activists," *St. Louis Post Dispatch*, July 3, 1978, p. 3H.

10. For an insightful treatment of this linkage see Paul Cameron, "Aborters as Participants in a Lethal Complex" (paper presented at a symposium on the psychological aspects of abortion sponsored by the Department of Obstetrics and Gynecology of the Stritch School of Medicine of Loyola University, Chicago, Illinois, October 31, 1978.

PART III. THE ALLIANCE OF THOUGHT AND ACTION

1. In this connection, see especially Paulo Freire, *Pedagogy of the Oppressed* (New York: The Seabury Press, 1970), and Ivan Illich, *Deschooling Society* (New York: Harper and Row, 1970).

2. In fact, in her own research she saw no exceptions at all. See Mary M. Wilcox, *Developmental Journey* (Nashville: Abingdon, 1979), p. 146.

3. Gandhi asserts, "It seems to me as clear as daylight that abortion would be a crime." From *All Men Are Brothers: Life and Thoughts of Mahatma Gandhi*, compiled and edited by Krishna Kripalani (Mystic, Connecticut: Lawrence Verry, Inc.). Quoted in Thomas W. Hilgers and Dennis J. Horan, eds., *Abortion and Social Justice* (New York: Sheed and Ward, 1972), p. ii.

4. For a more detailed treatment of this idea, see my essay "Abortion and the Cognitive Foundation of Dehumanization," in *The Psychological Aspects of Abortion*, ed. by David Mall and Walter F. Watts (Washington, D.C.: University Publications of America, 1979), pp. 139–51.

5. For practical suggestions concerning basic teaching methodology, see Clive Beck, *Moral Education in the Schools*, Profiles in Practical Education No. 3 (Toronto: The Ontario Institute for Studies in Education, 1971).

6. See especially Peter Scharf, "Creating Moral Dilemmas for the Classroom," in *Readings in Moral Education*, ed. by Peter Scharf (Minneapolis: Winston Press, Inc., 1978), pp. 76–81.

7. David P. Gauthier, "Moral Action and Moral Education," in *Moral Education: Interdisciplinary Approaches*, ed. by C. M. Beck, B. S. Crittenden, and E. V. Sullivan (New York: Newman Press, 1971), p. 146.

8. See especially Carl R. Rogers, *Counseling and Psychotherapy* (Boston: Houghton Mifflin Company, 1942).

9. For an excellent treatment of this simultaneity, see Lucy O'Keefe, "Abortion: A Framework of Inclusive Love," *Peacework*, No. 77 (July–August, 1979), unpaged. This is a monthly newsletter sponsored by a New England chapter of the American Friends Service Committee.

10. Stanley Milgram, *Obedience to Authority: An Experimental View* (New York: Harper and Row, 1974).

11. See John Rawls, *A Theory of Justice* (Cambridge: Harvard University Press, 1971), and the following commentaries: Brian Barry, *The Liberal Theory of Justice* (London: Oxford University Press, 1973); Norman Daniels, ed., *Reading Rawls* (New York: Basic Books, Inc., 1975); and Robert Paul Wolff,

Understanding Rawls (Princeton, New Jersey: Princeton University Press, 1977).

12. See especially *Furman* v. *Georgia*, 408 U.S. 238 (1972).

13. Adapted from an unpublished paper by Peter Heinbecker, M.D., contained in private correspondence with the author.

14. See Sandra Kathleen Mahkorn, "Pregnancy and Sexual Assault," in Mall and Watts, *op cit.*, pp. 53–72.

15. Note especially the revealing editorial in the official journal of the California Medical Association, "A New Ethic for Medicine and Society," *California Medicine*, CXIII, No. 3 (September, 1970), pp. 67–68.

16. Peter Scharf, *Moral Education* (Davis, California: Responsible Action, 1978), p. 106.

17. There are some who would argue that a moral consideration should be extended only to those who can return it, or that if a cognitively immature individual cannot reciprocate an empathic concern, then there is really no moral situation involved in the relationship. One commentator presents this argument as follows: "Given the foetus's lack of an independent psychological viewpoint, it is difficult to conceive of it as an appropriate object for role-taking." What those who argue this way fail to realize, however, is that though the empathic relationship is apparently one way (i.e., in the absence of an ability to measure accurately total fetal awareness and thus empathic response), it would appear that a psychologically healthy mother certainly has a concern for the welfare and continued existence of her unborn child. For such a mother, the mere presence of a baby *in utero* would naturally tend to create an imaginative "as if" interaction until that baby could reciprocate in a less passive way. The mother, in anticipation of birth, simply forgoes or postpones the more complete interaction which she knows will result at the end of the gestational period. I agree with the commentator that this whole line of argument is decidedly question begging. The idea really seems to boil down to a matter of duration of time between stimulus and response. In this sense why would a nine-month time-span preclude an unborn child from being a moral object? See Joseph A. Diorio, "Cognitive Universalism and Cultural Relativity in Moral Education," *Educational Philosophy and Theory*, VIII, No. 1 (April, 1976), p. 46.

18. See Howard W. Fisher, M.D., "Abortion—Pain or Pleasure?" in Mall and Watts, *op. cit.*, pp. 39–52.

19. For a brief analysis of some of the rhetorical/philosophical commonalities of abortion, prohibition, and slavery, see my "Stalemate of Rhetoric and Philosophy," in Hilgers and Horan, *op. cit.*, pp. 199–214.

20. I am indebted to Thomas Gordon for calling my attention to the basic structure of this diagram. See his *Leadership Effectiveness Training* (New York: Wyden Books, 1977), and *Teacher Effectiveness Training* (New York: Peter H. Wyden, 1974).

21. See Judith Fink and Marjory Mecklenburg, "Developing Alternatives to Abortion," in *Facing the Future*, ed. by Gary Collins (Waco, Texas: Word Books, 1976), pp. 123–36.

22. Richard H. Hersh, Diana Pritchard Paolitto, and Joseph Reimer, *Promoting Moral Growth* (New York: Longman, Inc., 1979), p. 170.

23. I have developed a decalage-type rhetorical analysis in my essay "Toward an Understanding of the Abortion Debate: Rhetoric as a Reticulate Structure." See *New Perspectives on Human Abortion*, ed. by Thomas W. Hilgers, Dennis J. Horan, and David Mall (Frederick, Maryland: University Publications of America, 1981), pp. 305–31. My essay is followed by another which indirectly touches upon this theme. See also Gordon Zahn, "Abortion and the Corruption of Mind," *ibid.*, pp. 332–44.

24. For a brief discussion of the empirical and pedagogical problems regarding decalage, see Peter Scharf, "Evaluating the Development of Moral Education: A Response to the Critiques of Flowers, Sullivan, and Fraenkel," Scharf, *Readings in Moral Education, op. cit.*, pp. 290–91.

CONCLUSION

1. For an outstanding analysis of the relationship between love and justice, see Gérard Gilleman, *The Primacy of Charity in Moral Theology*, trans. by William F. Ryan and André Vachon (Westminster, Maryland: The Newman Press, 1959), pp. 330–41.

2. Lincoln recognized this relationship well. When criticized for making friends with the South (the North's supposedly implacable foe), he replied that if he made them his friends, they would no longer be his enemies.

3. Paul Tillich, *Theology of Culture* (London: Oxford University Press, 1959), p. 144.

4. Among those writers who have dealt perceptively with the need for a healing vision are Dykstra and Hauerwas. Both stress the role of imagination in moral growth and show in various ways how a purely cognitive developmental approach is limited. I would be the first to admit such limitations, as this book has tried to indicate, and would also hope to be among the first to acknowledge, at least within the context of a social movement, the usefulness of a visional ethics tied to the growth of character and virtue. See Craig Dykstra, *Vision and Character* (New York: Paulist Press, 1981), and Stanley Hauerwas, *Vision and Virtue* (Notre Dame, Indiana: University of Notre Dame Press, 1981).

5. See *Congressional Record*, 97th Cong., 1st sess., CXXVII, No. 131 (September 21, 1981), pp. 10194–98.

6. See Nancy Koster, "New Amendment Strategy Proposed," *Minnesota Citizens Concerned for Life Newsletter* (September, 1981), p. 1.

7. Elizabeth Léonie Simpson, "A Holistic Approach to Moral Development and Behavior," in *Moral Development and Behavior*, ed. by Thomas Lickona (New York: Holt, Rinehart and Winston, 1976), p. 170.

8. For an eloquent description of this theme, see Brian Crittenden, *Form*

and Content in Moral Education, Monograph Series No. 12 (Toronto: The Ontario Institute for Studies in Education, 1972), p. 61.

9. Gerald C. Treacy, ed. *Five Great Encyclicals* (New York: The Paulist Press, 1939), p. 164.

10. Abraham J. Heschel, *The Prophets,* I (New York: Harper and Row, 1962), p. 201.

BIBLIOGRAPHY

This bibliography is divided into two sections. The first section is a list of Kohlberg's published work which was accessible to me. It is arranged chronologically and identified for use in the text by the symbol in brackets at the end of each entry. The second section is a list of books, grouped under appropriate headings, which I feel will be helpful to the reader.

SECTION I

Kohlberg, Lawrence. "Moral Development and Identification." *Child Psychology*. Edited by H. W. Stevenson. Sixty-second Yearbook of the National Society for the Study of Education. Part I. Chicago: University of Chicago Press, 1963. [K63a]

Kohlberg, Lawrence. "The Development of Children's Orientations Toward a Moral Order: I. Sequence in the Development of Moral Thought." *Vita Humana*, VI (1963), 11–33. [K63b]

Kohlberg, Lawrence. "Development of Moral Character and Moral Ideology." *Review of Child Development Research*. Edited by Martin L. Hoffman and Lois Wladis Hoffman. Vol. I. New York: Russell Sage Foundation, 1964. [K64]

Kohlberg, Lawrence. "A Cognitive-Developmental Analysis of Children's Sex-Role Concepts and Attitudes." *The Development of Sex Differences*. Edited by Eleanor E. Maccoby. Stanford: Stanford University Press, 1966. [K66a]

Kohlberg, Lawrence. "Cognitive Stages and Preschool Education." *Human Development*, IX (1966), 5–17. [K66b]

Kohlberg, Lawrence. "Moral Education in the Schools: A Developmental View." *The School Review*, LXXIV, No. 1 (Spring, 1966), 1–30. [K66c]

Kohlberg, Lawrence. "Moral and Religious Education and the Public Schools: A Developmental View." *Religion and Public Education*. Edited by Theodore R. Sizer. Boston: Houghton Mifflin Company, 1967. [K67a]

Kohlberg, Lawrence, and Zigler, Edward. "The Impact of Cognitive Maturity on the Development of Sex-Role Attitudes in the Years 4 to 8." *Genetic Psychology Monographs*, LXXV (1967), 89–165. [KZ67b]

Kohlberg, Lawrence. "Moral Development." *International Encyclopedia of the Social Sciences*. Vol. X. [K68a]

Kohlberg, Lawrence. "Montessori with the Culturally Disadvantaged: A Cognitive Developmental Interpretation and Some Research Findings."

Early Education. Edited by Robert D. Hess and Roberta Meyer Bear. Chicago: Aldine Publishing Company, 1968. [K68b]

Kohlberg, Lawrence, Yaeger, Judy, and Hjertholm, Else. "Private Speech: Four Studies and a Review of Theories." *Child Development*, XXXIX (1968), 691–736. [KYH68c]

Kohlberg, Lawrence. "Early Education: A Cognitive-Developmental View." *Child Development*, XXXIX (1968), 1013–62. [K68d]

Kohlberg, Lawrence. "The Child as a Moral Philosopher." *Psychology Today*, II, No. 4 (September, 1968), 24–30. This article also appears in *Developmental Psychology*. Edited by John Sants and H. J. Butcher. Baltimore: Penguin Books, 1975; in *Moral Education*. Edited by Barry I. Chazan and Jonas F. Soltis. New York: Teachers College Press, 1973; and in *Readings in Values Clarification*. Edited by Sidney B. Simon and Howard Kirschenbaum. Minneapolis: Winston Press, 1973. [K68e]

Kohlberg, Lawrence. "Stages in Moral Growth." *International Journal of Religious Education*, XLIV, No. 10 (September–October, 1968), 8–9 +. [K68f]

Grim, Paul F., Kohlberg, Lawrence, and White, Sheldon H. "Some Relationships between Conscience and Attentional Processes." *Journal of Personality and Social Psychology*, VIII, No. 3 (1968), 239–52. [GKW68g]

Kohlberg, Lawrence. "Stage and Sequence: The Cognitive-Developmental Approach to Socialization." *Handbook of Socialization Theory and Research*. Edited by David A. Goslin. Chicago: Rand McNally, 1969. [K69a]

Kohlberg, Lawrence, and Kramer, Richard. "Continuities and Discontinuities in Childhood and Adult Moral Development." *Human Development*, XII (1969), 93–120. [KK69b]

Rest, James, Turiel, Elliot, and Kohlberg, Lawrence. "Level of Moral Development as a Determinant of Preference and Comprehension of Moral Judgments Made by Others." *Journal of Personality*, XXXVII, No. 2 (June, 1969), 225–52. [RTK69c]

DeVries, Rheta, and Kohlberg, Lawrence. "The Concept Assessment Kit—Conservation: Review One." *Journal of Educational Measurement*, VI, No. 4 (Winter, 1969), 263–66. [DK69d]

Kohlberg, Lawrence. "Education for Justice: A Modern Statement of the Platonic View." *Moral Education: Five Lectures*. Edited by Nancy F. Sizer and Theodore R. Sizer. Cambridge: Harvard University Press, 1970. [K70a]

Kohlberg, Lawrence. "The Moral Atmosphere of the School." *The Unstudied Curriculum: Its Impact on Children*. Edited by Norman V. Overly. Washington: National Education Association, 1970. [K70b]

Kohlberg, Lawrence. "Moral Development and the Education of Adolescents." *Adolescents and the American High School*. Edited by Richard F. Purnell. New York: Holt, Rinehart and Winston, Inc., 1970. [K70c]

Kohlberg, Lawrence. "Reply to Bereiter's Statement on Kohlberg's Cognitive-Developmental View." *Interchange*, I, No. 1 (April, 1970), 40–48. [K70d]

Kohlberg, Lawrence. "Psychological View of Moral Education." *The Encyclopedia of Education*. Vol. VI, s.v. "moral education." [K71a]

Kohlberg, Lawrence. "From Is to Ought: How to Commit the Naturalistic Fallacy and Get Away with It in the Study of Moral Development." *Cognitive Development and Epistemology*. Edited by Theodore Mischel. New York: Academic Press, 1971. [K71b]

Kohlberg, Lawrence. "Stages of Moral Development as a Basis for Moral Education." *Moral Education*. Edited by Clive M. Beck, Brian S. Crittenden, and Edmund V. Sullivan. New York: Newman Press, 1971. [K71c]

Kohlberg, Lawrence. "Cognitive-Developmental Theory and the Practice of Collective Moral Education." *Group Care: An Israeli Approach*. Edited by Martin Wolins and Meir Gottesmann. New York: Gordon and Breach, 1971. [K71d]

Kohlberg, Lawrence, and Turiel, Elliot. "Moral Development and Moral Education." *Psychology and Educational Practice*. Edited by Gerald S. Lesser. Glenview, Illinois: Scott, Foresman and Company, 1971. [KT71e]

Gilligan, Carol, Kohlberg, Lawrence, Lerner, Joan, and Belenky, Mary. "Moral Reasoning about Sexual Dilemmas: The Development of an Interview and Scoring System." *Technical Report of the Commission on Obscenity and Pornography*, Preliminary Studies, I, No. 5256-0002. Washington, D.C.: U.S. Government Printing Office, 1971. [GKLB71f]

Kohlberg, Lawrence. "The Concepts of Developmental Psychology as the Central Guide to Education: Examples from Cognitive, Moral, and Psychological Education." *Proceedings of the Conference on Psychology and the Process of Schooling in the Next Decade: Alternative Conceptions*. Edited by Maynard C. Reynolds. Minneapolis: University of Minnesota National Support Systems Project, 1971. [K71g]

Tapp, June L., and Kohlberg, Lawrence. "Developing Senses of Law and Legal Justice." *Journal of Social Issues*, XXVII, No. 2 (1971), 65–91. This article also appears in *Law, Justice and the Individual in Society*. Edited by June Louin Tapp and Felice J. Levine. New York: Holt, Rinehart and Winston, 1977. [TK71h]

Kohlberg, Lawrence, and Gilligan, Carol. "The Adolescent as a Philosopher: The Discovery of the Self in a Postconventional World." *Daedalus*, C, No. 4 (Fall, 1971), 1051–86. This article also appears in *Twelve to Sixteen: Early Adolescence*. Edited by Jerome Kagan and Robert Coles. New York: W. W. Norton, 1972; in *Adolescents' Development and Education: A Janus Knot*. Edited by Ralph L. Mosher. Berkeley, California: McCutchan Publishing Corporation, 1979; and in abridged form in *Basic and Contemporary Issues in Developmental Psychology*. Edited by Paul Henry Mussen, John Janeway Conger, and Jerome Kagan. New York: Harper and Row, 1975. [KG71i]

Kohlberg, Lawrence. "Indoctrination Versus Relativity in Value Education." *Zygon*, VI, No. 4 (December, 1971), 285–310. [K71j]

Kohlberg, Lawrence, Scharf, Peter, and Hickey, Joseph. "The Justice Structure of the Prison—A Theory and an Intervention." *The Prison Journal*, LI, No. 2 (Autumn–Winter, 1972), 3–14. [KSH72a]

Kohlberg, Lawrence, and Mayer, Rochelle. "Development as the Aim of Education." *Harvard Educational Review*, XLII, No. 4 (November, 1972), 449–96. [KM72b]

Kohlberg, Lawrence. "A Cognitive-Developmental Approach to Moral Education." *The Humanist*, XXXII, No. 6 (November–December, 1972), 13–16. [K72c]

Kohlberg, Lawrence, and Whitten, Phillip. "Understanding the Hidden Curriculum." *Learning*, I, No. 2 (December, 1972), 10–14. [KW72d]

Kohlberg, Lawrence. "Continuities in Childhood and Adult Moral Development Revisited." *Life-Span Developmental Psychology*. Edited by Paul B. Baltes and K. Warner Schaie. New York: Academic Press, 1973. [K73a]

Kohlberg, Lawrence. "Moral Psychology and the Study of Tragedy." *Directions in Literary Criticism*. Edited by Stanley Weintraub and Philip Young. University Park: The Pennsylvania State University Press, 1973. [K73b]

Kohlberg, Lawrence. "Moral Development and the New Social Studies." *Social Education*, XXXVII, No. 5 (May, 1973), 369–75. [K73c]

Boyd, Dwight and Kohlberg, Lawrence. "The Is-Ought Problem: A Developmental Perspective." *Zygon*, VIII, Nos. 3–4 (September–December, 1973), 358–72. [BK73d]

Kohlberg, Lawrence. "The Claim to Moral Adequacy of a Highest Stage of Moral Judgment. *The Journal of Philosophy*, LXX, No. 18 (October 25, 1973), 630–46. [K73e]

Kohlberg, Lawrence. "The Contribution of Developmental Psychology to Education—Examples from Moral Education." *Educational Psychologist*, X, No. 1 (Winter, 1973), 2–14. [K73f]

Kohlberg, Lawrence. "Stages and Aging in Moral Development—Some Speculations." *The Gerontologist*, XIII, No. 4 (Winter, 1973), 497–502. [K73g]

Kohlberg, Lawrence. "Comments on 'The Dilemma of Obedience.'" *Phi Delta Kappan*, LV, No. 9 (May, 1974), 607+. [K74a]

Kohlberg, Lawrence. "Discussion: Developmental Gains in Moral Judgment." *American Journal of Mental Deficiency*, LXXIX, No. 2 (September, 1974), 142–44. [K74b]

Kohlberg, Lawrence. "Education, Moral Development and Faith." *Journal of Moral Education*, IV, No. 1 (October, 1974), 5–16. [K74c]

Kohlberg, Lawrence. "The Relationship of Moral Education to the Broader Field of Values Education." *Values Education: Theory, Practice, Problems, Prospects*. Edited by John Meyer, Brian Burnham, and John Cholvat. Waterloo, Ontario: Wilfrid Laurier University Press, 1975. [K75a]

Blatt, Moshe M., and Kohlberg, Lawrence. "The Effects of Classroom Moral Discussion upon Children's Level of Moral Judgment." *Journal of Moral Education*, IV, No. 2 (February, 1975), 129–61. [BK75b]

Kohlberg, Lawrence. "The Cognitive-Developmental Approach to Moral Education." *Phi Delta Kappan*, LVI, No. 10 (June, 1975), 670–77. This article also appears in *Moral Education*. Edited by David Purpel and Kevin Ryan. Berkeley, California: McCutchan Publishing Corporation, 1976. [K75c]

Kohlberg, Lawrence. "Counseling and Counselor Educating: A Developmental Approach." *Counselor Education and Supervision*, XIV, No. 4 (June, 1975), 250–56. [K75d]

Kohlberg, Lawrence, Kauffman, Kelsey, Scharf, Peter, and Hickey, Joseph. "The Just Community Approach to Corrections: A Theory." *Journal of Moral Education*, IV, No. 3 (June, 1975), 243–60. [KKSH75e]

Kohlberg, Lawrence, and Elfenbein, Donald. "The Development of Moral Judgments Concerning Capital Punishment." *American Journal of Orthopsychiatry*, XLV, No. 4 (July, 1975), 614–40. A somewhat longer version of this article also appears in *Capital Punishment in the United States*. Edited by Hugo Adam Bedau and Chester M. Pierce. New York: AMS Press, 1976. [KE75f]

Kohlberg, Lawrence. "Moral Education for a Society in Moral Transition." *Educational Leadership*, XXXIII, No. 1 (October, 1975), 46–54. [K75g]

Kohlberg, Lawrence. "Moral Stages and Moralization: The Cognitive-Developmental Approach." *Moral Development and Behavior: Theory, Research, and Social Issues*. Edited by Thomas Lickona. New York: Holt, Rinehart and Winston, 1976. [K76a]

Gibbs, John, Kohlberg, Lawrence, Colby, Anne, and Speicher-Dubin, Betsy. "The Domain and Development of Moral Judgment: A Theory and a Method of Assessment." *Reflections on Values Education*. Edited by John R. Meyer. Waterloo, Ontario: Wilfrid Laurier University Press, 1976. [GKCS76b]

Kohlberg, Lawrence. "This Special Section in Perspective." *Social Education*, XL, No. 4 (April, 1976), 213–15. [K76c]

Kohlberg, Lawrence. "The Quest for Justice in 200 Years of American History and in Contemporary American Education." *Contemporary Education*, XLVIII, No. 1 (Fall, 1976), 5–16. [K76d]

Haan, Norma, Langer, Jonas, and Kohlberg, Lawrence. "Family Patterns of Moral Reasoning." *Child Development*, XLVII, No. 4 (December, 1976), 1204–6. [HLK76e]

DeVries, Rheta, and Kohlberg, Lawrence. "Relations between Piagetian and Psychometric Assessments of Intelligence." *Current Topics in Early Childhood Education*. Edited by Lilian G. Katz. Vol. I. Norwood, New Jersey: Ablex Publishing Corp., 1977. [DK77a]

Kohlberg, Lawrence. "Moral Development, Ego Development and Psychoeducational Practices." *Pupil Personnel Services Journal*, VI, No. 1 (1977), 25–39. [K77b]

Colby, Anne, Kohlberg, Lawrence, Fenton, Edwin, Speicher-Dubin, Betsy, and Lieberman, Marcus. "Secondary School Moral Discussion Programmes Led by Special Studies Teachers." *Journal of Moral Education*, VI, No. 2 (January, 1977), 90–111. [CKFSL77c]

Kuhn, Deanna, Langer, Jonas, Kohlberg, Lawrence, and Haan, Norma S. "The Development of Formal Operations in Logical and Moral Judgment." *Genetic Psychology Monographs*, XCV, First Half (February, 1977), 97–188. [KLKH77d]

Kohlberg, Lawrence. "The Implications of Moral Stages for Adult Education." *Religious Education*, LXXII, No. 2 (March–April, 1977), 183–201. [K77e]

Kohlberg, Lawrence, and Hersh, Richard H. "Moral Development: A Review of the Theory." *Theory into Practice*, XVI, No. 2 (April, 1977), 53–59. [KH77f]

Kohlberg, Lawrence. "Foreword." *Readings in Moral Education*. Edited by Peter Scharf. Minneapolis: Winston Press, 1978. [K78a]

Kohlberg, Lawrence. "The Cognitive Developmental Approach to Behavior Disorders: A Study of the Development of Moral Reasoning in Delinquents." *Cognitive Defects in the Development of Mental Illness*. Edited by George Serban. New York: Brunner/Mazel, 1978. [K78b]

Kohlberg, Lawrence. "Revisions in the Theory and Practice of Moral Development." *Moral Development*. Edited by William Damon. New Directions for Child Development, No. 2. San Francisco: Jossey-Bass, Inc.: 1978. [K78c]

Turiel, Elliot, Edwards, Carolyn Pope, and Kohlberg, Lawrence. "Moral Development in Turkish Children, Adolescents, and Young Adults." *Journal of Cross-Cultural Psychology*, IX, No. 1 (March, 1978), 75–86. [TEK78d]

Kohlberg, Lawrence. "Moral Education Reappraised." *The Humanist*, XXXVIII, No. 6 (November–December, 1978), 13–15. [K78e]

Kohlberg, Lawrence. "Foreword." In Richard H. Hersh, Diana Pritchard Paolitto, and Joseph Reimer. *Promoting Moral Growth*. New York: Longman, Inc., 1979. [K79a]

Kohlberg, Lawrence. "Foreword." In James R. Rest. *Development in Judging Moral Issues*. Minneapolis: University of Minnesota Press, 1979. [K79b]

Kohlberg, Lawrence. "Justice as Reversibility." *Philosophy, Politics and Society*. Fifth Series. Edited by Peter Laslett and James Fishkin. New Haven: Yale University Press, 1979. [K79c]

Kohlberg, Lawrence. "The Young Child as Philosopher: Moral Development and the Dilemmas of Moral Education." *Taking Early Childhood Seriously: The Evangeline Burgess Memorial Lectures*. Edited by Marianne Wolman. Pasadena, California: Pacific Oaks College and Children's School, 1979. [K79d]

Kohlberg, Lawrence. "The Future of Liberalism as the Dominant Ideology of the West." *Moral Development and Politics*. Edited by Richard W. Wilson and Gordon J. Schochet. New York: Praeger Publishers, 1980. [K80a]

Kohlberg, Lawrence. "High School Democracy and Educating for a Just Society." *Moral Education: A First Generation of Research and Development*. Edited by Ralph L. Mosher. New York: Praeger Publishers, 1980. [K80b]

Power, F. Clark, and Kohlberg, Lawrence. "Religion, Morality, and Ego Development." *Toward Moral and Religious Maturity*. Edited by James W. Fowler and Antoine Vergote. Morristown, New Jersey: Silver Burdett Company, 1980. [PK80c]

Kohlberg, Lawrence. "Educating for a Just Society: An Updated and Revised Statement." *Moral Development, Moral Education, and Kohlberg*. Edited by Brenda Munsey. Birmingham: Religious Education Press, 1980. [K80d]

Bar-Yam, Miriam, Kohlberg, Lawrence, and Naame, Algiris. "Moral Reasoning of Students in Different Cultural, Social, and Educational Settings."

American Journal of Education, LXXXVIII, No. 3 (May, 1980), 345–62. [BKN80e]

Kohlberg, Lawrence, and Wasserman, Elsa R. "The Cognitive-Developmental Approach and the Practicing Counselor: An Opportunity for Counselors to Rethink Their Roles." *Personnel and Guidance Journal*, LVIII, No. 9 (May, 1980), 559–67. [KW80f]

Kohlberg, Lawrence, and DeVries, Rheta. "Don't Throw Out the Piagetian Baby with the Psychometric Bath: Reply to Humphreys and Parsons." *Intelligence*, IV, No. 2 (April–June, 1980), 175–77. [KD80g]

Kohlberg, Lawrence. "The Meaning and Measurement of Moral Development." Vol. XIII, 1979 Heinz Werner Lecture Series. Worcester, Massachusetts: Clark University Press, 1981. [K81a]

Kohlberg, Lawrence. *Essays on Moral Development*. Vol. I: *The Philosophy of Moral Development*. New York: Harper and Row, Publishers, 1981. [K81b]

Most of the preceding were gleaned from mimeographed bibliographies supplied by the Center for Moral Education at Harvard University.* A slightly larger version can be found at the end of the last entry cited. This work, the initial installment of a proposed three-volume series, is Kohlberg's first book. When completed, the series will have explicated his theory of moral development mainly through representative reprints of some of his previously published essays. I for one, however, prefer reading scholarly analysis directly from the original sources, where certain companion essays sometimes contain competing points of view which can help the reader understand moral-developmental theory with greater precision. For a review of this last entry, see Daniel Callahan and Sidney Callahan, "Seven Pillars of Moral Wisdom," *Psychology Today*, XV, No. 8 (August, 1981), p. 84, and Werner J. Dannhauser, "How to Be Good," *New York Times Book Review*, August 9, 1981, p. 11.

---

* Moral Education Resource Fund, Roy E. Larsen Hall, Appian Way, Harvard University, Cambridge, Massachusetts 02138.

SECTION II

Abortion

Bajema, Clifford E. *Abortion and the Meaning of Personhood.* Grand Rapids, Michigan: Baker Book House, 1974.

In this book the author grapples with a problem central to the abortion debate, the idea of personhood for the unborn. The book considers abortion from both a scientific and a religious perspective (the author is an ordained minister of the Christian Reformed Church). Each major argument favoring abortion is analyzed in capsule form, and the author evinces sympathy for the problems of pregnant women by advocating alternatives to abortion.

Brody, Baruch. *Abortion and the Sanctity of Human Life: A Philosophical View.* Cambridge, Massachusetts: The Massachusetts Institute of Technology Press, 1975.

A logician's perspective orients the thrust of this book. The author, a professor at MIT, analyzes the premises and hidden assumptions of the abortion debate, tests their validity, and presents the most frequently used arguments in their strongest versions. He stresses the moral nature of the controversy and claims that his own views were changed through careful analysis.

Cooke, Robert E., Hellegers, André E., Hoyt, Robert G., and Richardson, Herbert W., eds. *The Terrible Choice: The Abortion Dilemma.* New York: Bantam Books, 1968.

This book could be viewed as part of the anti-abortion counterattack of the late sixties. It is based on the proceedings of an international conference on abortion sponsored by the Harvard Divinity School and the Joseph P. Kennedy Jr. Foundation. An introduction by Pearl S. Buck, some spectacular photography by Lennart Nilsson, and a glossary and index help make the book a minor classic.

Daughters of St. Paul, eds. *Yes to Life.* Boston: Daughters of St. Paul, 1977.

Those who are looking for shortcuts in researching the historical attitude of the Catholic church toward abortion will find this book helpful. It is a compendium of basic church documents extending from the earliest beginnings of the Christian era to the present. The book has an imprimatur.

Denes, Magda. *In Necessity and Sorrow.* New York: Basic Books, Inc., 1976.

With a title that reflects the psychic trauma involved, this book deals with the complex emotional problems surrounding the decision to abort. It is a revealing look inside an abortion clinic by a clinical psychologist and psychoanalyst who personally experienced an abortion. The book is based on a series of interviews with patients, medical personnel, including physicians, nurses, and social workers, and husbands and boyfriends.

Francke, Linda Bird. *The Ambivalence of Abortion.* New York: Random House, 1978.

As its title suggests, this book concerns the underlying psychic difficulties that often surround the decision to abort. Using the interview technique, the author, who is a nonspecialist but confirmed abortion advocate, describes the process of making the abortion decision and discusses the special problems of abortion as it affects single or married women, sexual partners, teenagers, and parents. Her analysis concludes that abortion does not solve all problems.

Gardner, R. F. R. *Abortion: The Personal Dilemma*. 1st rev. ed. New York: Pyramid Books, 1974.

The author, a practicing gynecologist and clergyman in Great Britain (United Free Church of Scotland), addresses a global audience on abortion while discussing the special problems of England and America. The book is painstakingly detailed, with a special index containing numerous scriptural references from both the Old and New Testaments. A highlight is the chapter on the spiritual status of the fetus.

Granfield, David. *The Abortion Decision*. 1st rev. ed. Garden City, New York: Doubleday and Co., 1971.

In this book, published when the turmoil over abortion in the state legislatures was reaching its zenith, the clergyman/author discusses the many aspects of the problem including the historical, moral-sociomedical, scientific, and legal. These aspects are integrated within a finely written whole. The book is an excellent early work on the subject.

Guttmacher, Alan F. *The Case for Legalized Abortion Now*. Berkeley, California: Diablo Press, 1967.

Compiled at the height of the pressure on state legislatures to revise their anti-abortion statutes, this book is a representative sampling of pro-abortion thinking. Many of the writers were, and some still are, active in the movement to reshape the nation's attitude toward abortion. Their views cover most of the pertinent issues.

Hardin, Garrett. *Mandatory Motherhood*. Boston: Beacon Press, 1974.

This book comes closest to being a handbook for the pro-abortion advocate. The author, a professor of biology, analyzes most of the pertinent arguments while often employing *reductio ad absurdum*. His forceful conclusions leave no doubt where he stands.

Mohr, James C. *Abortion in America*. London: Oxford University Press, 1978.

The social forces that shaped the pre-*Roe* v. *Wade* anti-abortion statutes are the major theme of this book. As a perspective on American history, it attempts to account for the widespread anti-abortion sentiment of the late nineteenth century. Starting with the early 1800s, the book analyzes public attitudes toward abortion and the groups behind the anti-abortion drive.

Potts, Malcolm, Diggory, Peter, and Peel, John. *Abortion*. London: Cambridge University Press, 1977.

This is one of the more scholarly of recent books advocating induced abortion. Bolstering their arguments with considerable detail, including extensive use of tables and charts, the authors see abortion as an inevitable part of humanity's future. Historical and demographic aspects of the problem are given special treatment.

Ramsey, Paul. *Ethics at the Edges of Life*. New Haven: Yale University Press, 1978.

This book is an expanded version of the author's Bampton Lectures at Columbia University. While writing at times almost as a legal scholar, he extracts the underlying moral content of some recent court decisions. The book's careful analysis of the Edelin Case is perhaps the best in print.

Sarvis, Betty, and Rodman, Hyman. *The Abortion Controversy*. New York: Columbia University Press, 1973.

A writer/researcher and a social scientist collaborated to produce one of the more authoritative books favoring abortion to emerge prior to the *Roe* v. *Wade* decision. With some help from careful documentation, the book attempts to deal with major anti-abortion arguments which were articulated during the early seventies. The bibliography is excellent.

Sumner, L. W. *Abortion and Moral Theory*. Princeton, New Jersey: Princeton University Press, 1981.

The author of this book, a professor of philosophy at the University of Toronto, discusses the established views on abortion, which he labels liberal and conservative, and comes up with a third way. His alternative locates moral standing for the unborn somewhere in the second trimester of pregnancy, with sentience a necessary requirement. The book, which is more a treatise about ethics than about abortion, could be considered a philosophical foundation for *Roe* v. *Wade*, which it attempts to anchor in moral theory.

Ethics

Brandt, Richard B. *A Theory of the Good and the Right*. New York: Oxford University Press, 1979.

The author considers contemporary psychological theory regarding motivation and behavior to help bolster his traditional philosophical account. Along with this central theme, he emphasizes the rationality of rule utilitarianism. This is much more than a reformulation of his earlier work.

Dyck, Arthur J. *On Human Care: An Introduction to Ethics*. Nashville: Abingdon, 1977.

This book is an excellent general treatment of the science of moral decision-making. The author uses a number of dilemmas in medical ethics, including abortion, to reveal some of the underlying bases for moral choice. His treatment of relativism and account of the quest for the ideal moral judge are rewarding analyses of competing ethical theories.

Fletcher, Joseph. *Situation Ethics*. Philadelphia: The Westminster Press, 1966.

The thesis of this book has invited widespread support and condemnation. Simply stated, it is that circumstance or context should govern the outcome of moral decision-making. The author sees love as the final arbiter, i.e., the best solution to moral problems, including human abortion.

Hare, R. M. *The Language of Morals*. London: Oxford University Press, 1952.

At some point in every analysis of ethics that claims to be complete there must be a confrontation with language. Hare's confrontation, because of its scholarly rigor, is an intellectual treat. This book was written for the serious reader who likes to be challenged but not overwhelmed.

Rosen, Bernard. *Strategies of Ethics*. Boston: Houghton Mifflin Company, 1978.

Borrowing a metaphor often associated with competition and winning, the author clarifies and evaluates several approaches to the study of ethics—from normative to relative to meta-ethical. His analysis is enhanced by insights from anthropology, psychology, and physics. With short, partially annotated bibliographies accompanying each chapter, this book is for the serious beginning student of moral philosophy.

Psychology/Structuralism

Gardner, Howard. *The Quest for Mind*. New York: Alfred A. Knopf, 1974.

In a refreshingly readable style, the author discusses the structuralist movement through its chief architects, Claude Lévi-Strauss and Jean Piaget. The revolutionary import of structuralism is evaluated primarily within the context of the social sciences. Origin and prospects, strengths and weaknesses, are brought together in an engaging analysis of a new scientific world-view.

Lévi-Strauss, Claude. *Structural Anthropology*. Translated by Claire Jacobson and Brooke Grundfest Schoepf. New York: Doubleday, 1967.

Probably the author's most representative work, this book looks for and analyzes the isomorphism between language and social structure in nonliterate societies. Owing much to the science of linguistics, it offers a comprehensive view. As a major classic, the book should help one understand some of the structural underpinnings of Piagetian-Kohlbergian thought.

Pettit, Philip. *The Concept of Structuralism: A Critical Analysis*. Berkeley, California: University of California Press, 1975.

Although this book presupposes some familiarity with linguistics and the work of Lévi-Strauss, its value lies in the fact that cognitive-developmental models of moral reasoning are basically structural. The book evaluates the structural model as a research tool for studying a wide range of subjects. The reader who can make the necessary connections with moral development should profit greatly.

Piaget, Jean. *Structuralism*. Translated by Chaninah Maschler. New York: Basic Books, Inc., 1970.

This book summarizes the main features of Piagetian epistemology. Its relationship to the Kohlbergian moral-stage paradigm is obvious. Stages are structures that move, i.e., that undergo transformation while mediating the human mind's relationship with the physical and social worlds.

Sullivan, Edmund V. *Kohlberg's Structuralism: A Critical Appraisal*. Monograph Series, No. 15, Toronto: The Ontario Institute for Studies in Education, 1977.

The author examines the Kohlbergian system candidly and discusses its basic limitations with insight. This generally sympathetic treatment of both strengths and weaknesses analyzes the growth metaphor underlying the developmental mode. A sizable list of additional references is helpful.

Moral Development and Education

Cochrane, Donald B., Hamm, Cornel M., and Kazepides, Anastasios C., eds. *The Domain of Moral Education*. New York: Paulist Press, 1979.

This book discusses the major facets of its subject from every critical angle, while proceeding from delimitation to controversy. In ever-tightening circles, it begins with the limitation and nature of moral education, progresses to the troublesome problem of form and content, and ends with an evaluation of the developmental hypothesis itself. Composed of both original essays and classic reprints, this edited volume is one of the best currently available on the subject and should be read by every serious moral educator.

DePalma, David J., and Foley, Jeanne M., eds. *Moral Development: Current Theory and Research*. Hillsdale, New Jersey: Lawrence Erlbaum Associates, 1975.

While the issues raised are still largely unresolved, this book is a good description of the state of the subject in the mid-seventies. Possibly because the papers were first presented in a symposium (Symposium on Moral Development held at Loyola University of Chicago in December, 1973), the book does not strive to be comprehensive. The diversity of the sampling, however, adds breadth to these studies geared to those who are familiar with the field.

Dewey, John. *Theory of the Moral Life*. New York: Holt, Rinehart and Winston, 1960.

This book is a redaction from an earlier work—*Ethics* (with Tufts), 1932 revised edition—and worth reading for useful background. It is difficult (if not impossible) to read Dewey without appreciating his developmentalism. Kohlberg and Piaget were heavily influenced by him.

Durkheim, Emile. *Moral Education*. Translated by Everett K. Wilson and Herman Schnurer. New York: The Free Press, 1961.

Based on a course he taught at the Sorbonne, this book represents a central concept in Durkheim's investigation of the human sciences. Morality from the viewpoint of sociology is a necessary background perspective for any serious Kohlberg scholar. The book is one of the great classics in the field.

Graham, Douglas. *Moral Learning and Development*. New York: John Wiley and Sons, 1972.

This book offers a comprehensive review and analysis of the chief psychological theories of moral growth, including the psychoanalytic, learning, and cognitive-developmental approaches. Each school is described and its chief architects identified. Intelligence, religion, sex, and social class are studied for their impact on moral growth.

Hennessy, Thomas C., ed. *Values and Moral Development*. New York: Paulist Press, 1976.

Inspired by the developmentalism of Piaget and Kohlberg, this book is a collection of essays from prominent scholars in the field. It provides several critical views of moral development and uncovers some weaknesses in the developmental perspective. A rather extensive bibliography is appended.

Hollins, T. H. B., ed. *Aims in Education: The Philosophic Approach*. Manchester: Manchester University Press, 1964.

Six outstanding original essays help make this book a classic. Contributions by Hare and Peters, plus excellent discussions of utilitarianism and neo-Thomism, give the book a four-star rating. The book analyzes some of the fundamental issues in educational goal setting.

Joyce, Bruce, and Weil, Marsha. *Models of Teaching*. Englewood Cliffs, New Jersey: Prentice-Hall, 1972.

Without singling out the developmental model specifically, this book helps place the Piaget-Kohlberg system in perspective as one model among many. As its title indicates, this is a discussion of how to use models in teaching. Copious background material and a solid overview of the subject, including treatments of social interaction, information processing, and behavior modification, should benefit the Kohlberg scholar.

Kuhmerker, Lisa, Mentkowski, Marcia, and Erickson, V. Lois, eds. *Evaluating Moral Development*. Schenectady, New York: Character Research Press, 1980.

This book is a compilation of the conference papers presented at a 1979 conference of the Association of Moral Education. It includes a discussion of perspectives and directions, alternative modes of assessment, and evaluation strategies. In considering the state of the art, it proceeds with both caution and optimism.

Langer, Jonas. *Theories of Development*. New York: Holt, Rinehart and Winston, 1969.

This book is an excellent overview of three major models or hypotheses about human development, labeled by the author: the psychoanalytic, the mechanical mirror, and the organic lamp. Each perspective is described and criticized, its basic assumptions discussed, and its heuristic power evaluated. The book also points to a more comprehensive justification for psychological development.

Peters, R. S. *Psychology and Ethical Development.* London: George Allen and Unwin, 1974.

The author's analytic and speculative approach is especially effective in discussing and evaluating those theories on the borderline between ethics and psychology. He criticizes behaviorism and believes that Piaget and Freud developed theories that are complementary to each other. This collection of previously published work is important, since the author is one of Kohlberg's chief European critics.

Phenix, Philip H., ed. *Philosophies of Education.* New York: John Wiley and Sons, Inc., 1961.

After reading this book, one should be able to conclude that the Kohlbergian model, though fitting some better than others, is compatible with many educational philosophies. In thirteen essays the book allows the reader to examine basic assumptions behind educational practice. Authoritative spokespersons present the best features of a wide variety of educational approaches, from classical to experimental.

Stevens, Edward. *The Morals Game.* New York: Paulist Press, 1974.

Erudite, insightful, and clever are words easily applied to this book. The author discusses the world-views of several philosophers, including Dewey, Marcuse, and Sartre, and devotes a chapter to the Kohlberg stage sequence. An index would have made the book an even greater pleasure to read.

Wilson, John, Williams, Norman, and Sugarman, Barry. *Introduction to Moral Education.* Baltimore: Penguin Books, 1967.

This book, quoted often in the literature, is an excellent general introduction to the subject of moral education. It was written by a psychologist, a sociologist, and a philosopher from England, each of whom brings his discipline to bear. The reader should find its short reading list helpful.

Wright, Derek. *The Psychology of Moral Behaviour.* Baltimore: Penguin Books, 1971.

The author examines his subject from many angles. One chapter is devoted to the contributions of Piaget and Kohlberg. This book provides a panoramic view with copious citation of pertinent empirical data—and is well written.

General

Festinger, Leon. *A Theory of Cognitive Dissonance*. Stanford, California: Stanford University Press, 1957.
   Cognitive dissonance is a communication theorist's attempt to describe the mechanism of attitude change. Like the Piagetian concept of equilibration, it can aid one's understanding of how the individual moves through the Kohlbergian stages of moral development. The book is a much-quoted classic.
Habermas, Jürgen. *Communication and the Evolution of Society*. Translated by Thomas McCarthy. Boston: Beacon Press, 1979.
   One may gauge the spreading influence of a developmental morality by reading this book by an influential German sociologist. The book might be difficult reading but should be well worth the effort. The chapters on moral development and ego identity and the development of normative structures are particularly revealing.
Herskovits, Melville J. *Cultural Relativism: Perspectives in Cultural Pluralism*. New York: Vintage Books, 1973.
   No study of either Kohlberg or the abortion debate would be complete without some appreciation of the meaning of cultural relativism. The reader will confront that meaning squarely in this series of essays written over a twenty-year period. While the author opposes an absolutist ethic, his ideas should provide a certain stimulation for those who might not.
Hudson, W. D., ed. *The Is/Ought Question*. New York: St. Martin's Press, 1969.
   In 23 essays from a distinguished group of British, Canadian, and American philosophers, one of the central problems in ethics is discussed from a variety of aspects. Since Kohlberg's theory claims to solve the problem through the facts of moral-developmental psychology, this book contains important insights. A knowledge of the is/ought relationship will help illuminate the findings of cognitive moral developmentalism.
Lewis, C. S. *The Four Loves*. New York: Harcourt Brace Jovanovich, Inc., 1960.
   Since love begins where justice leaves off, this book is helpful in understanding what Kohlberg fails to discuss. Like justice, charity, an important aspect of love, is needed for a smoothly functioning society and has a certain prescription for success. The background of love brings the foreground of justice into sharper focus.
Mead, George H. *Mind, Self, and Society*. Chicago: The University of Chicago Press, 1934.
   As a part of the early history of social psychology, this book is good background for the study of Kohlberg. The author's ideas about the importance of role-taking and the emergence of the "generalized other" are classic. He asserts that the self is generated through a social process and that role-taking helps the individual to develop morally.
Niebuhr, H. Richard. *The Responsible Self*. New York: Harper and Row, 1963.
   In what some say is the author's most representative work, the

metaphor of responsibility implying an unlimited concern in accepting the consequences of one's actions is used to help explain the meaning of the moral life. The book is derived largely from the Robertson Lectures delivered at the University of Glasgow, while an appendix contains selected passages from the Earl Lectures delivered at the Pacific School of Religion. It is introduced by James M. Gustafson.

Perelman, Ch. *The Idea of Justice and the Problem of Argument.* Translated by John Petrie. London: Routledge and Kegan Paul, 1963.

Perelman brings together two important areas of knowledge useful to an understanding of both Kohlberg and the abortion debate: jurisprudence and rhetoric. This collection of previously published essays discusses types of justice as well as problems relating to language and communication. The book is a classic interdisciplinary work containing some useful background insights.

Pieper, Josef. *The Four Cardinal Virtues.* Notre Dame, Indiana: University of Notre Dame Press, 1966.

Kohlberg's exclusive reliance on the virtue of justice ignores the companion virtues of prudence, fortitude, and temperance. This book is an important corrective to that neglect. In a series of studies made in the 1950s and now united in a single volume, the author, who is a respected German academician, shows how the cardinal virtues are interrelated.

Smart, J. J. C., and Williams, Bernard. *Utilitarianism: For and Against.* London: Cambridge University Press, 1973.

Two extended essays by two British academicians comprise this philosophical inquiry. Both deal with the arguments and assumptions of a subject important to any student of Kohlberg. Utilitarianism is part of the foundation for the postconventional realm of cognitive developmental moral-stage theory.

This bibliography should not end without reference to a new quarterly journal which has become an important expositor of the Kohlbergian viewpoint. Along with some excellent feature articles, it contains reviews of significant books, and each Spring issue includes a comprehensive, up-to-date bibliography of pertinent articles and books. Consult the *Moral Education Forum*, c/o Editor Lisa Kuhmerker, Hunter College of the City University of New York (221 East 72nd St., New York, N.Y. 10021).

INDEX

NAME

ABOUT THE AUTHOR

David Mall is a scholar/activist who has written extensively about the cultural transmission of biomedical ethics. Educated at the University of New Mexico, Michigan State University, and the University of Minnesota, he has taught speech communication at a number of institutions, including Fordham, Purdue, Temple, and Villanova, as well as the University of Arizona and New York University. Some of his teaching responsibilities also involved coaching intercollegiate forensics.

Since the mid-1960s David Mall has been a participant/observer of the American pro-life movement. He helped found Minnesota Citizens Concerned for Life (MCCL) and was instrumental in establishing two pro-life youth organizations, Save Our Unwanted Life (SOUL) and the National Youth Pro-Life Coalition (NYPLC). He was also the executive director of two nonprofit educational foundations, the Illinois Right to Life Committee (IRLC) and Americans United for Life (AUL).

The author's chief academic interest is the rhetoric of social movements. He has co-edited *Death, Dying and Euthanasia*, *The Psychological Aspects of Abortion*, and *New Perspectives on Human Abortion* (all published by University Publications of America).

Library of Congress Cataloging in Publication Data

Mall, David.
    In good conscience.

    Bibliography: p.
    Includes index.
    1. Abortion—Moral and ethical aspects.
I. Title.
HQ766.2.M34   1982   363.4'6   82-9918
ISBN 0-9608410-1-6   AACR2
ISBN 0-9608410-0-8 (pbk.)

This book is dedicated to the proposition that rhetoric makes a difference in human affairs. It is part of a proposed trilogy investigating the abortion controversy from the perspective of communication. By analyzing how the mind comprehends the moral aspects of important contemporary issues, the author attempts to construct a theory of persuasion for social movements.

When completed, the trilogy will deal extensively with a critical but little-discussed dimension of the abortion controversy, that of rhetoric. No book has yet addressed itself to the problem of audience psychology as applied to the strictly moral aspects of a social movement. **In Good Conscience** is the first sustained analysis of moral persuasion from the pen of a scholar-practitioner. It helps the reader understand one of the great issues of our time with the added bonus that it can be used by those sensitive to the problem of audience adaptation.

Drawing upon the pioneering work of Piaget and Kohlberg, **In Good Conscience** deals with the structural transformation of moral thinking. It is more than an extension of previous theorizing, however; the book makes its own invaluable contribution by successfully unraveling the tangle of moral arguments surrounding abortion through use of the powerful tool of cognitive developmental analysis. This new dimension allows any perceptive reader to discuss moral thinking more intelligently.

The book proceeds from theory to practice and is divided into three parts:

- I. The Development of Conscience
- II. The Modes of Moral Discourse
- III. The Alliance of Thought and Action

At the core of the author's rhetoric is a theory of moral decision-making that emphasizes the principle of justice. Using the topic of abortion as a content area, the book shows how the human mind makes moral distinctions and how these can be stimulated through effective educational techniques. The book is thoroughly documented and contains a useful appendix and bibliography.